Gray Hill

With the Beduins

A Narrative of Journeys And Adventures in Unfrequented Parts of Syria

Gray Hill

With the Beduins
A Narrative of Journeys And Adventures in Unfrequented Parts of Syria

ISBN/EAN: 9783744759649

Printed in Europe, USA, Canada, Australia, Japan

Cover: Foto ©Andreas Hilbeck / pixelio.de

More available books at **www.hansebooks.com**

WITH THE BEDUINS

GÛDR, SON OF SHEIK SALEH OF KERÂK, AND HIS SERVANT.

*A NARRATIVE OF JOURNEYS AND ADVENTURES
IN UNFREQUENTED PARTS OF SYRIA*

BY

GRAY HILL

> "Already through each nerve a flutter runs
> Of eager hope, that longs to be away;
> Already 'neath the light of other suns
> My feet, new winged for travel, yearn to stray."
>
> — MARTIN's "*Catullus*"

SIXTY-EIGHT ILLUSTRATIONS AND A MAP

London
T. FISHER UNWIN
PATERNOSTER SQUARE
MDCCCXCI

𝔍 Dedicate

THIS BOOK

TO

MY WIFE.

PREFACE.

BEFORE we made the journeys of which an account is given in the following pages, my wife and I had long felt attracted towards Syria. Many years ago we had visited Beyrout and Damascus; and on two occasions we had landed through the rolling waves at Jaffa while the coast steamer lay off the Port for the day, and had looked longingly towards Jerusalem. After we had in our various autumn vacation trips coasted all round the Mediterranean Sea " from the Levant to the Pillars of Hercules," and from the gates of " the Propontic and the Hellespont " to the mouths of the Nile and the shores of Carthage, a time at last came when I was enabled to obtain a longer respite from the toils of a laborious profession, and we thus became free to choose our own season for an annual flight from the east winds and leaden skies of England. Then we determined that we would explore the wished-for country. And so, in 1887, we had travelled by the beaten track with which all travellers must begin, and with which so many are either contented or compelled to end, visiting Jerusalem, and traversing the hills and valleys of Palestine to Shechem, Samaria, and the wide plain of

Esdraelon; to Nazareth, the Sea of Galilee, Cæsarea Philippi, and the sources of the Jordan; and to Mount Hermon, Damascus, Baalbek and Beyrout.

In a month of riding and camping we had found new health and life, opened a fresh source of happiness, and imbibed somewhat of the spirit of the country. And from that time forth we have been drawn by an overpowering force, to which we have now learnt gladly to yield ourselves, to devote all the time which we can spare from work-a-day existence to journeying in Syria.

That which had charmed us most was the glimpse which we had gained into the life of the Arab Nomad tribes, and the silent impressiveness of the great Solitudes. To see something more of the simple pastoral existence of the Beduins, and to breathe the air of the wilderness; to sit with Father Abraham under the great tent, and to behold Isaac and Jacob "in their habits as they lived;" to watch the flocks and herds go forth to feed at dawn, and come home to the protection of the tents by the light of the setting sun; to camp alone in solitary fastnesses, or upon boundless plains; to gaze up into the starry depths of a Syrian night; to see the great disc of the full moon rise across the "eastern desert lone" until the splendour of its light irradiates the barren gorges, and changes the dark and silent surface of the Dead Sea into a "luminous floor of water," was what we now most ardently longed for.

In each succeeding year we have found greater and greater delight in the pursuit of our desire; and although the fascinations of travel have brought some anxious experiences, and involved some serious risks,—

and indeed in the spring of the present year was the cause of our finding ourselves on more occasions than one in a situation of a most disagreeable and alarming kind,—we still look forward with all the pleasures of hope to again and again revisiting that strangely attractive land, and to the glad welcome at the little landing-place at Jaffa of those servant-friends whose fidelity and affection have added so greatly to the enjoyment of our wanderings.

The things which we have seen and the little adventures which have befallen us have proved so interesting to ourselves, that we have thought that they might also interest the public. Whether they will do so depends much upon the manner of relating them, and unfortunately I am inexperienced in authorship. I can "only speak right on." But if, as I fear, I cannot succeed in making what I have to say attractive, I will, at any rate, try to make it clear ; and I will do my best to avoid the "limbs and outward flourishes" of tediousness. And the illustrations, which are principally from sketches and photographs taken by my wife, may in some imperfect way hold as "'twere the mirror up to nature" in some places where nature has not yet been reflected.

I am keenly alive to the shortcomings of my narrative. It does not report the discovery of any long-lost inscription, or record the survey of any unmapped hill, valley, or stream. It will not serve the purposes of an ordinary guide book ; nor has it scholarship to recommend it to those readers who, being unable to visit the Syrian land in the flesh, can only travel through it in imagination. The places which it describes are known to travellers, though many of them are but rarely visited; and the events which it records are not of public interest. It simply tells the story of journeyings which have been delightful to us, and of vicissitudes on which memory dwells happily; for "as it is pleasant to see the sea from the land, so it is pleasant for him who has escaped from troubles to think of them." If, then, critic or reader be disposed to think the recital of our wanderings superfluous I shall not quarrel with his judgment. One portion at least—the "Stories of Abou Suleyman" of which I place a selection before the reader calls for no apology. They were written down by me as I heard them, and are as far as possible in the words of the narrator; for they seemed to me as interesting in matter as they are quaint in style.

MERE HALL, BIRKENHEAD.
October, 1890.

CONTENTS.

	PAGE
PREFACE	7
TABLE OF CONTENTS	11
LIST OF ILLUSTRATIONS	24

PART I.

1888.

EAST OF THE JORDAN.

CHAPTER I.

THE JOURNEY TO THE JORDAN 29

We send for the Adwan Sheiks—George Mabbedy our Dragoman—The making of the contract for our safe conduct—We set out—The new road to Jericho—The hermits' caves—A stormy night—Bathing in the Dead Sea under difficulties—A header into the Jordan—The lessons of experience.

CHAPTER II.

THE CAMP OF THE ADWAN 39

The bridge over the Jordan—Ascending from the plain—Views of the Judæan hills—"Is London as big as Jerusalem?"—The Jewish ruins at Arak el Emir—Oleanders—Ascending the hills of Gilead—The Adwan camp at Hesbân—Ali Diab—His allowance of wives—

A feast in the great tent—A Beduin bride—Miss Finkelstein's lectures—A ride on the bride's camel.

CHAPTER III.

MOUNT NEBO 51

The Spring of Moses—Rainy weather—The land of milk and honey—Natural facilities for the cultivation of the Jordan valley—An offer to purchase it from the Sultan.

CHAPTER IV.

MASHITA 55

Objections of our Adwan guides to take us to Mashita—Description of our guides—Reconnoitring—On the look out for the Beni Sokr—Description of the ruins at Mashita—We proceed to Ammân—A supposed spy—The Adwan propose to kill him.

CHAPTER V.

AMMÂN AND ES SALT 61

A pleasant country—Old tombs—Abou Seyne steals a horse—Roman remains at Ammân—The Circassians—They decline to wash for Christians—The citadel—The Persian building—Uriah the Hittite—Strange geological formation—We give our guides a sheep—Their manner of cooking the meat—We set out for Es Salt—Misdeeds of Abou Seyne—Description of Es Salt—The Kaimakâm threatens to arrest us—Ali Diab comes to plead for a murderer—We proceed to 'Ain Roman—The Turcomans—The gorge.

CHAPTER VI.

JERASH 68

Over hill and dale—We cross the Zerka and camp amongst the ruins of Jerash—The Circassians—The street of columns—The Adwan men leave us—A fantasia—The Sheik of Sûf becomes our guide—Moonlight at Jerash—The Beni Sokr and their Remington rifles.

CHAPTER VII.

AJILÛN AND EL. HUSN 73

The forest land of Gilead—A rocky glen—Ajilûn—The Kaimakâm—How he pacified the district—The natural richness of the country—The Greek priest—The Crusader's castle—The shoemaker—The bridal procession—Gainsborough's country—The plain of the Western Hauran—Damascus in the distance—Fever and an anxious night—Is this our journey's end?—A removal to a healthier spot—St. Lazarus' Day—Representation of the miracle—A wild night—The wedding procession again—A cave for the horses and mules—The dead mare—A blood feud.

CHAPTER VIII.

GADARA—A NIGHT ATTACK 81

Umkeis—A charming country—The gorges of the Yarmûk—Old tombs—The ruins of Gadara—We encamp in view of the Sea of Galilee—Bad repute of the people of Umkeis—We are awaked by firing—Rats in a trap—The assailants driven off—The negro of Irbid—The moon rises—We depart betimes and ford the Yarmûk.

CHAPTER IX.

THE SEA OF GALILEE 85

The sulphur springs of Amatha—The "warawaras"—A bathe in the lake—Dangers of the Jordan where it leaves the lake—We ford the river and reach Tiberias—Heat and flies—A remedy—The missing lady—Khan Yubb Yusef—Capernaum and Bethsaida—The Jordan where it enters the lake—Different aspects of the lake—Safed—Extensive view—The Jews of Safed—Descent to the Sea of Galilee—The Indian Dervish—Ravines and caves—The land of Gennesaret—The Wâdy Hammâm—The Robbers' Castle—The village of Hattin.

CHAPTER X.

THE DRUSES—HATTIN AND MOUNT TABOR . . . 93

The Mount of the Beatitudes—George has fever—A Druse guard—Awakened again with firing—Only a hyena—The mosque of the Druses—Their regrets that Russia had taken India—The late Laurence Oliphant—A procession of Druses—The Horns and plain of Hattin—The sea of barley—The merry muleteer—We ascend Mount Tabor—The view from the top—Deborah—We proceed to Nazareth.

CHAPTER XI.

FROM NAZARETH TO CARMEL 99

Religious intolerance—The plain of Esdraelon—The woodland borders of the Kishon—Haifa—The German colony—Mount Carmel—The monastery—Too hot to get to Acre—Our waiter proposes—The medicine of the monastery proves of value—The work of the German colonists—A stormy night.

CHAPTER XII.

WE END OUR JOURNEY—GEORGE AND HIS FAMILY . . 104

We descend to the sea and travel southwards—The Crocodile River—Athlit—The last holding of the Crusaders—Kaisariyêh—The plain of Sharon—Fear of the Beduins—Mutual distrust—Haram Sidin Ali Ibn 'Alim—The mad woman—We are reported to be murdered—George's nephew—The last evening in camp—The last ride—George's family—Last view of Jaffa.

PART II.

1889.

PHILISTIA AND PALMYRA.

CHAPTER I.

THE JOURNEY TO GAZA 113

Arrival at Jaffa—Across the plain of Sharon to Ramleh—We turn to the South—El Mûghâr—Esdûd—Askalon—Gaza—George's opinions about the stars—The missionary—A Moslem funeral—Mount Muntâr.

CHAPTER II.

TO BEERSHEBA AND BEIT JIBRIN 118

The Beduin and the soldier—Tell Sheriah—A crane-like shepherd—Flights of storks—A barren land—Abraham's well—"What is a picture?"—Supper and breakfast by moonlight—The complaint of the Nubian—Long ride to Beit Jibrin.

CHAPTER III.

BY HEBRON AND 'AIN JIDY TO JERUSALEM . . . 123

Ruins at Beit Jibrin—Journey to Hebron—Mamre—A wild night—The cave of Macpelah—We leave Hebron—A Beduin camp—A quarrel—Magnesium light—The pass of 'Ain Jidy—Magnificent view—'Ain Jidy—A Syrian night—Journey through a rugged country to Bethlehem—Jerusalem.

CHAPTER IV.

FROM JERUSALEM TO BEISAN, MUZEYRÎB, AND DAMASCUS . 130

From Jerusalem to Jenîn—Jezreel—Beisan—Across the Jordan and up the eastern hills—A thief—His brother seized—Muzeyrîb—The Hadj station—Damascus.

CHAPTER V.

FROM DAMASCUS TO PALMYRA 136

Difficulties of the journey to Palmyra—A garden of roses—No one allowed to go to Palmyra this year—Sheik Nasr undertakes to conduct us—Our departure—The gardens of Damascus—A rocky gorge—The source of a stream—Saidnâya—Our muleteers lose their way, and we pass the night in a village—Sheik Nasr finds us—Rocky heights and cold winds—Ma'lula—Great heat—Nebk—Mahîn—Karyatên—The waterless desert begins—" Why had we come without an escort ? "—Expedition against the predatory Beduins—We are offered an escort—An evening start—Out into the desert—The Sirocco—Who are these ?—The escort—Riding through the night—The illusions of the desert—Giants become goats—A welcome draught of milk—El Bêda—A bite from a horse—Palmyra at last.

CHAPTER VI.

TADMOR IN THE WILDERNESS 147

Did Solomon build Palmyra ?—The rise of its greatness—The caravan track—Public monuments—The great arcade—Appearance of the streets—The great tombs—Zenobia—Her defeat at Emesa, and capture—Taking of Palmyra by Aurelian—Palmyra re-discovered by English travellers—Present state of the ruins—Recent discovery of sweet water—Underground conduits—Digging for water—The Téskeré—The French lady—Newly discovered sculptures—The trade in heads of statues—The governor speaks of the enormity of it, and offers us a good one—Destruction of our photographs.

CHAPTER VII.

THE RETURN JOURNEY 158

The heat drives us away—A last look—Seven hundred camels—Nasr kisses his brethren—El Bêda again—A burning sand-laden wind—Shelter at last—The old irrigation pits—An extra guard—A long ride—High hills and bitter winds—We leave the desert and part with the soldiers—A Beduin outpost—"Come you in peace, or come you in war?"—The Sheik on the white horse—Preparing for an attack—The men behind the hill—Shelter from the blast and a fire of cow dung—Homs—The country house of Lady Ellenborough—Sheik Nasr—The curiosity of the women—The Orontes—Back to Damascus and Jerusalem—Our last ride—The sagacity of a dog—Werdie's fate.

PART III.

1890.

ADVENTURES SOUTH AND EAST OF THE DEAD SEA.

CHAPTER I.

OUR JOURNEY TOWARDS PETRA—ARAR'S MESSENGER . . 171

The difficulty of getting to Petra—We are warned against the attempt, but are obstinate—Sheik Selim Abou Dahook—A long negotiation—The Jehalîn men—Our attendants—We leave our valuables behind—Precautionary measures—Letters and presents for the Sheik of Petra—The tribes reported at peace—The Kaimakâm of Hebron—Journey to the Dead Sea—We get within two days of Petra—Arar's messenger—Arar's seal—Fighting amongst the Beduins—We cannot proceed—How Arar had known of our coming—The scene at Zuweireh—We meet the Petra men there who take the Consul's letter to Arar—The messenger pursued by Howeytát men—We return to 'Ain el Bêda and determine to proceed to Kerâk.

CHAPTER II.

THE HOWYETÁT—A VERY ANXIOUS NIGHT . . . 180

A desolate country—We encamp at 'Ain el Bêda—The thicket of reeds—Arrival of Howeytát men—Their arms and their behaviour—"The cry is, Still they come"—How many more, and will they attack us?—The camp fires of the Howeytát—Will our Jehalín escort be firm?—Preparations for a defence—A watch all night—The dawn appears at last—Backsheesh—Circuitous route across the Ghôr—Another Howeytát—We enter the territory of the Ghawàrineh.

CHAPTER III.

The Ghawàrineh — We are threatened again — Arar assists us 186

Arar's cousin threatens Sheik Selim—"*I* will take you to Petra"—The villainous Sheik of the Ghawàrineh demands 100 medjidiés—Arar's brother arrives—Unpleasant situation—We send messengers to Kerâk—A brawl arises—Arar's brother stills it—Sunset on the red mountains—Mosquitoes—Arar's conduct—The Sheik of the Ghawàrineh raises his demand—We refuse to pay him—Journey to Nimeirah—The east shore of the Dead Sea—A red gorge—The heat—A messenger returns and the Keraki arrive.

CHAPTER IV.

The Keraki—Trap No. 1—Sheik Saleh . . . 193

The Keraki are most polite—The Jehalín men leave us—The journey to El Draa—The Keraki induce us to camp there—Arrival of Mejelli—Impracticability of reaching Petra *viâ* Kerâk and Ma'an—Isolation of Kerâk—More Keraki arrive—Another red gorge—Beauty of the scene—"What do you intend to give us?"—Excessive demands—Lies—The Christian scamp—Sixty napoleons the lowest—Letter from Sheik Khalíl—His position at Kerâk—We prefer to go back—"You shall not stir until you pay sixty napoleons"—Appeals to the honour of a man who has none—Impossibility of resistance—Saleh agrees to take us through his territory—We ascend the pass of Wâdy Kerâk—Strange caverns—Quarrelling over the booty—Strong position of Kir of

Moab and the Kerâk territory—The fighting strength of the tribe and number of the population—Experiences of previous travellers.

CHAPTER V.

THE ENGLISH MISSIONARIES 204

Mr. Lethaby—We enter Kerâk—Mrs. Lethaby and the mission room—Mr. Lethaby's history—Heroic conduct of the missionaries—The perils and annoyances to which they are exposed—The difficulty of communication with the outside world—Sheik Saleh's manœuvre to get all the money for himself—No sleep for George—Messages from Sheik Khalîl—His two sons—We manage to keep back a portion of the money—We descend the hill—My wife's strength fails—Mrs. Lethaby accompanies her—Sheik Khalîl and his followers.

CHAPTER VI.

THE KERAKI—TRAP NO. 2—SHEIK KHALÎL . . . 212

Ar of Moab—Ancient ruins—The encampment of Sheik Khalîl—We are forced to stop—We eat with Khalîl—Deceitful meat—The Hamèydeh men will come next—Khalîl demands sixty napoleons—We call on Saleh to perform his agreement—Consultations and appeals—The lying of Saleh—He will not divide with Khalîl, and satisfaction must come from our pockets—An unsatisfactory present—A compromise agreed on—But Saleh gallops off with the money, and leaves us in Khalîl's hands—Threatening aspect of affairs—The greedy Ibrahim—The cry for the money—We have not got it—Mrs. Lethaby returns to Kerâk—The insolence of Ibrahim—A paternal rebuke—They will starve us into payment—The Christian boys supply us with food—No money to be obtained from Kerâk—We are allowed to send to Madeba or, failing success there, to Jerusalem—We write our letters—A new proposal—The offer of the Christian shepherd—He is driven away—They must have the money—Our

"Holy Man" leaves for Jerusalem—More threats—The old muleteer—Preparations for an escape.

CHAPTER VII.

WE AWAIT THE RETURN OF THE "HOLY MAN" . . . 224

My wife's speech to the Sheiks—Its success—Sheik Faris wishes to go to England with us—Things go more smoothly—We take some portraits—Tempestuous weather—Anxiety about the messenger—The Christian boys—A murder at Kerâk—The rain—George ill—We are invited to build a house at Kerâk—The Christian shepherd makes a propitiatory feast—A welcome piece of ham—The Hamèydeh men are waiting for us—The return of the "Holy Man."

CHAPTER VIII.

WE GET FREE FROM THE KERAKI AND CROSS MOJÉB . . 231

We are forced to pay in advance, and surrender the presents intended for Arar, &c.—My wife puts an end to Ibrahim's demands—We have to make a *détour*—Uncertainty whether we shall really get away—The Hamèydeh—We descend Mojéb and cross the Arnon—The mares and their foals—The pride of Moab—How to bring Kerâk into order—The Keraki hand us over to the Hamèydeh.

CHAPTER IX.

THE HAMÈYDEH—WE DECLINE TO BE STOPPED AGAIN . 237

The number and equipment of the Hamèydeh—A pleasant lunching place—The Keraki reascend the pass on the south side—Our toilsome ascent on the north side—The Hamèydeh try to stop us, but we show fight and push on—An exciting half-hour—Eleven hours in the saddle—An eventful Good Friday—Will the Hamèydeh send for more men?—An early start—We pay only what we had promised, and give them a truthful certificate—A Christian would-be robber.

CONTENTS.

CHAPTER X.

MADEBA AND MOUNT NEBO ONCE MORE 243

In sight of Madeba—Peace at last—Senah the Sheik of Madeba—Kind reception—The City of Refuge—Roman remains—Easter Sunday—We take tea on Pisgah, and our good old cook offers up a thanksgiving.

CHAPTER XI.

ABOU SEYNE—THE KAIMAKÂM OF ES SALT AGAIN . . 246

Senah's efforts to assist us—He urges us to ask for redress—We send to Jerusalem and proceed to Hesbân—Death of Zatam el Faiz—We revisit Mashita and Hesbân where Turkish soldiers find us—We revisit Ammân—Abou Seyne joins our party—His skill in horsemanship, &c.—The Beni Sokr chiefs—Complimentary speeches—We enter Es Salt and visit the Kaimakâm—Curiosity of the people—Taking down the deposition—An adventure of Abou Seyne.

CHAPTER XII.

GEORGE'S PATRON SAINT—THE GOVERNOR OF THE HAURAN . 256

El Bukeia—The Beni Hassan—Og's dominions—St. George—Jerash—Tekitty—The governor of the Hauran—The Beni Sokr sheiks again.

CHAPTER XIII.

THE HAURAN—THE DRUSES 262

Our guards—Wooded country—Destruction of trees—Rantha—Abou Seyne's compliment—Og.'s capital—Busrâh—Strange nature of the country—Ruined towns—Roman remains at Busrâh—Bartering bottles for eggs—Stormy weather—The Roman road to Salkad—Difficulty of the journey—The Castle of Salkad—The filthy streets—A staring crowd—A blood feud—The Druses threaten to kill Abou Seyne, and we retrace our steps—His proposed revenge—Horses fighting—We cross the Hadj road and revisit El Husn—The Greek priest.

CHAPTER XIV.

THE JOURNEY BACK TO THE JORDAN VALLEY — THE OLD
  PRIEST OF AJILÛN 272

  Ride to Ajilûn—Our patients—The old priest—An opening for a medical practice—The beautiful Wâdy Ajilûn—Descent to the plain of the Jordan—The Dolmens—A patron saint of the Beduins—A present from a sheik—"Tells" in this neighbourhood.

CHAPTER XV.

WE FORD THE JORDAN—A NIGHT MARCH . . . 277

  The ride to the Jordan—The Sheik of the ford—Crossing the river—Regret at leaving the east side of the Jordan—Shakespeare's birth and death-day—We get up too soon—A dance—Abou Seyne leaves us—Riding in the dark—The coming of the day—A man of the Keraki—We end our journey and encamp on our own freehold—"Why should you leave us?"

PART IV.

THE STORIES OF ABOU SULEYMAN.

An Ill-assorted Marriage	285
The Daughter of the Sheik	286
The Circassians	289
The Refugees	290
The Bandit	291
Sheik Goblan	292
A Gospel Precept	294
SNAKES —I. The Man of Nablous	294
II. By the Jordan	296
III. The Man of Jaffa	298
IV. Abou Suleyman	298
V. The Snake and the Baby	299
Crossing the Jordan	300
The —— Consul	300

	PAGE
The Thieves and the Donkey	302
The Slave and his Lord at Tiberias	302
GHOSTS—I. The Black Dog	304
II. The Strange Knock	304
III. Royal Ghosts	305
The Quarrelsome Man	305
Cholera	306
Abou Suleyman's Grandmother	306
The last Words of a Beduin Sheik	307
RELIGIOUS ANIMOSITIES IN JERUSALEM—	
I. Jews and Copts	308
II. Jews and Copts	309
III. Mahommedans and Copts	309
IV. The Copts—A House divided against Itself	310
V. The Copts—A Reconciliation	311
VI. The Conversion of the Jews	312

FABLES.

I. Abou Seyne (the Father of Naughtiness)	314
II. The Mouse's Visit	316
III. The Donkey and the Sheep	317
APPENDIX	319

LIST OF ILLUSTRATIONS.

PART I.

		PAGE
1.	Gudr, son of Sheik Saleh of Kerâk, and his servant *Frontispiece*	
2.	Detail of sculpture—Mashita. (*Drawn from an imperfect photograph by F. Wiltshire*) . *To face page*	29
3.	Platform of the Dome of the Rock, Jerusalem . .	29
4.	George Mabbedy	32
5.	The River Jordan . . . . *To face page*	38
6.	Mashita	55
7.	Part of south front of enclosure wall, Mashita. (*Drawn from an imperfect photograph by F. Wiltshire*) . .	60
8.	Cattle in the Zerka near Ammân	61
9.	Jerash	72
10.	South end of the Sea of Galilee	85
11.	North end of the Sea of Galilee	92
12.	Haifa and the Bay of Acre from Mount Carmel .	102
13.	Nahr el Auja, a river near Jaffa	104
14.	Leaving Jaffa	110

PART II.

15.	Palmyra in 1750. (*From Wood and Dawkins,* "The Ruins of Palmyra") . . . *To face page*	113
16.	Nearing Jaffa	113
17.	Fountain near Jaffa } . . . *To face page*	114
18.	The Plain of Sharon }	
19.	The Dead Sea from the Pass of 'Ain Jidy . .	118
20.	The Sheik of Hebron . . . *To face page*	122

LIST OF ILLUSTRATIONS.

		PAGE
21.	Hebron	123
22.	Group of Arabs, Hebron	129
23.	The Jordan Valley	130
24.	Muzeyrîb	135
25.	Riding in the Desert	136
26.	Nebk	140
27.	Small Temple, Palmyra	*To face page* 146
28.	Gateway and part of Colonnade, Palmyra	147
29.	Part of Colonnade, Palmyra	*To face page* 148
30.	Arab entrance to the Temple of the Sun, Palmyra	152
31.	Great Temple of the Sun, Palmyra	*To face page* 152
32.	Sculpture, Palmyra	155
33.	Column, Palmyra	157
34.	Last View of Palmyra	158
35.	Werdie crossing the Desert	167

PART III.

36.	Keraki discussing the division of the spoil. Mountains of Wâdy Kerâk at the back	*To face page* 171
37.	Petra (after Roberts)	172
38.	Passing Jebel Usdum (Mountain of Sodom)	*To face page* 174
39.	Sheik Abou Dahook and his Slave	
40.	West of the Dead Sea	*To face page* 176
41.	East of the Dead Sea	
42.	On the march near where Arar's messenger turned us back	*To face page* 178
43.	Mare and foal in the Desert	
44.	Zuweireh el Tahta	179
45.	A halt—Looking out for Beduins	
46.	'Ain el Bêda. Beduins of the Howeytát tribe come out of the reeds	*To face page* 180
47.	A Wâdy south of the Dea Sea	185
48.	The Dead Sea from Nimeirah	186
49.	We enter the territory of the Ghawàrineh	*To face page* 188
50.	Arar's brother assists us against the Ghawàrineh	

LIST OF ILLUSTRATIONS.

		PAGE
51.	Ghôr es Safiyeh	} *To face page* 188
52.	Wâdy south of the Dead Sea—Our Jehalîn escort	
53.	Some of our faithful servants	192
54.	Isa Senah of Kerâk	193
55. 56.	Walking for a change	*To face page* 196
57.	Sheik Faris of Kerâk and his Brethren	204
58.	Mr. Lethaby, Missionary at Kerâk	*To face page* 204
59.	Encampment of Sheik Khalîl, where we were detained	212
60.	Sheik Khalîl of Kerâk and another of his tribe	222
61.	Young Christians at Sheik Khalîl's encampment. (*Drawn from an imperfect photograph by Leslie L. Brooke*)	224
62.	A drink in the Desert	242
63.	Busrâh-Eski-Shâm	260
64.	Druse Sheik of Salkad and his servant	270
65.	Jerusalem from the north end of the Mount of Olives	*To face page* 276
66.	Adieu to Syria	281
67.	The Summer Pulpit. Dome of the Rock, Jerusalem	*To face page* 284
68.	View from the Palace of the Copt Bishop, Jaffa	318

ERRATA.

Page 86, last line, *for* "Tiberia" *read* "Tiberias."

Page 188, Note, *for* "Tel" *read* "Tell."

Page 196, line 8, *for* "who just" *read* "who had just."

Page 197, line 11, *for* "man's" *read* "mind's."

Page 217, line 2, *for* "conducting safely" *read* "conducting us safely."

Page 280, line 21, *for* "that stands" *read* "that stand."

PART I.

1888.

East of the Jordan.

DETAIL OF SCULPTURE—MASHITA.

PLATFORM OF THE DOME OF THE ROCK, JERUSALEM.

PART I.

1888.

East of the Jordan.

CHAPTER I.

THE JOURNEY TO THE JORDAN.

"Who that has ever travelled in Palestine has not longed to cross the Jordan valley to those mysterious hills which close every eastward view with their long horizontal outline, their overshadowing height, their deep purple shade?"—Stanley's "Sinai and Palestine."

HAVING arranged for our intended tour by correspondence with our Dragoman beforehand, we had no sooner reached Jerusalem in 1888 than we got him to send off a horseman to the encampment of the Adwan tribe (which until the summer heats set in is to be found by the brook of Hesbân—the ancient Heshbon), to summon one of their sheiks to the Holy City, in order that the necessary arrangements might be made for our visit to the tribe, and for our safe conduct in their territory.

Before the messenger returns may I introduce to my readers a faithful friend, and our guide and companion in all our travels.

George Mabbedy is in his way one of the most interesting men I know. He is by race and religion an Egyptian Copt, but was born in Jerusalem, and educated at the English Bishop's school there. Having learnt our language through instruction in the Bible, he speaks a kind of sixteenth-century English, which is often quaint and expressive. And yet he has a habit of omitting the definite and indefinite articles and other unessential words which tend to that brevity which the present age prizes. He is very proud of his descent from the ancient inhabitants of the land of the Pharaohs, and is fully convinced that the Copts (who form the smallest of the Christian sects), are the chief depositaries of the Christian virtues, and are now, in succession to the Jews deposed, the chosen people of the Almighty.

He is short, strongly built, with a broad forehead, a very dark rather fierce-looking and handsome face, and in general appearance he bears a considerable resemblance to the great Italian tragedian, Signor Salvini. Indeed, in telling a story or when labouring under excitement, in look, voice, and action, he often reminded us strongly of Salvini in the character of

Othello, and the resemblance is the more striking as his dress is very similar to that which the great actor wears. He is a splendid horseman, of great muscular strength, very brave, absolutely honest, faithful, indeed devoted to us, and as careful of us, as watchful over us, as if we were his parents or his children. I have had some experience of dragomen, but never have I met one who in any way resembled George. You must, however, make a friend of him if you want to have the full advantage of his services. He cares less for money than for proper treatment, and that you may fall into his humour and look at things with his eyes. And, indeed, we have often found it difficult to get him to do himself justice in the money arrangements for the journey.

George is much puzzled to understand what I do when I am at home, and how I earn my living. After much pondering—for he is a taciturn man, slow to speak [1]—he proposes this question to me: "When one man kill another and come to see you, what you tell him?"

"When one man kills another he does not come to me. He runs away; if he is caught he will be hanged."

"But if he bribe the judge?"

"Judges in England do not accept bribes."

"Well it is different in Syria."

And then he tells us how a man in a certain city of that country killed both his wives to satisfy another woman, who made these murders part of her bargain to marry him, and how this man went to see the judge

[1] "Men of few words are the best men" ("Henry V.").

"with fifty Turkish pounds in his hand, and the judge tell the people, This murder not this man's business at all. These women kill one another."

George wants to come to England with us and to help me at my office.

"What would you do there, George?"

"I stand at the door with my sword. This man come in, I let him come—this man go out, I put him out."

GEORGE MABBEDY.

His main idea is that I must be constantly engaged in divorce and murder cases, and that those whom I am opposing must always be seeking my life; and he wants to be my guard against avenging knives. George has travelled much amongst the Beduins—having traded with them in earlier years, and is a great favourite with the Adwan tribe.

On the second day after the messenger departed

Sheiks Fallach and Ali Abdul Aziz returned with him to Jerusalem. A small carpet was spread in the hall of Howard's Hotel for their reception, the sheiks arranged themselves upon it, and after they had consumed the large bowl full of mutton and rice which was placed before them, Mr. Howard and George sat down beside them to make the bargain. We placed our chairs near that we might enjoy the sight; coffee and cigarettes were brought ("Coffee very good," says George, "bring mind in head") and the negotiation was entered upon. Of course the sheiks began by demanding an extravagant sum; of course Mr. Howard and George jumped up several times with horror-struck and indignant looks, as if the proposal to visit the lands of Moab and of Gilead were at once and for ever withdrawn; and of course after an hour's gesticulation all was happily ended for a reasonable sum. We did not understand what they said, but when the sheiks and our negotiators suddenly kissed one another on the cheek we felt that a satisfactory treaty had been made, and we accompanied the former to the British Consul, where a contract was drawn up and sealed by impressions from their silver signet rings dipped in ink. For the sum of sixteen napoleons and a backsheesh (the latter expressly repudiated by the contract, but secretly understood to be paid if all went to our satisfaction, for it is impossible really to exclude backsheesh from any money arrangements with Arabs), we were to spend nineteen days in their camp.

Accordingly the next morning, the thirteenth of April, we departed from Jerusalem after listening to an earnest conjuration from a kind-hearted lady staying at the hotel not to trust our lives to such a wild-looking man as George, and such obvious cut-throats as the sheiks.

Then with thoughts of the country beyond Jordan and the Beduin life gladdening our hearts, we rode on past the Damascus Gate, the Virgin's Fountain, the Garden of Gethsemane, the Jewish Cemetery, up the western slope of Olivet, past the village of Bethany, on to the bare and arid country, the wilderness of desolation which leads at first in rise and fall, but latterly in one continuous descent (for the Jordan valley and the Dead Sea are about three thousand seven hundred feet below Jerusalem), to the plain of Jericho. The way is not much safer in the present day for the *solitary* traveller than in the days of the Good Samaritan, but in addition to our own men we had six Beduins with us, and had paid our " scot and lot " to the Jericho Sheik. So that we had nothing to fear.

George enlivened the way by telling us of a Greek merchant going down to Jericho the year before with a large number of piastres, who was robbed of his money. " And they fire at him and hit his leg ; but it do not matter much because it is only the *meat* of his leg what is hurt." [1]

There will probably soon be a change in regard to the safety of this route, for now (1890) a good carriage

[1] In June, 1890, a caravan of the Keraki (the people who in that year detained and extorted money from us, as related in these pages) journeying to Jerusalem with butter and sheep for sale, were themselves robbed of all they had with them, including their horses, mules, weapons, and clothes, at a spot close to the Khan called the " Inn of the Good Samaritan," about half way between Jerusalem and Jericho.

road is nearly finished from Jerusalem to Jericho. The report we heard was that it had been ordered by the Sultan in the expectation of the visit to the Holy Land of the Prince of Wales and one of the German Princes. The road is of course made by forced labour, but many of those who work on it being peasants of the neighbourhood, will benefit by it if it should lead to peaceable traffic, and the abolition of insecurity and blackmail.

We descended the gloomy gorge that leads to Jericho and the valley of the Jordan, and found our tents pitched at the clear spring known as "Elisha's Fountain." Near here are numerous caves in the sides of the steep hills and cliffs inhabited from of old by anchorites. The modern anchorites (for some of the holes are still inhabited) cannot be wholly given up to the pious contemplation; for a little time before our visit one of them, having in vain demanded money of the Greek Patriarch at Jerusalem, shot at him and wounded him in the hand. And we met some soldiers who told us that in consequence of this affair they had been engaged in removing certain hermits out of their caves.

The weather was very windy and showery, and lightning was playing about when we went to bed, but we fell comfortably to sleep at once. Indeed, there is nothing much pleasanter than sleeping in a tent when you are pleasantly tired with the day's exercise, and the wind rushes through the canvas; provided, that is, that you keep yourself warm, and that the tent does not blow away. Often have we slept under a perfect torrent or cascade of air, wrapped in flannel clothing, and with our heads covered with flannel shawls. The air you breathe is so exquisitely pure that you sleep as soundly and happily as a child, and if you dream at all it is of such things "as give delight and hurt not," and your slumber is of a kind that wraps a man all round like a cloak, as Sancho Panza says.

About midnight, just as I was engaged in a charming flight of fancy, in which I was about to conclude a bargain for the purchase of three rooms full of splendid old Italian pictures and furniture at an unheard-of sacrifice on the part of the seller, I became aware of a swaying motion as of a ship at sea; there was a cry from without, a great flapping within, and over went the table that served as washstand, with the tin jugs and basins; chairs and clothes were tumbled together; and my wife's voice, buried under folds of raging canvas, appealed to me for help. In a moment, before I could get up to assist, George, always watchful, accompanied by some of his men, was inside the tent holding up the pole which was just about to fall, while the rest tightened the pegs and made fast the ropes without, so that we still had a roof over our heads. Whatever the weather, George has always contrived to keep that for us.

Many tourists while at Jericho bathe in the Dead Sea and the Jordan, and for very shame I could not pass by without doing so. But my experience was peculiar. I had with me one of the Jericho sheiks, and one of our muleteers, and we rode first to the Dead Sea. Its waters are generally perfectly still, and of a splendid blue colour, about equally compounded of the sapphire and the aqua-marine stone. But now owing to the storm they were very rough, the waves ran high, and for some two hundred yards from the shore were of an ugly muddy brown. It seemed for all the world like the English Channel on a raw and gusty day in October. I looked askance at it as I undressed, but felt bound to go in. The waves very promptly knocked me down, and filled my mouth, nose, and eyes with their strong brine. Again I tried, and again; picking up one after another of the bare branches of trees which are carried down by the Jordan and washed on to the shores of this strange lake, with which I tried to steady myself as I walked in. But the force of the waves, aided by the great floating power of the water twisted the branches out of my hands, and knocked me down time after time; until feeling that I had done enough for principle I acknowledged that the victory did not lie on my side, and scrambled out smarting most unpleasantly all over my face.

Then we galloped off to the Jordan, where I thought I should succeed better. So I cast about for a suitable place to jump in, for I did not like to crawl in ignominiously at the Roman Catholic pilgrims' bathing-place, near which we were, and which would have been the wisest course to adopt; I wanted to take a header. So procuring a long stick I ascended the stream a little, and made sure by sounding with it of a deep spot under an overhanging tree. In I plunged, intending to swim down to the regular bathing-place, where I knew there must be a good bottom for getting out. Down I came with the fast-flowing yellow flood striking out in the fullest enjoyment: but when I was just about to put my foot to the ground I was brought up sharp with a tremendous blow on my right breast; if it had struck me on the heart it would I think have killed me on the spot. I had come down on to the end (fortunately not very sharp) of a stake pointing up-stream, and driven in to mark the upper boundary of the bathing-place, but which was hidden owing to the rains having raised the surface of the river. I had some difficulty in crawling out again, and was black and blue in the chest for a month afterwards. There is nothing like a little experience to teach one wisdom. I shall not do that again, and I shall remember that "Jordan overfloweth all his banks all the time of harvest." [1]

[1] Joshua.

THE RIVER JORDAN.

CHAPTER II.

THE CAMP OF THE ADWAN.

"His substance also was seven thousand sheep, and three thousand camels, and five hundred yoke of oxen and five hundred she-asses, and a very great household; so that this man was the greatest of all the men of the East."—JOB.

AFTER staying two nights at Jericho, we struck the tents in the interval between two heavy showers, and started for the wooden bridge which was erected over the Jordan a few years ago to the north of the pilgrim bathing-places. Our way lay for the most part over low hills composed of soil, which is in appearance like heaps of the refuse of chemical works, with intervening scrub of the so-called juniper bushes which afford cover for snakes. These hills were extremely slippery after the rain, and baggage-mules and horses—even the mares of the Beduins—had much difficulty in keeping their footing; indeed several of them fell down. This was succeeded by scrub, and then appeared the yellow rushing Jordan, on the further or east edge of which was a thick jungle of trees and bushes.

The wooden bridge is fastened by a gate at each end to facilitate the collection of tolls, and the gatekeeper lives in a little hut on the west side. We took our lunch in a small courtyard in front of this wretched place in company with Beduin dogs and cats and a puddle of ill odour; and there wrapped up in my warm cloak, I had a pleasant little nap *al fresco* in spite of mud and rain.

Then crossing over the bridge we entered upon a wooded country with some cultivated land. We kept near to the banks of a stream which falls into the Jordan, and by the side of which we saw many storks and kingfishers. Then we began to ascend the foot hills of the mountains of Gilead, getting splendid views backwards of the Dead Sea, the Plain of Jericho, the Valley of the Jordan, and the Judæan mountains beyond, in a Constable-like effect of cloud and sunshine, and found our camp fixed at Tell Nimrin. To the east of us were the rugged hills up which our next day's journey was to lead us, and upon whose summits we had so often longed to wander.

We had six Adwan men with us, and two more sheiks of that tribe came to see us here. One, a very pleasant-looking old fellow, had had in past years to go to Constantinople to obtain pardon for killing a Turkish officer and eight soldiers who had visited the tribe on a tax-collecting expedition. But the Adwan are now on friendly terms with the Government, the party against peace having come to an end with Sheik Goblan's death.[1] The sheiks asked what news from London. Would there be war between Turkey and Russia? Was London as big as Jerusalem? They certainly did not believe me when I told them that

[1] See page 292.

London had about one hundred and fifty times the population of El Kuds.

We saw a wild boar running by the stream below, and at sunset heard the sharp, whining, cat-like bark of the jackals, always a delightful sound to us, as it reminds us that we are on our happy gipsy wanderings in the Syrian land.

The next day we journeyed to Arak el Emir, following the windings of a very rough mountain track through a grassy country, and ascending a good deal, for this place is two thousand seven hundred feet above the Dead Sea. The day was cool, cloudy, and pleasant, the air exhilarating, and the ride delightful. But the rain had fallen very heavily at Arak el Emir, and the camping ground there was very damp. The ruins at this spot (the ancient Tyrus) are placed on an admirable site, and are particularly interesting as being, according to Major Conder, the only relic remaining of the Jewish architecture of the days of Judas Maccabæus. The stones of which they are composed are of great size, so that three courses carried the wall of the temple up to the roof, and the capitals of the great pillars are remarkable for their resemblance to Egyptian work. Not far from the ruins are extensive caves two stories in height, which I entered, in the upper tier of which, according to the same authority, there are mangers for one hundred horses. It was very cold at night here, and blew hard, but we were none the worse for that.

Down the steep slope of the hill, on which what remains of Tyrus still stands, we scrambled on our sure-footed little horses to the stream below. It flows through thickets of oleanders, then all covered with red blossoms, which swept past us, under our hands, against our faces, and over our heads, as we pushed down to the edge of the water, passed through it, and mounted up the opposite side. All the streams in the lands of Gilead and Moab are fringed with oleanders in full bloom in the spring, and nothing is more beautiful than the red blossoms. The flowers of the oleanders do not keep fresh for long after they are gathered, for the plant being of a thirsty nature, they are very sensitive to the heat of the sun; but when the supply is so abundant that does not matter much. We stick them into the headgear of our horses, and often cover the tent-pole with them, from the top of the table upward as high as we can reach, until they make a splendid show. It is said that snakes will never come near the oleander, which is an important point, as snakes are somewhat numerous in this country.

We climbed up a steep hill side and along a winding track; then down into a deep valley and across another track fringed in like manner; then up an extremely sharp ascent for one thousand or fifteen hundred feet, from near the top of which we obtained more splendid views of the Dead Sea, the Jordan Valley, and the Judæan hills. The country through which we were passing was most charming. The hills were covered with grass, except a few patches of barley, most of it wild. We passed Syrian oaks in full leaf, and many-hued kingfishers and blue pigeons were flying by. For the most part there was no track; and of course no enclosures of any kind exist in this wide, open country; and we simply followed our Beduin guides wherever they led the way, enjoying the glorious air and view, and with well-deserved confidence in the sure-footedness of our horses' feet.

At last we entered a large, narrow, grassy valley, and groups of camels, cattle of the small Beduin kind, sheep and horses grazing, told us that we were approaching the camp of the Adwan. Soon a turn of this valley brought us into a larger one, and the " black booths " of the Beduins appeared before us on the slope above the west side of the clear, bubbling brook. On the east side of the stream, and about half a mile from the great tent of the Sheik Ali Diab, we saw our own tents pitched.

The Adwan are celebrated amongst the tribes of the Beduins. They can bring about eight hundred horsemen into the field, and although they are much less in number than the Beni Sokr and the Aenezeh, who in Bible and Beduin language are "like the stars of heaven for multitude" (*i.e.*, can show as many thousands as the Adwan can hundreds of warriors), they are much respected and feared for their fighting and cattle-lifting powers.

Several of the sheiks came to visit us in our hut, and amongst them the head of all, Ali Diab. His father is still living, being, according to Beduin report, a hundred and fifteen years of age, though probably not really over eighty; but he has surrendered the government to his son. Ali Diab looks about sixty, and is a man of very remarkable appearance. A high Roman nose, shaped almost like an eagle's beak, sunken cheeks, heavy eyebrows, " an eye like Mars to threaten and command,"—and a peaked beard, give him a most haughty, aristocratic look. One might take him for some mediæval warrior king, stern, even ruthless, accustomed to command and to be obeyed, and yet capable of generous acts. Many are the stories of his fights and adventures.

> "And to that dauntless temper of his mind
> He hath a wisdom that doth guide his valour
> To act in safety."

Now (1890), owing to the death of the head of the Beni Sokr, whose sons are yet young, Ali Diab has become a kind of leader amongst all the tribes that dwell beyond Jordan between the Jaulan and the Hauran on the north and the river Arnon on the south; and is in particular the chief amongst the Beduins of this district, who adopt the policy of semi-submission to the Turkish Government. We found him polite in manner, but taciturn; but as George says, "A high man do not speak much."

Ali Diab is somewhat liberal in the matter of wives, marrying a new one every three or four months. He divorces old ones as frequently, and generously bestows them upon the less important members of his tribe. He has one chief old wife who looks after his harem and domestic affairs. But even she cannot keep absolute order in the female quarter of the great tent; for he complained to my wife that his wives were always quarrelling, and that it made his head ache. What did she advise him to do? She suggested that it might be best to reduce the establishment to one. But if he had only one, what could he do when she got old? She observed that with age would come wisdom, but the old reprobate did not seem to think much of that.

We asked what he thought about the weather. Was the rainy season over? He replied, "If it please God to send rain, it is well. If it please him not to send rain, it is well also." He was feeling ill. Could we give him a little medicine? The damp had affected him, and we thought a little chlorodyne was the right thing for him. He liked it so well that he sent for several more doses. You must not give more than one dose of medicine at a time to a Beduin. If you give him a bottle full nothing will induce him not to take it all at a draught if he thinks it good, so as to get well at once. He asked how the Queen of England was. Had she any children? Yes, many. And grandchildren? Yes, many more. "May God bless them," said the old sheik, and, mounting his beautiful mare, departed with a lordly air, inviting us to a feast in his great tent.

An hour or two later we mounted our horses and rode with George to the feast. The tent was about eighty feet long, open on the whole length of that side of it which looked towards the valley, except for one end which contained the apartment of the women. I will describe the scene, which is similar to what we found in the tents of the sheiks of other tribes.

Ali Diab sat on a carpet with his back towards the closed back of the tent, his youngest son on his right, and his nephew on his left, and the more important members of the tribe near to him. Others were placed according to their several ranks in the estimation of the tribe on carpets laid opposite to, and on each side of him, so as to form a small square. In the middle of this square was a heap of hot wood ashes, from which an old slave picked live embers, which he held with a pair of little tongs to any one who wished to light narghilé or cigarette. Ali Diab sent for some cushions from the women's apartment to be put at our backs, beautiful Persian rugs having already been spread where we sat. Our place was on the sheik's left, next to the nephew. The tent was full of people, and just in front of it the sheik's mare was tethered; many Beduins came and went, sitting, smoking, and staring at us for a little while, and then departing as if to make room for more; and when an important man came into the little square Ali Diab rose up in honour of the comer, and all rose with him.

Lemonade was brought in a bowl, and then poured into glasses, and little cups of coffee without sugar (Beduin fashion) was handed about, first to us, and then to the rest sitting in the square. From where we sat we could see not only all the people in the tent and without, but beyond them the valley which was spread out before us. Ali Diab was silent, and we enjoyed sitting still and looking about us. Presently a great bowl was brought in containing a whole sheep stuffed with rice and pistachio nuts, excellently cooked, and laid upon Arab loaves of bread made in the form of pancakes. A few spoons were stuck into it for our use, and we were invited to be the first to put our hands in the dish. With some anxiety we did so, but found it very good—a most savoury mess. We forebore to eat more than two mouthfuls, however, wishing to acquire a reputation for good breeding, and when we had eaten, Ali Diab motioned to the Beduins to draw near. He then stood up and withdrew a little from the place where he had been sitting, as if to remove restraint from the feast; and (except just in front of us, where a lane or opening was left, lest, as we supposed, any one should turn his back to us) men sat all round the bowl, eating heartily and fast, and then withdrawing so as to leave room for others. They sat edgeways close to each other, the face of each towards the back of his neighbour, and each held his right arm stretched towards the dish. The most important ate first, and were followed by the others according to their degrees, and in a very short time the great mass of food had disappeared.

One of the head men told us that he would like to go to England. We asked him what he would do there. He explained that he should first go to stay with the Queen, and then he would go to visit Napoleon, King of France. The Beduins do not read the newspapers, and he was a little behind the time. No doubt he thought that the Queen and Napoleon III. lived in great tents like Ali Diab, where all could come and go at pleasure, and eat of the hospitable dish.

George whispered to us that the sheik had killed two sheep in our honour, and that we must, according to Beduin custom, make him a suitable present; so, having nothing with us, we asked the sheik's son to come back with us to visit us in our tent. He came, and we gave him a small revolver, which he took away rejoicing.

That night the whole of the Adwan camp was alive with fires, but before they were ablaze we saw by the fading evening light a long string of camels with their little ones returning from the pasture grounds. They were not the hard-worked beasts of burden with the hair worn off their sides and daubed with a composition smelling like tar, which are so plentiful on the way between Jaffa and Jerusalem, and on the caravan route from Jerusalem to Damascus, and which still keep up a doubtful contest for existence with the well-managed French waggons on the great road between the latter city and Beyrout. These were the beautiful camels of the Beduins, kept for breeding, for milk, and for meat.

The next day the chief wife of Ali Diab came to call upon my wife and examined her with a critical eye. She mentioned that there had been a wedding in the camp the evening before, and that the bride ran away in the night, and escaped up a narrow valley to the east of our tents (which I afterwards explored), and that fifteen horsemen being sent in pursuit she was found in the morning and brought back. The poor girl was only fourteen years of age, and probably had not been consulted about the marriage. She must have passed close to our tents which were placed at the entrance of this valley.

We learnt from the Adwan that Miss Finkelstein, whose interesting lectures on Bible life, as illustrated by modern Syrian customs, are well known in England, had often visited them, and we understood that she had purchased from them the tents and appliances which she exhibits to her audiences.[1]

---

[1] If our ministers of religion had attended these lectures and listened to them with "an attent ear," we should not so often hear them speak of the grand old sheiks of the old Testament as if they were a kind of superior Sunday-school teacher.

I rode up to the top of a hill about one thousand feet above the valley to see the ruins of Heshbon. Here are hewn stones strewn over, a space of forty or fifty acres, but I found nothing of very particular interest. Upon returning Sheik Ali Abdul Aziz begged us to visit the tents of his family, at the distance of about a mile from the main encampment, as he wished my wife to see his latest bride. We were received with a hearty welcome by his chief wife, all his relations, and various dogs and donkeys. After the usual coffee and cigarettes, a remarkably fine camel appeared, caparisoned with many carpets arranged like a howdah amongst which the bride sat. It was the animal with the trappings which had been used in her marriage procession. She made the camel kneel down, descended from the seat, and placed my wife on his back in her stead; and the camel rose again and bore her off to our tents amidst the applause of the Beduins, who sang a bridal song as the beautiful creature moved off.

The Adwan men are, for the most part, fine, tall, and handsome, and, like all the Beduins whom we have seen, have remarkably well-formed noses.[1] The women would be handsome if they were not tattooed about the chin and mouth. They do not cover their faces. The children are pretty, but terribly dirty. My wife had given the chief wife of Ali Abdul Aziz a pair of scissors, and he called in the evening to say that his

[1] In the tribes to the south and east of the Dead Sea—the Howeytát, Hamèydeh, and Keraki—the handsome Jewish character of the nose is very observable, and we noticed the same characteristic in the Beduins of Sûf near Jerash.

bride would also like a pair. We had not another to spare and offered a coloured silk handkerchief as a substitute. But he maintained that this was not so good as scissors. However, upon our expressing our willingness to take the handkerchief back, he slowly put it into his pocket and departed.

CHAPTER III.

MOUNT NEBO.

"We will, if the day be clear, show you the Delectable Mountains."—"PILGRIM'S PROGRESS."

OUR path to Pisgah (Mount Nebo) lay along the mountain side, and after about an hour's ride a turn in the valley brought us in full view of the plain of the Jordan and the Judæan hills, under the unwonted aspect of cloud and sunshine, chasing one another as on a changeful April day at home. Then we passed along the side of a deep gorge, and by a very rough track to the so-called Spring of Moses, which issues forth from the rock just above the head of a narrow gully, and runs down the face of the cliff into the ravine below. Another branch of it rushes abundantly out of a little cave a few yards further on. As we went along we could see the clouds gathering on the Judæan hills on the other side of the Jordan valley. They seemed to form in four great columns in order to cross the valley to the eastward, and between these dark columns we could see the sunlit slopes—an extremely strange and beautiful sight. But soon all united for the attack, hill and valley were blotted out from view, and our cloaks were wet through. So we took shelter under an over-hanging rock and ate our lunch. The rain ceasing we hung out our cloaks to dry, and walked back to the spring, noticing as we did so a wolf steal down the ravine below us.

An hour more brought us to the summit of Mount Nebo, which is in spring a grass-grown hill, and is but little raised above the high land from which it springs. On the top are the remains of a building supposed to be a Christian Church, and just below them is a large vaulted cistern now empty, but capable of holding a large supply of water.

All travellers in this country in the spring must be surprised at the contrast in regard to fertility between Gilead or Moab, and Judæa. One feels inclined to say to the Beni Israel :

> "Have you eyes ?
> Could you on this fair mountain leave to feed
> And batten on this moor ?"

The best of the milk and honey are on the east side of the Jordan now. It is obvious that only a very distant and partial view of the fertile plains beyond the Judæan hills could have been obtained from Nebo. The view is principally bounded by their barren slopes. And even the vegetation in the Jordan valley is now, for the most part, very poor and uninviting. There is a striking passage in Macaulay's essay on Bacon in which he compares the author of the "Novum Organum" to the great Hebrew lawgiver standing on Pisgah, with a wilderness of dreary sands and bitter waters behind him which the multitude alone could see, while he beheld the long course of fertilizing rivers running through ample pastures. If Macaulay had ever stood there himself, he would have modified this passage. And yet what Moses did see was no doubt striking enough, for the Jordan valley is capable of the highest cultivation, and in all probability at the time of the Hebrew invasion received it.

The distance from the Sea of Galilee to the Dead Sea is about sixty miles and the fall in elevation, or rather I should say in depression, for both are below the line of the Mediterranean, is about six hundred feet. The valley is nowhere more than eight or ten miles broad; the Jordan winds so much that it runs over a course of about one hundred and eighty miles; and several large streams join it (coming principally from the east side), so that it would be a very easy thing to irrigate the valley. And as may be seen in the garden of the clean and comfortable little inn recently erected at Jericho, and in other cutivated spots near to that place, wherever the water is carried the vegetation is most abundant. And yet there is, speaking practically, no irrigation throughout this great depression of the Jordan valley, which has an almost tropical climate, and would return to the cultivator a thousand-fold. Nearly the whole of the land is said to be the private property of the Sultan; and the story goes that some years ago a French company offered to buy it from him, that the price was agreed upon, but that the bargain went off, because the company made a stipulation that the Turkish Government should keep a thousand soldiers in the valley to keep off the Beduins; for it is useless to sow if the marauder is to reap.

The basin of the Sea of Galilee is another barren

place, which must once have been extremely fertile and could readily be made so again. But the insecurity caused by a weak and inert government "dulls the edge of husbandry" throughout Syria, except in the Lebanon where a different state of things prevails.

MASHITA.

CHAPTER IV.

MASHITA.

" My name is Ozymandias, King of kings ;
Look on my works, ye mighty, and despair ;
Nothing else remains. Round the decay
Of that colossal wreck, boundless and bare,
The lone and level sands stretch far away."
SHELLEY

FROM Mount Nebo a very pleasant journey of an hour and a half's duration over uplands which reminded us much of the country about Stonehenge, brought us to the little town of Madeba ; and from Madeba we were to visit Mashita.

Mashita, or Umshetta, as we have always heard it called by the Arabs, is a very extensive ruin which was first discovered by Canon Tristram in 1872; and is supposed to be the remains of a Persian palace of the seventh century A.D., built by Chosroes II., of the Sassanian Dynasty. It is not in the territory of the Adwan, but in that of Beni Sokr Beduins. We were, however, very anxious to visit it, and had had it specially mentioned in the contract made before the Consul, as one of the places to which our guides were to take us. Only very few travellers have seen it, and indeed when we revisited Mashita in 1890, the Adwan men who then accompanied us told us that only one other traveller (an American) had been conducted by them to the place. He must, I think, have been Dr. Merrill, who visited Mashita in 1876.[1]

Although our Adwan had agreed to take us to the place, yet they made objections when it came to the point. Mashita is four hours' ride from Madeba, and there was the risk of an attack by the Beni Sokr. Notwithstanding the recent establishment of more friendly relations between the two tribes by means of the marriage of the daughter of the reigning sheik of one to the Ruler of the other, blood feuds still exist amongst certain families on both sides, and our guides did not at all like the journey. We, however, insisted upon their carrying out their agreement, and got them to make an early start on the morning of the twentieth of April.

The number of Adwan whom we had with us was now reduced to four. The head of the party was Sheik

[1] Dr. Merrill's "East of the Jordan."

Ali Abdul Aziz, who was a big, heavy man with an enormous appetite. Another, whose real name I will not give, lest by any possibility the tales I have to tell of him should get him into trouble, but whom I will call Abou Seyne (the Father of Naughtiness), was a fine, tall, handsome fellow, wonderfully skilful and active with his spear, sword, and gun, who rode his mare with the most perfect command over her, without the use of bit, stirrups, or girths, and who was probably the most accomplished horse-stealer and cattle-lifter of the tribe. With him we became very friendly, and he travelled with us again during part of our journey in 1890. The third member of our party was named Shebeeb, a man of quite another type—of the bluest blood of the tribe, tall, thin, and elegant, with most beautifully formed hands, and a very charming manner and address, the very type of a wily attractive Beduin. The fourth man had nothing about him worthy of particular notice.

The country through which we had to pass was undulating, and it was curious to see how these men reconnoitred the country. On approaching each eminence they separated, and mounted it from different parts, rushing up at a gallop. On the top they dismounted and examined the country round, and my fieldglasses were called into use, although I could not see much better with them, powerful as they were, than they with their unaided sight, and they did not seem to be able to use them satisfactorily. Being satisfied that no one was in sight they descended, and proceeded to the next eminence up which they rushed in like manner. We met no one on the way, but when our guides reached the ruins they mounted on the walls, and kept an anxious look-out on all sides for the Beni Sokr.

The ruins at Mashita cover a large extent, and consist of a walled enclosure about one hundred and sixty yards square, at the north end of the inside of which are the remains of a large building, supposed to be a palace. A great part of the enclosure wall which faces the south and contains a large gateway, is most elaborately ornamented with carvings of designs of a Persian character, consisting of an embossed pattern of zig-zags and rosettes, and of delicate tracery of foliage, animals, and fruits. The string courses are also most beautifully adorned by tracery. The lower ones are so near the ground, that they give one the impression that the land round the building has been raised since it was erected, which is very likely to have been the case by soil blown in from the surrounding country during the dry season. To the east of the main gateway I noticed a cavity, looking down into which I saw courses of stone descending for several feet below the surface of the ground; and this particular spot had apparently been used for the purpose of burial as I observed a skull and some human bones there.[1] The main erection and enclosures are built to the cardinal points of the compass; and the appearance of the ruin fully supports the theory that the buildings were never finished, as there is nothing like the requisite amount of material on the spot for completion of the work;

[1] "So vast,
So sumptuous, yet withal so perishing;
Even as the corpse that rests beneath their walls" (Shelley).

nor are there any other buildings near enough to make it probable that they were used up in construction elsewhere. The outside of the west and inside of the east walls of the enclosure are much worn and decayed, whilst the inside of the west and outside of the east walls are fresh looking. The state of the parts exposed to the west is, no doubt, due to the westerly gales and rains.

After we had walked over the ruins, our guides only allowed us sufficient time for my wife to make a sketch, and for us both to take a little lunch, and then hurried us off towards Ammân (Rabbath Ammon). Our course lay again over the open country, and up and down low hills. Our guides again proceeded with extreme caution, and on approaching the first hill, three of them rode off to reconnoitre it in the usual fashion, galloping up, and spreading themselves out as they ascended. My wife and I rode together at some distance behind, and George was between us and the Beduins.

I noticed a man suddenly appear on the side of the hill, and come a little way down it in our direction. Then three of our Beduins, who had previously passed by the place where he appeared without having seen him, galloped back to him, and the fourth, who was a little behind, galloped forward to join them, and they all surrounded the man. George hurried forward; there was evidently something in the wind, so I followed at full speed to learn what it was. Then I found that they had caught the man, who was an Arab bearing a heavy club in his hands, such as is generally carried by Beduins on foot. Our guides thought he was acting as a spy for some of the Beni Sokr, whom they supposed to be lying in ambush for them, and they were proposing to kill him at once. But fortunately George knew the man, and the latter ran to George for protection, and kissed his foot, entreating his interference, which was promptly given. He was in a very excited state when I came up. He was soon allowed to go free on my request, and we passed on.

PART OF SOUTH FRONT OF ENCLOSURE WALL, MASHITA.
(*Drawn from an imperfect photograph by F. Wiltshire.*)

CATTLE IN THE ZERKA (JABBOK) NEAR AMMÂN.

CHAPTER V.

AMMÂN AND ES SALT.

"With nodding arches, broken temples spread,
The very tombs now vanished like their dead."
                                                POPE.

AS we approached Ammân (Rabbath Ammon), we saw plenty of cultivated land. The sun was bright, the clouds were magnificent, the air fresh and exhilarating, though a little cold; the wild flowers were abundant, and in the fields red with poppies the storks were walking about, except when they rose lazily into the air and floated round and round in the strong sunlight; and the riding was most delightful. Two or three miles before we got to Ammân we came to some sarcophagi, and some rock-tombs lying below the surface of the ground, in which latter we could see the " loculi " as we passed; and we noticed many openings in the rocky ground which appeared to be old cisterns.[1]

Here we had a taste of Abou Seyne's marauding powers. Seeing a horse tethered by the track as we neared Ammân he rode quietly up to it, dismounted, and took possession of it. He was just walking away with it, and I was telling George to let him know that I would have no horse-stealing while he was with us, when the proprietor appeared; and Abou Seyne handed the horse back to him with a graceful air, as if he had been anxiously looking for the true owner. We learnt afterwards, that that night, while all slept he arose, took his arms, and mounting his mare rode to the place where this horse had been tethered, cut the rope, and brought it away.

At Ammân there are very extensive Roman remains, and a great theatre with numerous rows of seats cut out of the side of the hill. A colony of Circassians has been allowed to settle here by the Turkish Govern-

[1] In many parts of Syria, especially in places at a distance from perennial streams, are found ancient disused cisterns, most of which require nothing beyond recementing to make them serviceable; but even those round Jerusalem, where the land is valuable, are neglected. The number and extent of these cisterns give one a strong impression of the former fertility of the country.

ment within the last few years. They, their cattle, and horses form a strange contrast to the Beduins and their animals. The Circassians, instead of being handsome, dignified, and graceful, are hard-featured, surly, and angular; and in place of flowing robes they wear tight-fitting, long white woollen coats. Their horses are little creatures, perhaps as useful, but not nearly so good-looking as those of the Beduins. Their cattle are much larger than any which the latter possess, and their little carts with solid round wheels are objects of wonder in a country otherwise quite devoid of vehicles. We wanted to have some clothes washed here, but the Circassians absolutely declined to wash for Christians.

On the hill above the town of Ammân, there are the remains of a castle or citadel which must once have been an extremely strong place. The hill is steep on all sides, and the walled enclosure is built with large hewn stones without cement.[1] In the middle of the enclosure is a square building, plain outside, but very beautifully ornamented within. It has been described as having been a Byzantine church, but is thought by Major Conder to be a Persian erection of the Sassanian age. The town is situated in a narrow valley, on both sides of a clear stream which flows through it. On the

[1] It would seem to have been in assaulting this citadel that Uriah the Hittite, being placed by David's orders "in the forefront of the hottest battle," was killed when David's men "were upon them (the children of Ammon), even unto the entering of the gate," and when "the shooters shot from off the wall" upon the Israelites (2 Samuel). The position of the gateway can be identified at the point where a neck of land connects the citadel with high land beyond.

slopes of the hills are numerous small caves, some of which have been used as tombs. One of the latter has a very beautiful and stately front of Roman work.

The geological formation in the neighbourhood is very strange, the strata being much curved and twisted; and the hills are extremely steep on every side; so that the numerous caves, the tops of which follow the curves of the strata, look forth upon the valleys like eyes peeping out from under the overhanging eyebrows of the arched tops.

At Ammân we presented our Beduins with a sheep, so that they might make a feast and be merry. In order to roast the meat they dug a hole in the ground, covered it over with large stones, and made a wood fire inside. When it ceased to burn in a flame, they laid the meat upon the embers, and covered up with mud the entrance and all the holes through which smoke issued, and left the meat in the oven to roast for about two hours. The oven was then opened, and the meat was picked out with the fingers, and washed in a dish containing salt water, and then placed in a large bowl from which it was eaten. We tasted a morsel, and found it very good. Sheik Ali Abdul Aziz managed to eat three-quarters of the whole sheep himself, and his three companions, who had gone to the little town to make purchases while the work was in progress, were much disappointed on their return with the remnant which he had left for their share.

The following day we set out for Es Salt. There was not a cloud in the sky, and the country looked delightfully green and fresh after the recent rains.

Our route lay over a very pleasant country with much cultivated land and pasturage on which large flocks browsed. On the way our charming friend Abou Seyne stole some clothing from a poor peasant which we made him give back, and later on I found him flourishing his sword over the head of another man from whom he wanted to take his cloak.

A little over three hours' quiet riding brought us to a fine ash tree, standing alone on a high hill, around which were some Arab graves. Here we rested under the shadow of the tree and took our lunch, while we enjoyed the wide view of hill and dale which lay before us.

Two hours more of up and down work brought us to Es Salt, which is two thousand seven hundred and fifty feet above the Mediterranean, but lies sheltered in a narrow valley. It is a strange looking place. The houses are built in terraces one above another on the steep side of two hills, and there are very beautiful gardens and orchards where the fresh green leaves of the fig-trees and pomegranates gladdened our eyes. The people were much interested in our arrival, and seem to pass the afternoon in watching us from their house-tops, except a considerable number of them who squatted on the ground in our immediate neighbourhood. Abou Seyne would not enter the town as he owed money there, and was also "wanted" by the Governor for some misdoings; for this town has a Turkish Governor or Kaimakâm.

In the evening we took a walk in the town with George and Sheik Ali Abdul Aziz, and then leaving it, crossed the brook at the bottom of the valley and sat by the side of the road while my wife made a little sketch. As we were thus engaged, the Kaimakâm, accompanied by his attendants, came bustling up to us, and asking in angry tones where we had come from, who we were, and what we meant by sketching, requested us to produce our passports, and told us to go to our tents, to consider ourselves under arrest, and not to leave them without his permission. We could not understand what had offended him in my wife sketching, as there is no kind of fortification at Es Salt. However, George called on him in the evening and soon put the matter right.

We found Sheik Ali Diab at Es Salt. It appeared that one of the people of his tribe residing there had had the misfortune, as he put it, to kill his servant for stealing. It struck us as rather an unreasonable thing for a Beduin to kill any one for that. The man had already been in prison for twenty-one days, and Ali Diab had come to pay something to the parents of the murdered man, and arrange matters with the Governor, and hoped to have his man out of prison shortly.

The next day we travelled to 'Ain Roman, a most delightful ride, in perfect weather, over a beautiful country of hill and dale, strewn with scarlet anemones. We passed many flocks of sheep, goats, and cattle. Many of the Beduin cattle here are extremely small, some of the cows being not much larger than a large Southdown sheep in England. 'Ain Roman is a spring which trickles down a gorge and joins the river Zerka—the Old Testament Jabbok—an important tributary of the Jordan. Near this place is a settlement of Turcomans. They have a larger and better breed of cattle than the Beduins, much resembling the Alderney in size, colour, and general appearance. The Turcomans, like the Circassians, are well armed, and are able to protect themselves against attacks from marauding tribes.

In the evening we walked down the gorge, through which the stream runs. Oleanders fringed its banks, and big rocks were strewn about on each side. It is a very picturesque place, and reminded us of a Dartmoor glen. Here were many of the large blue pigeons of Gilead, and other birds.

CHAPTER VI.

JERASH.

> "I sat beneath an olive's branches grey,
> And gaz'd upon the site of a lost town."
> SHELLEY.

ANOTHER most delightful day opened with the morrow. Again we were riding in air like an elixir of life over a charming country abounding in wild flowers.

We wound round the mountain sides looking down into the deep valleys, and following the steepest of paths, mounted over hill-tops, a long descent from which brought us to the river Zerka, where the red oleanders were in greater masses than ever, and stretched away by the sides of a long reach of the stream which we could see before us winding to the westward. We forded the little river and ascended the steep hill opposite, looking eagerly for the first sight of the ruins of Jerash. We passed outlying remains which gave us an idea of the extent of the suburbs of the ancient city, and in an hour after leaving the Zerka we had passed by the great gateway and ridden up the street of columns.

With some difficulty we found a convenient camping

place in the midst of the ruins, but when we revisited this place in 1890 the Circassians, who are settled here, compelled us to put our tents away from the most interesting part. They have happily built their own houses on that side of the stream which contains fewest remains, but they have ploughed up and enclosed much of the space on the other side, and grow corn in all the available spots, so that it is more difficult to get about than it was before their time. But by the aid of a little backsheesh all difficulties vanish. The situation of the city is delightful, the country round consists of fine rolling hills, and views of it are commanded from every part of the ruins.

The street of columns must have been a splendid and delightful place in the day of Jerash's glory. Many pillars still stand, although the majority have fallen; but the latter have simply been shaken down by an earthquake, and have only separated into the sections or drums of which they were originally composed; and the entablature which crowned them all still lies beside them. With small exception the whole is simply disjointed by the fall.

It would be a pleasant task to take up one's residence here for a time, and to rebuild this splendid street. It could easily be done, and would cost very little money. The climate is pleasant. The place is seventeen hundred feet above the Mediterranean Sea, and the heat cannot therefore be overpowering in the summer season. The Circassians would no doubt want something in the way of backsheesh to permit the rebuilding, but they would be more easily dealt with than the Beduins, and the offer of employment to them would be readily accepted. In residing at Jerash, however, one would have to look out for the snakes which are very numerous there.

Here we parted with our Adwan friends. The night before they left us we had a fantasia in the dining tent, consisting of singing, dancing, smoking, and pistol firing. Including both our own men and Beduins we had fourteen all smoking at once in the tent, so that the atmosphere was a little oppressive. Abou Seyne and four of our men performed several dances, and there was singing with a chorus in Arab style, accompanied by much clapping of hands. At frequent intervals some of the men fired off pistols from the tent door into the air, greatly to the satisfaction of the rest.

At Jerash we contracted with the Sheik of Sûf to accompany us as far as Tiberias for the price of five pounds sterling, nine days being allowed for the journey. When we were here again in 1890 we found that the Circassians had taken the conducting of the parties of the few tourists who visit Jerash into their own hands, and had driven the poor Sheik of Sûf off the field.[1]

The moon was nearly at the full when we were at Jerash, which enabled us to enjoy moonlight rambles amongst the ruins, and I would recommend travellers

---

[1] Perhaps it served him right, as travellers give him a bad name. But we had no complaint to make of him. This was the man who amongst the other testimonials from travellers of which he was proud had one which he was sure was good, as the Franghis always laughed when they read it. It was in these words, " I was a stranger and he took me in " (Dr. Merill's " East of the Jordan ")

to endeavour to arrange their visits so as to obtain this advantage. The effect of the moonlight pouring down upon the street of columns, the pillars of the Forum, the temples and theatres, is magnificent—a thing never to be forgotten. But the inhabitants are not accustomed to visitors, and the first night whilst we were wandering about enjoying the sight, some Circassian shepherds came running out at us with their guns, thinking that we had come to steal their cattle.

The headman of the Circassians told us that in 1887 the Beni Sokr Beduins came in great numbers to Jerash and fed their horses upon the standing corn belonging to the Circassians; that the latter went forth with their flint-lock guns to defend their possessions, but had to submit, for the Beni Sokr (who they mentioned were "as the sand of the seashore for multitude") displayed their Remington rifles. The Turkish Government will not allow its own subjects to carry breechloaders, lest they should be able to resist the Turkish troops; but they cannot prevent the Beduins from obtaining them, so that the more peaceable and settled inhabitants are often at a disadvantage from the want of proper means of defence against the Ishmaelites.

The Remingtons have no doubt been smuggled through the desert from Egypt. Great numbers were taken by the Soudanese from the army of the ill-fated Hicks Pasha, and some of those obtained from Arabi's army by English soldiers in the Anglo-Egyptian Expedition, and sold to native dealers, were no doubt conveyed in the same way. All these rifles being taken in war would be sold very cheap, so that the richer tribes are well supplied with formidable weapons; and ammunition can always be obtained at Damascus for breechloaders of all kinds, although I suppose the trade is contrary to the law, as the price is high.

JERASH.

CHAPTER VII.

AJILÛN AND EL HUSN.

"And flowers azure black and streaked with gold,
Fairer than any wakened eyes behold."
SHELLEY.

"Heaviness endureth for a night, but joy cometh in the morning."—PSALMS.

FROM Jerash we turned to the north towards the Jebel Ajilûn, and rode over a country even pleasanter than any which we had yet traversed. For the first hour we passed through an upland partly covered with barley fields and partly overgrown with forest. After leaving the village of Sûf which is built on the slope of a steep hill, from whose side abundant waters issue, the woodland increased, and the cultivation came to an end. The country reminded us of the New Forest, save that the trees were not so large as in Hampshire; yet there were many of a good size with widespreading branches, amongst which were the large blue wild pigeons which I have mentioned.

Several hours of very delightful riding brought us to a rocky glen embosomed deep in trees. It was like one of Salvator Rosa's robber valleys, only much prettier. Here we noticed a large grey squirrel with black bars upon its fur gambolling amongst the branches. Just as this ravine opens out towards the little town of Ajilûn there is a large cavern also much in the style of Salvator, in which were a herd of black cattle; and into this we rode and sheltered for a little from the sun, while George lighted candles and showed us its recesses. Passing on to Ajilûn we pitched our tents in a grove of fine old olive trees just above a beautiful clear stream, and all the population came out to sit in rows in front of our tents, and enjoy a hearty stare at us.

The Kaimakâm, a pleasant mannered, but shabby old Turk, came to call upon us. He told us that the people of this district were very troublesome when first he came into it, but that he sent one hundred and fifty of them to prison at Damascus, *where one hundred and twenty had the misfortune to die*, and that since then the people had behaved better.[1] He said that the land is very rich, not only for agricultural purposes, but also in minerals; gold and silver even existing; there is, however, no capital or enterprise. The climate he considered delightful—not too hot in summer. The fig, olive, pomegranate, lemon, and vine are very productive here, but the grapes are used exclusively for raisins.

The old Greek Priest who looked miserably poor came to see us, and we gave him a little money. He seemed a kind-hearted old fellow.

At a great height above this valley stand the ruins

---

[1] I wonder if he was the Kaimakâm commended for his energetic conduct in Laurence Oliphant's "Land of Gilead." That book contains a good account of Ajilûn. See also Schumacher's "Northern Ajilûn," published in 1890 by the Palestine Exploration Fund.

of an enormous Crusaders' Castle (the Castle of Rubud), and I rode up with some of our servants to inspect it. It is difficult to get into, owing to the dangerous state of the bridge over the dry moat: but the view from the summit is magnificent. The valley of the Jordan, the plain of Esdraelon, the Sea of Galilee, and Mount Hermon are all clearly visible from it.

On coming down a man rushed up to me and kissed my hand, putting it to his forehead with much fervour, and began a rapid speech. He was a shoemaker who had mended a shoe for one of our muleteers, and done it so badly that the man, having easily pulled it to pieces with his hand, refused to pay anything, and this was an appeal to my intervention. On inquiry into the merits of the case I gave judgment that the work should be done again properly and then paid for, and both men went away satisfied.

As we were about to start the next morning (the twenty-seventh of April) we saw a very pretty sight. Along the path through the olive trees just above our camp came a procession of about twenty men on horseback, accompanying four camels with erections like howdahs on their backs, in which sat women and girls. This was a wedding party going to a neighbouring village. In the dappled morning light, with the guns and spears of the horsemen glancing in the sun, the light colours of the women's dresses, the trappings of the camels, and the joyous look of everything, the picture was a charming one.

We were still journeying in the same delightful woodland country through the forest trees and out into the glades. Stately hollyhocks of the most delicate colour, white and blue larkspur, scarlet tulips and anemones, the wild cherry in full blossom, primroses, and a little blue starred flower lined the way, whilst lilac scented the air. Almost the only human beings we saw were some pretty ragged Beduin children on donkeys, looking for all the world like Gainsborough's gipsies wandering in Gainsborough's wood. Then passing out of the forest we came to the brow of a hill from which we looked down upon the plain of the western Hauran which leads to Damascus, and the long snowy summit of Mount Hermon. From here George said that he could see a glittering spot which must be that oldest of all historical cities, but my eyes could not make it out. The men of Sûf who served us as guides were stirred here to show us their horsemanship, and whirled round one another in mimic sham hostility. Descending a long valley in which the afternoon sun was extremely oppressive, we found ourselves at the large village of El Husn, and pitched our tents in a grassy hollow hard by.

That night was one of the most anxious I ever passed. The heat had brought upon my wife a very severe feverish attack. Shiverings were followed by an extremely high pulse, and by midnight she was in a delirium. I never felt so helpless. We were several days' journey from the nearest doctor, and there seemed no possibility of getting her into a state of repose, as the mosquitoes which had not troubled us in any other place were here almost maddening. Very happily I had brought with me for emergencies a very strong dose of sleeping medicine, which I had saved out of a bottle prescribed for her in Jerusalem, where she had been seriously ill. This and a resolute holding of her hands enclosed in mine so to keep them from the wretched insects, while I covered her face with handkerchiefs, at last got her some sleep, and the restless tossing to and fro yielded after many hours to something like rest. All night long I sat in the chair by her side looking out into a splendid moonlight night (for the tent door was turned up to admit every breath of air), wondering if I was to bury her in this distant land.

At dawn I sent George to set up the dining tent on the hill above, for I thought that change of air was an important matter, and felt that we must get rid of the mosquitoes. And when it was ready we placed her wrapped in blankets on a donkey, and upheld by willing hands on both sides we managed to take her in safety to the higher ground where the air was fresh and cool. She began to mend at once, and all anxiety was over. I went out for a little walk, and when I came back, found a Greek Priest, belonging to the village of El Husn, kneeling by her side and praying over her.

This happened to be the day of St. Lazarus in the calendar of the Greek Church, and about five and twenty children of that community marched up the hill singing as they went, and drew up in front of our tents to give us a representation of the resurrection of the Saint. Six little girls stood on one side to represent Mary and Martha, and six little boys on the other for Christ and His disciples. One boy lay down between the two groups to counterfeit Lazarus in the tomb. He was completely covered with a large cloth or veil. The rest of the children stood by as spectators. The performers held stretched out between them and above the prostrate form of Lazarus a long ornamented MS. scroll, each group holding one end of it. From this boys and girls sang alternately, and in a touching, sympathetic way a verse of the New Testament narration of the event. At the right moment Lazarus sprang up, and running into our tent kissed our hands, and put them to his head.

After this our servants who had been most kind and helpful over the illness gave a fantasia in honour of the recovery. We had a wild night—a great storm arising—and lay down with our clothes on lest the tents should blow away from this exposed spot. But George watched over us, and our canvas, though the rain descended and the winds blew, fell not. But some little black kids pushed into the tent to get shelter from the storm, and were not at all inclined to go out again.

Early next morning all the camp ran out notwithstanding the rain to see the same wedding procession that had passed us at Ajilûn. This was the third day of the ceremonies. The horsemen made a great show on approaching El Husn, careering round and round over the plain with their drawn swords, and firing off their guns. The Sheik of El Husn killed four sheep, and made a great feast for the wedding, and George went off to witness the festivities, and fired off a number of shots in honour of the event.

On the first day of the ceremonies the friends of the bridegroom came to fetch the bride who was a daughter of the Sheik of Ajilûn, and her father invited the friends to feast and sleep at his house for two nights, and on the third day they returned with the bride to the bridegroom's village. The invitations of the Sheik of El Husn were given or "sealed" by the sheik tying a handkerchief round the neck of the bride's camel. There would afterwards be a feast and rejoicing at the village of the bridegroom, and then the bride would be led to the bridegroom's house where she would be left, and all the friends would then disperse. During the whole of this time the bridegroom does not appear, and it may be that the young people have never seen one another before the marriage.

We stayed another day here that my wife might gather strength, which she did very rapidly. We were troubled to get a little protection from the weather for the horses, mules, and donkeys, but we found a cave near the top of the hill, and after the entrance had been cleared a little, it made a good shelter for them all, and for some of the muleteers also. These poor fellows sleep outside generally, wrapt in their thick coverings, but in very wet weather they often get ill, and are glad of quinine.

On the evening of the last day which we spent on the hill near El Husn George told us that a fine mare had been stabbed a little way down the hill. We had lanterns lighted, and went down the hill to see the poor creature. A young peasant who had been supplying fresh grass for our horses came with us. He was the nephew of the man to whom the mare belonged. He led the way, and we soon came to the carcass, which was already disembowelled. A hyena stole off as we came up.

We brought the young man back with us, made him sit down in the tent, and gave him some coffee and bread. He said that he was sixteen years old. He had two long plaits of black hair hanging down on each cheek, and his manner and gestures were very gentle and winning. He told us that his uncle had killed a man of the village in a quarrel, and that the relatives of the deceased had in revenge killed the mare. He said that he and his relations would kill one of the men who had destroyed the mare, or failing an opportunity to do so, they would kill his horse. We urged him to let the matter drop, and to allow the mare's life to stand for the man's, " and there an end"; but he said the man's life was nothing, that his uncle had killed him by accident, meaning only to hurt him, and that they must revenge the death of the mare.

On the summit of this hill I counted eight small circular basins, each about six inches in diameter, cut in the rocks near to one another. We have seen many such east of the Jordan. They are mentioned in Major Conder's writings.

CHAPTER VIII.

GADARA. A NIGHT ATTACK.

"To-morrow is uncertain, and how knowest thou that thou shalt live till to-morrow."—THOMAS A KEMPIS.

THE next day (the thirtieth of April) we travelled to Umkeis, the ancient Gadara. It was a beautiful morning; all nature was radiant after the rain. Our path lay for a while across a wide plain covered with tall green barley. The larks were singing, and the storks were floating lazily in the air. Having crossed the plain we began to ascend hills of a moderate height, descending again into valleys, in which there was much barley, interspersed with red poppies and other wild flowers. The summits of the hills were covered with wild thyme and mint, the scent from which was very pleasant. Then passing some strange looking villages we got on to the tableland, where the barley was waving in the wind. Keeping along this we got glimpses to the northward of some rocky valleys, which we thought must have led to the great gorge of the Sheri'at el-Mandhûr or Yarmûk river; and then we entered a very pleasant park-like country covered with trees and grass, but with stone breaking out on the surface. As we advanced the grass became less and the rocks increased, until the road became very difficult for the animals, as it consisted to a great extent of flat rocks with a smooth surface.

After a ride of about seven hours we reached the entrance to the village of Umkeis, and caught a view of the south end of the Sea of Galilee, which lay about two thousand feet below us. Near the village are many ancient stone sarcophagi with classical ornamental devices on them, and there are a ruined theatre and other Roman remains.

Finding that from the village itself we could not get a view of the Sea of Galilee we passed by it, and encamped on a hill to the west of it, from which we could see the lake as far as Tiberias, and also the deep ravine of the Yarmûk, and some of the windings of that river as it moves westwards to join the Jordan. Some objection was made by the sheik of the village and several of the villagers to our setting up our tents in this spot, on the ground that our mules might escape from their tethers and get into the corn; but a small present and a promise to pay for any damage which was done seemed to satisfy them.

The people of Umkeis bear a bad character, the village being a place of refuge for the outlaws of Tiberias and other places to the west of the Jordan. But we had never been molested by any one in our journeyings up to this time, and did not think of any danger. We went to bed early, intending to rise with the dawn, and to explore the Yarmûk valley to the eastward; our ambition having been aroused by the late Mr. Laurence Oliphant's account of his ineffectual attempt to make this exploration.

About half-past eleven, when we had been asleep for two hours, we were awakened by the firing of guns and pistols, the running of feet close to the tent in which we slept, and a general hubbub. On jumping up and getting outside the tent, I found all our men firing away as fast as they could. I had no weapon with me, not having carried a revolver up to this time. I never before felt so much like a rat in a trap, and determined that I would not go to Syria again without carrying a weapon for our defence. One of our Beduin guides reported that he had seen a man creeping up to our sleeping tent, who had begun to lift up the canvas at the bottom at the side next to my bed, and also noticed other men about. The Beduin had presented his gun at the man, and threatened to shoot the first that moved onwards. At the same time George saw other men also creeping towards our tent, and threatened them in like manner. The assailants (for we afterwards found that there were eight men in all) replied by firing at George and the Beduin. The latter returned the shots, and then all our men came running out with their weapons. The robbers having fired about a dozen shots in all made off. A good deal of blood was found in the morning in the direction in which the men were seen, so that one or more of them must have been wounded, but no one of our men was hurt. One of the eight men who attacked us was a negro whom we had noticed when we passed through the village, and who followed us from a place called Irbid, which we passed on the morning of the same day, and he had collected other men with him from Irbid and from Umkeis. The negro and another of the company had come into the kitchen tent that evening, and one of them had shortly afterwards attempted to steal a horse. After all had gone to bed, one of our servants named Nakhli aroused George, telling him that he heard men about, and George then ran out with his gun just in time.

The attack was very well timed, as the night was then extremely dark, the moon not having risen. About half an hour after the robbers had been driven off the moon arose,[1] and cast a brilliant light all round us, and then we felt that danger was past; and leaving some one to watch we went to bed again. My wife very philosophically went to sleep, but I lay awake, thinking what was best to be done; and not feeling sure that the men might not return with a larger force, it occurred to me that if we remained another night at Umkeis we should run a great risk of being attacked again, and there was of course no assistance obtainable in this wild place. I therefore rose up before dawn, and finding that George agreed in this opinion, we had the tents taken down, loaded the mules, descended on foot the very steep hillside which led to the gorge of the Yarmûk: and forded the beautiful stream at the bottom fringed deep with red flowered oleanders which rose above our heads as we sat on horseback.

[1] The moon plays an important part in a desert country. "If the moon be with thee thou needst not care for the stars" (Burckhardt's "Arabic Proverbs").

SOUTH END OF THE SEA OF GALILEE.

CHAPTER IX.

THE SEA OF GALILEE.

"The gentleness of heaven is on the sea."—WORDSWORTH.

THE ford was a difficult one to cross, owing to the large stones and rocks forming the bed of the river, and the depth of the water caused by the recent rains. Ascending the bank on the other side we came to the sulphur springs of Amatha. Twenty or thirty Arabs were quartered here for the sake of the bathing. There is nothing in the shape of a bathing-house, although the remains of Roman buildings which, no doubt were once sumptuous bath-houses, exist; but some of the people had tents to shelter them. The baths consist of two large pools of perfectly clear hot sulphur water in which the patients sit, one being appropriated to the men, and the other to the women. There is an abundant supply of sulphurous water at a temperature of 115°.

Mounting up the cliffs above the baths on the northern side of the Yarmûk, we kept our path right along the precipitous sides of the gorge through which the river runs, and after about three hours' steady riding we descended to the plain of Jordan, where the Yarmûk turns to flow across it to join the Jordan ; and passing the south end of the Sea of Galilee we came to the spot where that river flows out of the south-west corner of it. Here we found a very sweet pastoral scene.

The lake was perfectly calm, and of a light blue colour, and the sparkling waters swept out of it with a very swift current down into the river bed. On the west side of the Jordan is a narrow promontory, covered with long grass, which stretches into the lake, and on it were pretty little black and white cows grazing. Swallows, water-birds, and the lovely yellow, blue and red " warawaras" were flying swiftly backwards and forwards. These birds are shaped like swallows, but have the most brilliant plumage. They live in the holes in the low sandy banks in this part of the lake. Here I had a bathe, swimming from the lake into the Jordan ; but on attempting to return I found it quite impossible to make headway against the stream, and had some difficulty in regaining a footing and scrambling out again, so very rapidly does the current flow. Dr. Torrance, the British Medical Missionary at Tiberias, afterwards told me that it was well I went no further down the river, as just below the ford is a dangerous part overgrown with weeds, from which if one gets swept into it there is no escape. He mentioned that three people belonging to Tiberia had been carried into this place and drowned during the preceding month. We then forded the river, the sheik of the ford leading the way; the water rose above the bellies of our horses as we passed over.

From this point we had a very pleasant ride for about an hour and a half along the west side of the lake, passing great quantities of oleanders, and large flocks of sheep and goats, and herds of cattle, which had been brought down to be watered. A shepherd's dog amused us by lying in the lake with the water up to his neck, and watching the flock as they drank in front of him.

On approaching Tiberias we felt at home, as we visited the place in 1887. But the weather was extremely hot, and the flies and mosquitoes were very troublesome; they are indeed in the summer months often so numerous here as to actually put out the candle by crowding into the flame. By the advice of a boatman of Tiberias, whose acquaintance we had made the year before, we got rid of both mosquitoes and flies by making a fire of cow dung in front of the tent, and letting the smoke blow through it; but after we had done so we were doubtful whether the remedy was not worse than the disease.

We learnt that the day before our arrival a large number of French pilgrims had come here, amongst whom was an English lady, who had disappeared in the night, and was supposed to have wandered up into the mountains. We were asked to look out for her on our way northward; and we did so, but without result. We afterwards heard that the lady's body had been found in the lake, but it was not known how she got there, and all sorts of stories were circulated in Palestine about the manner of her death. When we revisited Tiberias, in 1889, we found a tomb erected to this poor lady close to the place where we encamped.

After staying two nights at Tiberias we journeyed to a place called Khan Yubb Yusef, which is about twelve hundred feet above the lake at its north end, and from which there is a very fine view of its whole extent.

We took a circuitous route to this place, as we wished to see the spot where the Jordan enters the Sea of Galilee at the north-east end. We therefore kept along the north shore, revisiting Tell Hum, said to be the site of Capernaum, and another place believed to be that of Bethsaida, which we had seen in 1887. Our road passed the north end of the lake, amongst bushes and small trees, from which hundreds of birds rose as we passed. By the side of the Jordan we found a few Beduin huts, a herd of cattle, and some cultivation; and when we pitched our little luncheon tent there the Arabs soon surrounded us. Here I bathed in the river, the flow of which, though fast, is slower than where it leaves the south end of Galilee. From this spot the lake looked most sweet and peaceful, and the water seemed to be of the colour of pearl.

We have seen the Sea of Galilee from almost all points of view, and under every aspect of weather; from the mountains above it at the south-east end; from the level at the south end; from Tiberias, and from the lake hills above it on the west side; from the hills high above the lake to the north; from boats on its surface in every part; in clear weather; with rain-storms sweeping up it ; with a rainbow spread over it ; at sunrise ; at sunset ; and by the light of the full moon. And I know not from which side or under which state of the sky it looks the most gravely and quietly beautiful, or the more fitted for solitary thought and reflection.[1]

The next day (the fourth of May) we started for Safed, which is supposed to be the "City on the Hill" referred to in the Sermon on the Mount. It is one of the Holy Places of the modern Jews, and is at a height of about two thousand seven hundred feet above the Mediterranean. Our way lay at first up a kind of stone trough and through a narrow rocky hollow, in which we felt the heat a good deal, notwithstanding

---

[1] When passing the north end of the Sea of Galilee in 1889, we noticed a small red-tiled house near the beach, not far from Tell Hum. On riding up to it we found it was inhabited by two Germans, who had just built it and made a neat little garden round it. They told us that they were Bavarians, and were the pioneers of a Roman Catholic colony. The house consisted of but one room. Under the roof was a long wooden shelf with a ladder leading to it. They told us that they slept on this shelf, pulling up the ladder at night, in order to be out of the way of the snakes, as they had seen a large one in the garden. The considerable number of snakes about Galilee, and the great quantity of fish in the lake, give point to the Gospel question, "What man is there of you . . . if he ask a fish will give him a serpent?" (St. Matthew). We have seen a great many snakes in Syria, and several times found them in our tents, but neither we nor any of our men have ever been bitten, nor have we ever heard of any traveller being bitten by them. Perhaps there is truth in the following observation : " J'imagine que les reptiles sont les plus prudents des animaux, qu'ils ont des notions presque toujours claires et vraies, beaucoup d'ignorances et peu d'erreurs" ("Pensées de Joübert").

the early hour. But two hours' climbing up the steep hillside brought us to a very pretty valley, in which a clear spring rises from the hillside, and waters gardens containing figs, pomegranates, and other fruit trees, whose leaves and flowers are very refreshing to the eye in their luxuriant green. Here we found shade and fresh cold drinking water, and had a pleasant rest. Then a short scramble upwards brought us to Safed, and we climbed to the highest point, on which is the ruined site of an old castle, to take our lunch and look down upon the surrounding country. The view is very extensive, including the Sea of Galilee, Mount Tabor, and the peaks known as the Horns of Hattin—the supposed Mount of the Beatitudes. I went for a ride of about forty minutes to another hill to the eastward, from which I had a similar view, with the addition of Mount Hermon and the Lebanon Chain with their snowy summits.

The Jews of Safed are reputed to be very fanatical, and in 1875 an attack was here made on the members of the Palestine Exploration Survey. Many of the people scowled at us as we passed through the streets, but we were not actively molested in any way. The inhabitants were very picturesque in their various costumes, except the washed-out looking Polish Jews with their pale faces, side-curls, and slight figures, who are as numerous here as at Tiberias and Jerusalem. At a little distance from our camp was a Moslem cemetery, from which we had a splendid view of the Sea of Galilee, lying three thousand four hundred feet below us, and of the hill country both east and west of it, the Horns of Hattin, Mount Tabor, and much of the tableland on the top of the mountains of Gilead being particularly observable.

The next day (the fifth of May) we started at a very early hour. It was a glorious morning. Our path lay down a fertile hillside slope and valley, ending in a deep ravine, where were numerous caves high up on the cliff sides; many of them evidently shaped to a large extent by the hand of man. From some of these young owls looked placidly down upon us as we passed by. Here we met an Indian dervish, who told us that he was on his way from India *viâ* Baghdad to Jerusalem, as a pilgrim to the sanctuary of the Dome of The Rock. Rising out of this ravine we tried a short cut, and were brought up by another ravine still more remarkable. We passed along the edge of this, the rocky, perpendicular sides of which contain a great number of large caves, some with stories one above another, and apparently communicating internally. This appeared to be a most remarkable place, and I do not think we should have seen it if we had not lost our way a little. I have not come across any account of this ravine, which it would be very interesting to explore.

The track now brought us down nearly to the shore of the Sea of Galilee at the north-west end, which is believed to be the land of Gennesaret; but instead of continuing along the margin of the lake we turned to the west, and soon entered the Wâdy Hammâm, and after a ride of five hours stopped at the brook in this valley to lunch. Above us on each side rose very high cliffs, in which were numerous caves. Amongst these were the ruins of the Castle of Kal'at ibn ma'an, consisting of caverns in the rock several stories high, connected by passages and protected by walls. In the time of Herod this was the stronghold of a great robber chief, who with his crew spread terror all over the neighbourhood. They were only captured by soldiers who were let down by ropes from the top of the cliff. Our chief muleteer and I with some difficulty got our horses up to the bottom of the almost precipitous ascent to the castle, which begins at about one hundred yards below it, and scrambled up the rest of the way on foot. It was impossible to ride down again, and I had therefore to walk all the way, and was rather upset by the heat of the sun; but George put me to rights by pouring water over my head from the brook, while I sat under the shadow of a wild fig tree.

We set off again winding up the Wâdy Hammâm, until taking a turn to the left, we ascended a steep hill to Hattin, which is the very filthiest mud village that I ever saw. It is, however, surrounded with lovely orchards, in which the pomegranates in full flower were conspicuous. Passing through the village, we encamped above it on the slope of the hills behind it.

NORTH END OF THE SEA OF GALILEE.

CHAPTER X.

THE DRUSES. HATTIN AND MOUNT TABOR.

"From the top of Tabor you have a prospect which, if nothing else, well rewards the labour of ascending it. It is impossible for man's eyes to behold a higher gratification of this nature."—HENRY MAUNDRELL, A.D. 1697.

IN the evening some Druses came to call on us. They have a little mosque here, close to which our tents were pitched : and to this shrine pilgrimages are made by Druses from other parts of Syria. About twelve of these men came into our tent, sat down, and were served with coffee ; the Druses do not smoke. They were fine, handsome, pleasant-looking men, grave and sedate in manner, and very clean in person. They invited us to see their mosque, which we promised to do in the morning, and they insisted upon guarding our tents at night, and refused to accept any remuneration for doing so.

When they had gone I rode up the slope behind the village and round the head of a small valley at the foot of which it stands, to a steep, round hill just below the Horns of Hattin. I am no authority upon the matter, but it appeared to me that from its beautiful situation and pleasant, green look, for " there was much grass in the place," and leafy trees were pleasantly dotted about, this was more likely to be the Mount of the Beatitudes than the craggy-topped "Horns"; and it struck me that a large number of people could more conveniently sit and better hear a discourse at this place than would be possible at the other. From this spot there is a most lovely view. Safed sits glistening on its mountain-top ("A city that is set on an hill cannot be hid"), and the gap in the hills in the foreground forming the Wâdy Hammâm, and the other gap leading to Tiberias allow portions of the lake to be seen. Below are the fertile, peaceful plains, waving with green barley, and the rich orchards surrounding the village.

On returning to the camp I found George very ill with shivering fits which were followed by fever. My wife applied remedies and nursed him with the greatest care, and he threw off the attack after a night of delirium. The same night we had another kind of alarm, being awakened at two o'clock by the firing of guns. Learning that the shots proceeded from the Druse guard, who had only fired at a hyena prowling about the kitchen-tent, we went comfortably to bed again. We intended to stay the next day at Hattin, but at 6.30 A.M. it was already so hot, and our tents were so full of flies coming from the dirty village below that we determined to move on.

Before starting we went to see the mosque of the Druses, being conducted by a deputation of them, who arrived to bring us. They told us that it had been built by one of them, who was pointed out to us, at his own expense; and both he and they were evidently very proud of the erection. It stands at the top of a flight of steps, and is indeed a handsome little mosque, and very pretty and clean inside; it contains the tomb of a saint. We were ushered in and placed on a carpet, and the Druse men and boys all sat crosslegged in a semicircle in front of us, the women and girls, who, following the custom of the Druses, did not cover their faces fully, but only obscured one eye, sitting silent at a distance by themselves, and gazing at us, especially my wife, with the greatest interest.

The men told us that travellers seldom came to Hattin, and that we were the first this year. They asked many questions about England, which they said they looked upon as friendly to the Druses, because in 1860, after the massacre of the Maronites, it had prevented them from being exterminated. They had heard that Russia had taken India, and were very sorry for England. They were glad to learn from us that this news was not true. They told us that in the Hauran, where most of the Druses live, the Turkish Government left them alone; but that at Carmel, and the villages in Palestine in which many are scattered in small communities, it was very hard on them. Would we speak well of them in England, so that they might be helped against the Turks? They spoke much and with great affection of "Howadjah Oliphant" (the late Laurence Oliphant) and Sitt Alice (his first wife), whom they knew at their home on Mount Carmel. They gave us coffee and treated us in the most polite and considerate way, coming out of the mosque with us to say good-bye at the top of the flight of steps.

We rode at first to the hill where I had been the evening before, and from there we saw a great number of Druses, men and women in their picturesque costumes, coming on horseback from the direction of the Sea of Galilee towards the mosque. There must have been two or three hundred in all. This was their saint's day. I rode on with our chief muleteer to the Horns of Hattin from which the view is even more extensive than from the hill before mentioned, and then followed the others towards Mount Tabor.

Our journey lay across the plain of Hattin, the scene of that great defeat of the Crusaders which practically ended their dominion in Palestine. This plain descends gradually, and then rises slightly towards Tabor. We traversed a wide extent of tall barley, some of it coming as high as my knees as I sat on horseback; and as we brushed through it some gazelles passed quite close to us, but we lost sight of them almost immediately. After crossing the plain we ascended gradually up the valley leading to the foot of Mount Tabor [1] on the west side, and after four hours' riding we rested and took our lunch under a widespreading oak on the side of the hill.

One of our men, a very merry fellow, who was always skipping, singing, and laughing as he went along, immediately got up into the tree, singing very loudly and firing off his pistol in triumph. While passing through the barley he had, to amuse us and please

---

[1] "This strange and beautiful mountain is distinguished alike in form and in character from all around it. As seen from the northwest it towers like a dome. It is not what Europeans would call a wooded hill, because its trees stand all apart from each other. But it is so thickly studded with them as to rise from the plain like a mass of verdure. Its sides much resemble the scattered glades in the outskirts of the New Forest" (Stanley's "Sinai and Palestine").

himself, rolled over and over like a porpoise, and then dived as in the sea, appearing again on the surface of the corn a long way off shouting with laughter. This poor fellow walked nearly the whole way throughout our journey, only very rarely getting a lift on one of the mules, and slept in the open air—sometimes in the rain; but I think he was the happiest person of the whole party. After lunch and a little sleep we started in a very hot sun, and reaching the top of Mount Tabor, which is fifteen hundred feet above the plain, found our tents pitched in the courtyard of the Latin Monastery.

Later in the evening we visited the ruins of the churches on the highest part of the mountain, and had a most glorious sunset view of the country all round. To the north, we saw the "Horns," and the plain of Hattin, and in the distance Hermon; to the east, the mountains of Gilead, and the north end of the Sea of Galilee; to the south, the villages of Endor and Nain, the hill known as Little Hermon, and the mountains of Gilboa; and to the west, the plains of Jezreel and Esdraelon, the mountain range of Carmel, and the Mediterranean Sea. Below us was the scene of the victory sung by Deborah, when "the stars in their courses fought against Sisera," and the village of Debûrieh which would seem to perpetuate her name.[1]

[1] "There are instances in later history in which a defeated Arab has sheltered himself in the women's apartments, but such an infringement of Eastern etiquette has always been punished by death; and it is not improbable that, in revenge for such an insult, Jael seized the iron tent-peg, and drove it with the mallet used to fix the tents to the ground through Sisera's brain." ("Twenty-one Years' Work in the Holy Land.")

The next morning we walked down Mount Tabor, leading our horses as we descended; and, crossing the hill country by a rough track, we got to Nazareth by ten o'clock, the heat by this time being very great.

CHAPTER XI.

FROM NAZARETH TO CARMEL.

"The whole scene is studded with sites which carry us in retrospect through ages of history for three thousand years. That plain has been what Belgium is to Europe, the battlefield of Syria."—"PICTURESQUE PALESTINE."

AS soon as we had pitched our tents, a nice little boy from the Roman Catholic school who could speak French attached himself to us, wanting to show us about and earn backsheesh. Having visited Nazareth before we did not require a guide, but kept the little fellow near us to run messages. Our tents were placed close to a burial ground, and very shortly after we arrived the body of a boy belonging to the Greek Church was buried here. It was put in the grave without any coffin, and placed within little walls or rows of stones, other large stones being laid over it, but so as to rest on the walls, and not to touch the corpse. No one of the little assemblage seemed to grieve, and the earth was filled in, and all departed. The poor child was not, however, quite unmourned, for by half-past five the following morning women were sitting in a circle round his grave, singing a monotonous kind of chant and occasionally crying.

This circle was added to by fresh arrivals, until when we started soon after six there were over twenty women present.

I asked the Roman Catholic boy about the child that was buried, when he told me that he was only a little boy belonging to the "Greek Schismatical Church," and seemed perfectly indifferent to his fate upon this account. This is only a slight instance of the religious animosities to be found amongst different kinds of Christians in Palestine. There is something peculiarly repulsive in the exhibition of such feelings at Nazareth. But " graceless zealots " abound in this country, and the Greek and Latin Churches carry on a bitter rivalry at all the Holy Places.

Our way lay over the hills to the westward,— "solemn wastes of heathy hill,"—then down their slopes across a portion of the plain of Esdraelon, and then through a charming forest country with tall green barley growing in the open glades, reminding us again very strongly of English woodland scenery as painted by Gainsborough, Crome, and Constable. The illusion was heightened by our meeting a waggon drawn by a team of horses; the team was driven by a German waggoner, and the waggon contained several casks of wine brought from Haifa. This woodland borders on the course of a branch of " that ancient river, the river Kishon," where, as Major Conder points out, Sisera's army were driven by the Hebrews as the Turks were many centuries afterwards driven by the French in Napoleon's campaign in Syria, into the quagmire of the Kishon springs.[1]

[1] "And I will draw unto thee to the river Kishon Sisera, the

We lunched and rested under a tree for two hours; and then descending into the plain again, and crossing another branch of the Kishon (which branch was here but a muddy little brook running between sloping banks), we passed through the outskirts of Haifa, and entered its streets. It is but a small place; but it has a much cleaner and more modern appearance than any other town in Syria except Beyrout, which we have visited; a distinction no doubt due to the influence of the adjoining German colony. Here we found a telegraph office and despatched a message home reporting our arrival.

We then passed through the neat and pretty village of the German ("Temple") colony, with its little white houses with red-tiled roofs, and pious little German texts over the doorways, and ascended the hill to the Carmelite Monastery, and the Lighthouse, nearly five hundred feet above the sea, from which there is a delightful view. The hill is very steep on the west side, so that we seemed to look from our tents straight down into the blue waters of the Mediterranean. Opposite to us on the north across the bay was the town of Acre, towards which the white beach curved; and beneath us to the north-east was a promontory of lowlying land beautifully cultivated by the Germans, who had also planted vineyards up the side of the hill upon which the vines looked most flourishing. Their labours and those of the Fathers of the Monastery in their smaller piece of land enable us to understand what "the

captain of Jabin's army, with his chariots and his multitude; and I will deliver him into thine hand . . . The river of Kishon swept them away" (Judges).

excellency of Carmel" must once have been. The road from Haifa to Nazareth, which is fit for carriages, has been made by the German colonists, and it is now (1890), almost, if not quite, carried on to Tiberias.

The next day was very hot. I started to ride to Acre, but after descending into the plain, and getting some little way beyond Haifa, I was forced to return, on account of the great heat. A small party of Greek Christians came up the hill with their priest, leading a sheep, which he blest, and they killed, and cut up and cooked then and there. Amongst these people

HAIFA AND THE BAY OF ACRE FROM MOUNT CARMEL.

was a girl, who was so much admired by our long-legged waiter, that he immediately offered her his hand, and wanted to marry her on the spot; but she only laughed at him. He seemed to feel the disappointment keenly for the rest of the day, but became cheerful again by dinner-time. Later in the day we rode for some way along the wooded backbone of the ridge of Carmel to the south-east, and in the evening went down to the seashore and gathered some of the beautiful shells to be found there.

We stayed for three days on Mount Carmel, and on the third rode again along the forest-clothed [1] mountain range to the south-east. We had bought from the monks of the monastery some bottles of medicine which they prepare from herbs, and which has a great reputation in Palestine. Fortunately my wife happened to take a small bottle of this in her pocket, for as we rode we found a poor native of the country stretched on the ground crying out in great pain, suffering apparently from colic, and seeming to be almost at his last gasp. Some of this stuff being poured down his throat had a marvellous effect, and in about half an hour he was able to get up and walk away.

In the evening I had a ride all about the German settlement, and amongst the new roads and clearings which the industrious colonists had made. We were interested in this place owing to the various accounts we had read of it, written by the late Laurence Oliphant, and we intended to call on him, but to our disappointment found that he was then in America. It is most interesting and noteworthy to see what these few hundred Germans have done in turning a comparative wilderness into orchards, vineyards, and gardens. The soil on the hillside is red and rocky, very much in appearance like that of the best vine-growing parts of France ; and this is planted chiefly with vines.

That night a heavy storm of wind and rain swept up from the sea over our tents, which were again in danger ; but all the bad weather had cleared away by the morning when we started to ride along the coast to Jaffa.

[1] "I will enter into the forest of his Carmel" (Isaiah).

NAHR EL AUJA, A RIVER NEAR JAFFA.

CHAPTER XII.

WE END OUR JOURNEY.   GEORGE AND HIS FAMILY.

"This my son was dead and is alive again; he was lost and is found."—ST. LUKE.

ALONG slope brought us down to the level of the sea, and sometimes near the waves, and sometimes over the sandy hills we rode onwards, until we came to the castle of Athlit (Château des Pèlerins), an extensive ruin close to the sea, which encloses a Beduin village. On the land side, at a little distance from the castle, is a natural rampart formed by the rocks, through which a narrow winding cutting passes to the castle. It was the last place in Palestine surrendered by the Crusaders.

Passing from here we kept along the seashore, while a fresh wind blew, and a rough sea broke in upon the beach, and passing through the village of Tantura (supposed to be the ancient Dora), we kept along the sands until we reached the Nahr ez Zerka, which is also known as the Crocodile River. It has been disputed whether the river really contains any crocodiles, but Major Conder says that it does, and Mr. Howard of Jaffa and Jerusalem told us that he had seen some small ones—three or four feet long—there. Fording this about five in the evening of the eleventh of May, we reached Kaisariyêh (Cæsarea), where there are remains of Roman and mediæval walls and buildings, and where no doubt much of interest lies undiscovered beneath the surface. The stones of the walls are very rapidly being removed to Jaffa, where they are sold as building material; little trading schooners constantly plying backwards and forwards between the two places. Here St. Paul was imprisoned two years, and made his speech to Felix in answer to Tertullus, the advocate of the High Priest, and also his speech to Festus and King Agrippa.

As the plain of Sharon is frequently infested by marauding Beduins, the guide-books say that a guard of soldiers, or of Beduins should be taken on this route to Jaffa;[1] but we had not thought it necessary to follow this advice. On leaving Cæsarea, however, George said that we must use precautions, and required me to carry arms. I was accordingly furnished with a pair of flint-lock pistols, whilst he carried his double-barrelled gun and revolver, and the chief muleteer, who rode with us in advance of the camp, was also provided with a gun. Our way lay along the seashore, and the hard sand was very pleasant for cantering. As we reached a place where the cliffs came near to the sea, so as to leave only a narrow road (our muleteers

[1] It was on this route that Mr. Wade was attacked and wounded by Beduins early in 1890.

with the baggage mules being out of sight a long way behind), we met three mounted Beduins, who approached us with their hands on their guns, and their eyes fixed on ours. We watched them in like manner with our weapons in our hands, but they went by in peace. George fell in with one of these men in 1889, and learnt from him that he and his companions were then looking out for travellers, and would have attacked us but that they observed us to be equal to them in number, and to be as well armed as they were.

After this we turned inland a little, and continued our journey on the plain of Sharon, thinking it better to avoid narrow ways. We passed hundreds of camels with their young ones grazing, but very rarely met a human being. Five hours' riding brought us to a little hollow where there was still water for the horses, and at this spot we set up our little luncheon tent.

Here we had an instance of the distrust prevailing amongst travellers in this part of the country. It occurring to me that the hollow was the very place to be caught in by robbers, I ate my lunch rapidly, and ascending the hill on the south side, sat down on a rock, from which I could see the path on both sides, and kept a look-out against surprise. I had arranged with George that if I saw any men coming I should whistle and run down to the tent, and that he and the muleteer who was with us would at once come forth with their weapons. After sitting a long time, and seeing nothing but a young owl, who, gravely reposing on a tree near, stared steadfastly at me, I made out with my glasses three men on horseback, armed with guns, approaching. I at once blew my whistle loudly and ran down to the tent, and George and the muleteer coming out, we all stood ready to receive the enemy. After we had waited a little while, the first horseman appeared above the hollow on the north side, looking down at us in an uneasy and apprehensive manner, and approached us " delicately," then observing my European dress he came on as if reassured, and with many salaams passed by us and mounted the hill on the opposite side. The other two men never appeared at all. No doubt they thought we were lying in ambush for them and had changed their route.

We rested here until the muleteers with the baggage animals came up, and then went on with them to a place called Haram Siden Ali Ibn 'Alim. Here is a large and handsome mosque and a dirty little village. The former stands on a cliff about fifty feet above the sea, from which Jaffa is visible in the distance. Not far from this place is a ruin of a castle by the sea, which has been rent to pieces by some tremendous earthquake, portions of the immensely thick wall having fallen down on to the beach.

We found a poor mad woman at this village, who goes about neighing like a mare. She is under the impression that she is herself the very mare on which the saint buried here used to ride, and wanders over the country neighing and begging. This place is only three hours' ride from Jaffa, and very early the next morning we sent off one of the muleteers to get our letters and bring them back to us, as we had heard nothing from home for many weeks. He returned in the afternoon bringing not only the letters, but also news that there had been a report in Jaffa that my wife, George, and I, had all been murdered at Kerâk [1] (where we had then never been) and that George's wife and mother were in great grief, and had been throwing ashes over their heads for some days.

Presently two of George's nephews arrived, and then three others of his relations, all of whom seemed to be greatly pleased at finding him safe and sound, and each as he rode up descended from his horse and kissed George again and again on both cheeks. Amongst these was one nephew whom he knew before, who was in a great state of agitation. He burst into tears on meeting George, and then broke out again in our tent, crying "Sitt (lady), Monsieur, George," pointing to us one after another, and indicating that he had thought we were all murdered, and burying his face in his handkerchief. He said that he had telegraphed to Beyrout for news of us and could get no answer. I do not know how the report arose, but rumour should be painted fuller of tongues in the East even than in the West.

The evening was beautiful. We heard the muezzim rung out from the minaret of the mosque in the evening air, and watched the young moon rise. Our good cook sent up a magnificent repast for the last dinner, including a wonderful hard-bake erection, like those temples of barley-sugar which were fashionable at ball suppers when I was a boy. It bore on the front of it the words " Good-bye " and " Good health," inscribed in letters of sugar, and contained amongst its pinnacles a little roll of paper expressing the good wishes of all.

[1] It is strange that in 1890 we should have got into trouble at Kerâk.

How hard it was to leave this happy life, even with the hope of returning to it again at no distant period. How forbidding appeared in prospect the gloomy skies, the monotonous daily toil, the party cries, the striving contentious life of our native country, and how attractive that restful, acquiescent spirit of the East, which induced an old Syrian Sheik to make the following answer to an European traveller engaged in the aggressive occupation of collecting facts !

"Worthy friend ! joy of my life ! What you ask of me is wearisome and useless. Though I have lived all my life in this village, I never felt any curiosity to count the houses or the inhabitants. What my neighbour carries on his shoulders, or the merchant over the way puts in his ships, does not concern me. The former circumstances of this district are known only to Heaven, and I have no desire to learn what wickednesses were indulged in by the unholy Giaour before the sacred sword of Islam gave the place to the true believer. And yet, O light of my countenance, I am contented. Do thou likewise, and may thy day be bright and blessed."

We had yet one pleasant ride before us. The men being very impatient to get into Jaffa, we started before six in the morning of the fourteenth of May, and cantered along the sand of the seashore, which the long shadows from the eastern cliffs kept cool. Half way to Jaffa another nephew of George's met us, and both dismounted and kissed each other on the cheek. Then we forded the beautiful little river Nahr el Auja, having, as in the case of all the streams running into the shore from the Plain of Sharon, to be very careful to avoid quicksands. As we entered the outskirts of the town George's wife, sister, and little daughter, came out to meet him rejoicing in the news that he was safe; but his poor old mother, whose eyesight was very feeble, had extinguished its last rays for ever by the ashes which she had thrown over her head during her days of mourning. When he reached his home she "lifted up her voice and wept," and her first words were those of the text which heads this chapter.

Our revels now were ended, and a day or two afterwards as the steamer bore us away our faithful followers stood watching us from the little landing-place until they themselves had melted into thin air, and even the white houses of Jaffa, ceasing to sparkle in the light of sunset, had faded like the baseless fabric of a vision, and left not a wrack behind.

LEAVING JAFFA.

PART II.

1889.

Philistia and Palmyra.

PALMYRA IN 1750. From Wood and Dawkins' "The Ruins of Palmyra."

NEARING JAFFA.

1889.
Philistia and Palmyra.

CHAPTER I.

THE JOURNEY TO GAZA.

"For, lo, the winter is past, the rain is over and gone. The flowers appear on the earth, the time of the singing-birds is come, and the voice of the turtle is heard in the land."—SONG OF SOLOMON.

EARLY on the morning of the ninth of March we landed at Jaffa, and were received by George and some of our old servants, and by our good friend Mr. Howard, who keeps the hotels known by his name at Jaffa and Jerusalem. The kind welcome, the warm sunshine, the blue skies, the cooing of doves and chirping of birds, soon made us forget the little disagreeables of a rough voyage.

Having completed all our preparations, we started

the next day through the orange groves which encompass Jaffa on the land side, past the beautiful old fountain outside the town, between the long lines of cactus hedges, and so out on to the plain of Sharon, which seemed to overflow with the spirit of the spring. It was a lovely day, and the brilliant green of the young corn, now about eighteen inches high, the purple distance of the Judæan hills, and the white fleecy clouds lying above them made up a charming scene. But the sun was powerful and there was little wind to temper the heat. After riding for four hours we dismounted, rested, and lunched under a large olive tree at the edge of the Arab burial-place to the north of Ramleh.

At this place we left the Jerusalem road, and turning to the southward passed under a long line of olive trees, and through the young corn which they sheltered. We had another delightful three hours in the saddle, and about sunset reached our camp on the brow of a hill near a little village of mud-houses called El Mûghâr. We found the elders of the village seated on the roofs of their houses in patient expectation of our arrival, and a row of the younger ones arranged opposite to our tents. A more delightful camping ground could not have been chosen; for from our tents we had a lovely view over an extensive plain to the westward, rich with the young crops. The night set in without a cloud in the sky; there was no "husbandry in Heaven," and the young moon and stars shone brightly. It was a delightful beginning to our journey, and we felt as happy as larks.

We started very early the following day and saw the

FOUNTAIN NEAR JAFFA.

THE PLAIN OF SHARON.

first rays of the morning illumine the wide expanse of cornland, its brightness being heightened by a dark shadow from the hill behind. On we went over a gently undulating plain, partly cultivated, through a few plantations of olive trees, and past orchards of pomegranates and figs. Here for the first time we saw camels ploughing, some alone, others joined with an ox or a donkey. We stayed for our midday rest at Esdûd (the ancient Ashdod), and then continuing our ride over very much the same kind of country we arrived at Askalon, and encamped close to a small mosque and Arab graveyard, just below the ruins of the Crusaders' castle, and under some noble old sycamore trees.

It was a lovely evening, and we climbed up the slope to explore the ruins of the walls which look seaward and are half buried in the sand which has been blown in from the beach during the course of many centuries. Happening here to talk to George about the stars, their size and distance from the earth, and the time that it takes for light to travel from the more remote, we found him quite incredulous upon the subject. He was convinced that the heavenly bodies were only small things like candles, that the moon was next in size to the sun, and that we had been persuaded to the contrary by interested people who wanted to sell us telescopes. He has several times since begged us, as one pitying our mental condition, not to remain under such foolish delusions. At night we heard the jackals cry and the owls hooting to one another—pleasant assurances that we had really for a time put on "this our life exempt from public haunt," and had indeed "this wide and universal theatre" of nature alone before us.

Our next point was to be the ancient town of Gaza. We rode by the seashore through the old site of Askalon, which lies in a semicircle backed by rising ground, which is crowned with the ruined fortifications and faced by the sea. Here we noticed many columns lying about, and several excavations where men seemed to be digging for worked stone for building. Statues have been found here in this manner, and there is evidently a great field for discovery at Askalon.

After this we rode along the seashore for some hours, until we had to leave the sparkling waves of the Levant, and turn inland for Gaza. The sands were often firm and shelly, but sometimes heavy for the horses. At a point where lies the wreck of an English steamer, belonging to West Hartlepool, we wheeled round to the eastward, mounted a hillock, and crossed a little plain of beautiful pure yellow sand (thinking that it probably covered many buildings of an age long past), descended into a hollow full of vegetation, where the barley stood high and in full ear, and by a gently-rising ascent reached the town. We found our tents pitched just outside of it, between the Moslem burial ground and the English Protestant missionary's house and garden.

George lost no time in going to the Governor to ask for two soldiers to accompany us to Bir es Seba (Beersheba) and on to Hebron, but he could gain no admittance to the presence of the great man, and we decided to endeavour to obtain the assistance of the missionary. The latter (Mr. Huber) kindly wrote a note at once to the Governor; but the reply was that we could not have the soldiers for two days, as they were all dispersed collecting taxes.

Mr. Huber had been thirty-four years a missionary in this country and previously in West Africa. We went over the schools. It was a pretty sight to see the little child-faces at work, with the sun shining in at the doorway lighting up their intelligent countenances, and all as busy as they could be. There were many beautiful little girls amongst them, and some of them spoke English very well. They evidently had a kind good friend in Miss Huber. Mr. Huber told us that wherever there is digging at Gaza, foundations of old buildings and hewn stones are found.

On returning to our tents we saw a Moslem funeral procession come up to a grave just in front of us. A poor woman and her baby were to be buried together. The bodies were carried in an open bier with a cloth laid over them, and the mourners chanted in the monotonous eastern way. In the evening we rode to the top of Mount Muntâr, a little way to the south-east of Gaza, from which we had a wide view extending to the Judæan hills and the sea. This is the spot to which Samson is reputed to have carried the gates of Gaza, and there is a little mosque on the top which is much venerated by the Moslems.

THE DEAD SEA FROM THE PASS OF 'AIN JIDY.

CHAPTER II

TO BEERSHEBA AND BEIT JIBRIN.

> "All around
> The boundless, waving grass-plains stretch, thick starr'd
> With saffron and the yellow hollyhock
> And flag-leaved iris-flowers."
> MATTHEW ARNOLD.

WE determined not to wait for the soldiers to come before setting out as we had two Beduins with us; and when we started at an early hour the next morning these were soon joined by a trooper who said that another trooper was to follow; but no other came. We passed over the same kind of plain as before, only that we did not come upon any trees or orchards, and the soil appeared to be very poor. Soon a Beduin joined us carrying a long spear. He was evidently a friend of the soldier, for on coming up to us he dismounted, and, tying his mare's forelegs together to keep her from straying, he ran up to him and kissed him on both cheeks, and they then rode along talking merrily together. At last we came to the Wâdy es Sheriâh, at the bottom of which was a stream, and here we had to remain for the night, as there was no other water between this place and Beersheba, a journey of six hours.

We pitched our tents on the slope of the hill known as "Tell Sheriah," a little above the stream. It was very warm here, and the horses much enjoyed a swim in the water, and the men a good wash. It was a very lonely spot, not even a Beduin tent being within sight. We noticed a lad who had come to look at us — a shepherd boy clad in a sheep-skin. He had folded one leg up under his clothes out of sight, and stood in this position for such a long time that we thought he had but one. He looked more like a crane than a human being. Since then we have often seen the shepherds of the south stand in this way. We had another glorious night, the moon being at the full. It seemed to us more impressive shining over the silent country and the desolate hills than upon the most beautiful of cities.

The next day (the sixteenth of March) we left for Beersheba. We took a circuitous route following the soldier, who led us so as to avoid the Beduin camps, but on the whole we steered south-east. Gradually we mounted to higher ground. Many vultures hovered about, and we saw the beautiful storks, at first "single spies" and then "in battalions." A flight of several hundreds of storks is one of the great sights of Syria. They come up from Egypt in the spring and disappear from Syria when the summer sets in. They wheel round and round high in the air, seeming often to float without motion of their wings; then form a long line and fly away. After the sun has set upon the plain they will circle in its light while it still lingers in the sky, like a legion of Botticelli's angels; until when it has faded from their wings, and darkness is falling over the heavens, they trail off in one long flight disappearing in the night; then they descend earthwards, and rest upon the branches of trees, or amongst the long grass of some marsh or streamlet's side until the dawn.[1]

The following day, after a pleasant ride of four hours through a pathless land of barrenness, interspersed, however, with patches of barley and carpets of wild flowers, we stayed on rising ground to lunch, and to allow the baggage mules to pass us. But they took the wrong direction, and when we arrived at Abraham's wells they were nowhere to be found. George and the Beduin rode off at a hard gallop, and after being away for an hour, having found the missing men and animals, brought them to the right spot. We were very tired and hot, the thermometer stood 84° in the tent, and the water from out of the well was cool and welcome to the taste. The hard stone sides of the chief one, cut deep with the letting down and drawing up of the bucket ropes of many generations, give it an appearance of immense antiquity. In no place could water be more welcome. We had come through a true wilderness "void and empty" of man and beast, and could feel what a refuge for the thirsty and exhausted must be this place of cool springs of water which never fail.

[1] "Who bid the stork, Columbus-like explore
Heavens not his own, and worlds unknown before;
Who calls the Council, states the certain day;
Who forms the phalanx, and who points the way?"
POPE.

We saw no remains of the churches of which Sir John Mandeville speaks, or of any building whatever.[1]

The Beduins belonging to the neighbouring camp gathered round our tent, and the sheik asked us to eat with him, but we declined as politely as we could, feeling too tired for anything but rest. George told the sheik that we wished to make a picture of him (a photograph) if he would sit still on his horse. To which he replied " What is a picture ? " How should he know? He had never seen one. In the evening the Beduins and our own people ate their supper in the moonlight, and we sat and watched them in a kind of rapture of repose and peace.

We rose so early the next morning as to have the moonlight on our breakfast table as we sat in the open air. We were to reach Beit Jibrin (as some suppose the Gath of the Old Testament) that day ; and a very long journey it turned out to be. However early we might start the Beduins and the soldier always said their morning prayer on their little carpets with uncovered feet before they ate. We passed by the bare stone-encircled well of Abraham, of which I have spoken, and the broad dry river bed below it, and turned our horses to the northward. A Beduin from Bir es Saba joined us here, so that our escort was increased. For several hours the road was over a treeless

---

[1] "When you pass the desert on the way to Jerusalem, you come to Beersheba, which was formerly a very fair and pleasant town of the Christians, some of whose churches still remain. In that town, Abraham the Patriarch dwelt a long time. It was founded by Beersheba (Bathsheba), the wife of Sir Uriah the knight, of whom King David begot Solomon the Wise" (Sir John Mandeville, A.D. 1322). In this statement the worthy old traveller seems to be a little out in the order of events.

undulating plain, partially planted with barley; but the wild flowers increased in number and beauty, and we saw many storks. After five hours' riding we came to water at a place where was a wooden wheel set in motion by an emaciated horse, and here we made our midday halt.

As we rested a tall black Nubian came running up to us with wild speech and gesticulation—evidently complaining indignantly of something or somebody. It appeared from what he said that one of our muleteers who had gone forward with the baggage animals had struck him, and he asked for compensation. This we gave him in the form of a few piastres which comforted him at once.

Now the country became more interesting. We ascended low hills, and wound along a wâdy most of which was covered with barley, and by hills which were dotted with tamarisks. We expected the journey to take six or seven hours, but hour after hour passed and we were still in the open country, and could see nothing of Beit Jibrin. About sunset, however, timber trees began to appear, then olives in abundance, long trains of camels and cattle, flocks of goats and sheep with their young ones, well ploughed land, and finally we came to a small common covered with short grass and planted with ancient olives, a little below the town, and here we pitched our tents. We had been ten hours in the saddle, and we, our men and animals, were all very glad to come to the end of the day's work. How the mules revelled and rolled in the grass, and how we enjoyed the light in the heavens, and the fairy-like appearance of everything in the full brilliant moonlight!

THE SHEIK OF HEBRON.

HEBRON.

CHAPTER III.

BY HEBRON AND 'AIN JIDY TO JERUSALEM.

"He travell'd through wide, wasteful ground,
That naught but desert wilderness show'd all around."
SPENSER.

THE following day we were to reach Hebron, so after a sound sleep we rose again at six o'clock, and after taking a look at the outside of the celebrated caves of Beit Jibrin, for we had not time to descend into them, we started. Passing on the north side of the town amongst ruins of outbuildings, some Roman, some mediæval, we were soon again amongst the olive trees and corn fields. After a while we entered a narrow gorge, winding and rocky; a very difficult path for the horses, along which they had to pick their way as best they could. The track ascended and brought us gradually to the top of the hills above the gorge whence we had a very fine view; and descending thence through a long stony combination of lane and stream which extended all the way to Hebron, we found our encampment under the olive trees near the lazaretto, used for travellers coming from Egypt.

We were here about three thousand feet above the Mediterranean, the clouds were flying across the sky, a cold west wind was blowing, and the general effect was very gray and cheerless, if delicate in colour.

The old Sheik of Hebron came at once to welcome us, and to arrange about an escort for us to 'Ain Jidy. From here we made a little excursion to see the wonderful old oak called Abraham's, at Mamre, which is at a little distance from Hebron. It is supported on all sides by props, and the big hollows in it are built up with stones.[1]

We shall never forget the night we passed at Hebron under the olive trees. The wind blew in stormy gusts, and the rain fell in torrents. We thought that we and the tents must be blown and washed away, but the faithful George never wearied of watching for our protection. He was round and round all night, knocking in a peg here and tightening a rope there, and it was not surprising that in the morning although our tents stood fast, he had a bad sorethroat and cold. There

---

[1] The cavities in old olive trees are often built up in like manner. This plan might be adopted with advantage in the case of any valuable or favourite old tree at home. I suppose that the effect is to stop decay by excluding damp and the incursions of animals. It seems an analogous process to stopping a hollow tooth.

were two other parties of travellers encamped near to us, and their tents were carried away by the wind into the valley below, while the occupants had to take refuge, some in the Russian hospice close to the oak of Mamre, and the others in a Jew's house in the town.

In the morning it still rained so heavily, and the ground was so sodden that we thought it best to remain in bed till noon in order to keep warm and dry. The men made stepping stones between the tents, and did everything that care and forethought could do to make us feel comfortable; and in the afternoon the rain clearing off after sixteen hours' heavy downpour, we made an attempt to see the town, and took that furtive glance into the Haram from the street above, and up the steps which lead to the mosque covering the cave of Macpelah from the street below, which is all that Moslem fanaticism allows to the Christian. The streets were filthy beyond description, and the rain had made the rough stones so slippery that we could barely balance ourselves on them: so that we soon had enough of Hebron.

We settled to take two fresh Beduins (the old ones leaving us here) and a soldier to 'Ain Jidy. There were several German gentlemen also going to that place, and they brought another Beduin, so that we felt well protected.

We left Hebron as early the following day as we could, considering the difficulty of getting men and mules over the slippery muddy ground. We had soon to go up a kind of rocky staircase which ascended rapidly and made the footholding very difficult for the good horses. But once on the top of the hill the staircase came to an end, and there was no more marsh, the air was buoyant and fresh, and the wild thyme smelt deliciously after the rain. Passing this good ground we had soon to descend along the windings of a deep gorge like that of Marsaba; and after five hours of this work we came to a plain in which we found a large Beduin encampment where the sheik received us with a welcome; and here we settled to remain for the night. The Germans, pressed for time, determined to go on, and took our Beduins with them for protection, leaving us only with the soldier. The sheik, however, expressed a wish to accompany us on the morrow.

We were seated comfortably in our tents, resting after our ride, when all at once a great hubbub arose between the soldier and a Beduin who had come to have a good look at us. The soldier struck the Beduin; the latter struck back; the soldier picked up his rifle and aimed at the man; and the other Beduins ran up to assist their brother; but George and the sheik interfered in time, and after much talk and unpleasantness peace was restored. To make the peace good we invited the sheik to eat with us and offered food to all; at the sight whereof the soldier and the Beduins became friendly with one another. The sheik insisted on giving us a sheep which was killed and cooked, and our men sat down and ate it. When it became dark, in order to amuse the Beduins, we lighted some magnesium wire, but although they had never seen such a thing before they expressed no surprise. They mentioned casually to George, however, that they supposed we had shown them something which had fallen from the stars.

The next day the sheik and one of his men came with us, and after a ride of only two and a half hours we arrived at the top of the great pass which is above 'Ain Jidy, the Engedi of the Scriptures. Here we had a glorious view through the jagged gap in the mountains of the Dead Sea lying placid and blue far below us, and across its deep waters of the mountains of Moab. We wanted to descend to 'Ain Jidy, camp there, and follow the shore northwards to Ras el Feshka, a mountain at the north-west corner of the Dead Sea, but the Beduins told us that the lake was unusually full, the water being so high that it would be impossible to get past the mountain side in some places. We had, therefore, to go to Bethlehem direct. But I descended the extremely steep path to the Spring of the Kid ('Ain Jidy). A portion of the descent consists of mere ledges of slippery rock overhanging a sheer precipice, and other parts are much more like a broken staircase than a path. The sun striking against the face of the cliff made it very hot work.

I found the spring rushing out from under a rock, but although very clear the water is tepid. A few trees and bushes surround the stream, and there is some cultivation where it reaches, but nothing compared to what would be possible with proper attention and what must have existed in ancient times.[1] It was too hot to go further down to the shore of the Dead Sea which appeared to be several hundred feet below, and

---

[1] "My beloved is unto me as a cluster of camphire by the vineyards of Engedi" (Song of Solomon).

I rested here until the sun moving to the westward, the path was in the shadow cast by the cliffs, and then re-ascended. It was a most pleasant change to get to the top of the pass where our tents stood, for there the air was fresh and exhilarating, and the view extraordinarily beautiful and grand. After watching the purple light of sunset die out upon the mountains to the eastward, we went happy and tired to bed.

We awoke "in the dead vast and middle of the night," and stood at our tent door to gaze on the splendour of a Syrian night; on moon and stars resplendent in their majesty; on high and jagged rocks; on deep gorges, and precipices, and old hermits' caverns invested with wondrous Rembrantesque effects of light and shade; on the deep waters of the Dead Sea; and on the faint outlines of the Moabite mountains. An intense feeling of loneliness and awe and mystery wrapt us round, and held our very senses in a spellbound suspense; even "the inaudible and noiseless foot of time" seemed to be arrested.

In the morning we parted with Sheik Moussa, and giving him, in addition to his own backsheesh, a small musical box for his little son, started on our way to Bethlehem. We ascended a pass to the north-west, a very difficult and almost dangerous road, and added a stone to the heap at the top made by travellers who have arrived so far in safety. For two hours the country was a complete desert; not a bird or other creature, not a tree, nor any sign of vegetation; although later we passed some Beduin encampments and bits of cultivated ground. After nine hours of very fatiguing riding in a hot sun we climbed up a long rocky ascent to Bethlehem, and found rest and food at a spot at a little distance from the town, commanding a fine view of the Church of the Nativity, where we have encamped on several occasions: and the following day, the twenty-third of March, we reached Jerusalem.

GROUP OF ARABS—HEBRON.

THE JORDAN VALLEY.

CHAPTER IV.

FROM JERUSALEM TO BEISAN, MUZEYRÎB, AND DAMASCUS.

"Strike the innocent that the guilty may confess."
BURCKHARDT'S "ARABIC PROVERBS."

FROM Jerusalem we journeyed northward to Bethel, to Hawara, to Nablous (the ancient Shechem), where live about eighty-five Samaritans, the sole survivors of their ancient faith, and so to Jenîn. At Jenîn we obtained an escort of two soldiers, and turning to the eastward we rode through the plain of Jezreel, passing Ahab's Acropolis in a great darkness and storm of rain and wind, in which lightning flashes lit up the slopes of the hills, and illuminated the masses of cloud rolling up from Mount Carmel and the sea, as on the day when "Elijah girded up his loins" and ran before the king's chariot to the entrance of Jezreel; past Mount Gilboa, where Saul and Jonathan were slain; past the fountain of Gideon, to Beïsan (the ancient Bethshean—Scythopolis) a place containing some very extensive and interesting ruins; down to the valley of the Jordan; along the west bank to the old Roman bridge; over it; across the eastern side of the valley; up the slopes of the Eastern hills; down into the valleys, in which the streams flow, and the oleanders stand above our heads, as we push through the water on horseback; up again, slope beyond slope of rich but uncultivated land, carpeted with a wonderful profusion of wild flowers, cream-coloured, golden-yellow, and purple, until we encamped at the top of a high ridge, from whence we could look down upon the plain which leads to Damascus.

On this ridge was a village, and here a little incident occurred which throws light on the ways of the country. George engaged one of the villagers to bring water for us. He was seen to run away with a metal dish belonging to our cook, but on being charged with the theft denied it. When we got up the next morning we found that the soldiers who accompanied us had taken this man and chained his feet together, and were beginning to beat him with a stick to make him confess where the dish was. But we objected to this, and the man, being released, ran to me, kissing the hem of my coat, my hands and my feet, in spite of all my efforts to prevent him, and cried out that he was innocent. Thinking that perhaps there had been a mistake, and not feeling authorized to be judge in what was very like my own case, I told the soldiers to let him go, and very soon afterwards he was smoking a friendly cigarette with them.

Then the sheik of the village came and offered to pay the value of the basin; but we thought that he would reimburse himself by making exactions from the villagers, who looked very poor, and so we declined his proposal. We supposed the matter to be ended, and rode on our way with George and a Beduin guide, leaving the others to follow with the soldiers. But after we had started, the cook, who wanted his dish for use on the journey, and could not wait till we could buy him another, went to the village, found the man's house, and, searching it, discovered the stolen object hidden under some wood.

The soldiers now looked for the offender, but he had run off. So they seized his brother (an old man) instead, and, binding his arms behind him, began to lead him off to Irbid, a town seven hours' distant by the way we were going; and the old man's son followed him, lamenting and abusing the whole party. Soon the poor old fellow fell down, being unable, from infirmity, to walk; and at this stage we found out what was going on, and got the soldiers to release him. We were perhaps the first European travellers whom these villagers had beheld, and we should have been very sorry to have brought any trouble upon them.

We rode on from here in the beautiful morning light, the country looking radiant after the rain, passing olive trees, tall barley, and oaks which grew larger and more abundant as we descended. We passed down the eastern slopes of the hills and on to the great plain, and to the little lake and village of Muzeyrîb, where the great Hadj, or company of pilgrims going to Mecca, assemble and rest certain days, while the stragglers and late starters from Damascus and other places join the vast crowd, which then "flows due on" to the Holy City of the Moslems.[1]

[1] "The assembling of the pilgrim multitude is always by the

So, journeying on, we came by the pilgrim road (in many parts of which the Roman pavement still remains, and on which we saw the poor peasants forced to labour at the improving of the highway) to the ancient city of Damascus, which we reached on the sixth of April. Our journey up to this point had occupied twenty-six days, so that we had now settled well into our saddles, and felt encouraged to make the (to us) great attempt of the journey to Palmyra.

We had visited Baalbek in 1887, Jerash in 1888, but there remained Palmyra. For years we had talked about Palmyra. We longed and yet feared to undertake that difficult journey. Heat, cold, fatigue, thirst, sand storms, and Beduins seemed to threaten our path, and warn us from the attempt; and I must now frankly admit that if I had known of the obstacles which we had to surmount, and the discomforts (notwithstanding all that was done by our dragoman and other servants to assist us) that we had to endure, I for one should still have been "letting I dare not wait upon I would, like the poor cat i' the adage."

After we had pitched our camp at Damascus, which we did by the side of a clear stream springing from a

lake of Muzeyrîb in the high steppes beyond Jordan, two journeys from Damascus. Here the hajjies who have taken the field are encamped, and lie a week or ten days in the desert before their long voyage" (Doughty's "Arabia Deserta"). Any one interested in Beduin life should read this most admirable work. Even to those not interested in the subject, the very unusual but—when one gets used to it—extremely attractive literary style of the writer would be sufficient recompense.

basin, and in a certain garden of roses,[1] where we had been accommodated in 1887, the first intelligence which we obtained was that no one could go to Palmyra that year.

The Government authorities at Damascus, who are accustomed to send a guard of soldiers with travellers on the rare occasions when the journey is made, refused to allow of any escort, and two English gentlemen, who had come to that city for the purpose of making the expedition, had on this ground given up their intention and gone back to Beyrout. But George was determined that we should not be disappointed, and seeking out a Beduin sheik, called "Nasr," or the Victorious, belonging to the Aenezeh tribe, in whose country Palmyra is situate, brought him to our camp. We arranged with Sheik Nasr that he should be our guide and protector, as we supposed that if any Beduins were inclined to rob us, his authority would be sufficient to prevent them from carrying their intention into effect. He was not to set out with us, lest it should be known where we were going, but to join us at our first camping-place.

On the morning of the ninth of April we took our departure. Our company consisted of my wife, myself, the faithful George, Haleel our cook, Tanus our waiter, Selim our chief muleteer, three under-

---

[1] "A fountain of gardens, a well of living waters, and streams from Lebanon" (Song of Solomon).

"In that City of Damascus there is great plenty of wells, and within the city and without are many fair gardens, with diversity of fruits. No other city can be compared with it for fair gardens" (Sir John Mandeville, A.D. 1322).

muleteers, and the young man of all work, named Nakhli, who, with our dragoman, now accompanied us on our travels in Syria for the third season in succession. We had the usual provision of tents and baggage mules, and rode on horses. We left all the arrangements to George.

MUZEYRIB.

RIDING IN THE DESERT.

CHAPTER V.

FROM DAMASCUS TO PALMYRA.

"But is there for the night a resting-place?"
CHRISTINA ROSSETTI.

"I did hear
The galloping of horse?"
  * * * * *
"Were such things here as we do speak about?
Or have we eaten on the insane root
That takes the reason prisoner?"
"MACBETH."

AS we started for Palmyra George led the way, riding with great pride at the head of the procession, but he was careful to take us through some back streets; and I rather think that the Zaptieh, or police officer, who had been to our tent to see our passports, had left under the impression that we were going in a very different direction; for George told me afterwards that we should have been brought back if the police had known our real destination. And no doubt, from all that I heard, he was right.

Through the streets we passed into the gardens of Damascus, and then from below the grateful shade of the trees out into the open country. Then, ascending along the side of a swift running stream, we plunged into a rocky gorge, which was so narrow that we were as often riding in the bed of the stream as on the almost precipitous side of the hollow. Then we passed through a wider part of the valley, which was planted with trees, and reached the source of the rushing little river, and of all the vegetable life which clung close to its course, which we found issuing from the foot of a high rock, in a great bubble and rush of water. Then we passed into a bare hilly country, rising gradually to a summit, on which stands an old Greek nunnery, that towers above a village called Saidnâya, containing a population mostly of Christians. According to the usual custom, while we stayed for luncheon (which on this day we had eaten by the stream in the wooded valley) our muleteers and baggage animals had passed us, and proceeded on to the spot where George had arranged to pitch the camp for the night. But the country was strange to them, and they had wandered from the track, or rather from the direction, for there was no particular track.

We supposed the tents to be ahead of us, and kept riding on. Our way lay over a country regularly undulating like great waves of the ocean. There were crests with hollows between, and we rode on and on, up the sides, and over the crests, and down into the hollows, expecting from every little summit to see the welcome white tents with their flags fluttering in the breeze, and the tired mules tethered around.

The sun was getting lower and lower on the horizon, and the high and rocky hills which bounded the view to the west (we were going about north-east) began to cast long shadows behind us, which gradually crept up to us, and passed on enveloping us in the shades of evening, and still no tents were to be seen. George galloped on to a distant village, but returned without being able to learn anything of the camp. At last night fell, and the stars and moon shone forth, but still no prospect of food or bed appeared. Then we had to give up all thoughts of tents, and make for the nearest village; where, after much palaver, and after a congregation of curious shepherds and husbandmen had inspected us in the moonlight, we were ushered through a courtyard enclosed in mud walls (where men lay under a pent-house roof and camels reposed in the open air) into the family living room, of which the house proper alone consisted. It was about twenty feet square, the ceiling formed of trunks of poplar trees covered with a mud roof, and the walls fresh daubed with a kind of cement of mud, which was still not quite dry. The woman of the house lighted a fire of sticks and cow dung under a rude chimney, drew some coverlets and mats from a heap which lay in a corner of the room, placed a smoky little oil lamp over the fireplace, and sat down with all the rest of the family on the other side of the room, from whence they enjoyed a hearty and very long stare at us, queer and outlandish creatures no doubt in their sight, as they were in ours. Fortunately, we had some remains of lunch in a bag and a little cold tea, and we comforted ourselves with these refreshments (which were, however, not too abundant) as well as we could, and slept as much as possible, which was in truth but little, for the place was damp, and got very cold as the night dragged its slow length along.

The next day Sheik Nasr found us, and we all proceeded together, he leading us more to the north, until after a long ascent we got to the foot of a great precipitous range of rocky heights which appeared to crown the hills on that side. Then we passed through a very narrow winding cleft in them, and began another slow ascent up the sides of bare stony hills, and on to a ridge at the top of them where the wind blew very coldly and in great gusts, so that we could barely get our horses along it; then down a steep descent into a deep valley, where was the welcome sight of a stream of water, a few trees, a little verdure, a monastery, and a collection of rude dwellings mostly made out of old caves which are very numerous here. This was Ma'lula, a very curious looking place.[1] Even here deep in the hollow as we were, and surrounded by trees, the wind blew so hard at night that we expected the tents to be carried away, or to tear down the slender trees to whose trunks they were attached by means of ropes, and whose boughs

---

[1] A full account of Ma'lula and of the peculiar dialect spoken there (written by my friend Mr. F. Bliss) is to be found in the Quarterly Statement of the Palestine Exploration Fund for April, 1890.

bent over us with the blast. But in all the storms we have been in under canvas, George has managed by his watchful care always to keep a roof over our heads.

The third day we kept more to the east, getting the wind behind us, which was easier to bear. In three hours we came to a steep hill-side in which numerous caves had been cut, some apparently places of sepulture, others hermits' holes; then we moved

NEBK.

towards a white-coloured hill at the foot of which was a white-coloured village, all intensely staring in the heat, for it had now become extremely hot. The people of the village stared at us even more than their houses and the hill-side, and plodding on through the white heat we got to Nebk, where our tents were pitched.

The next day of nearly eight hours' riding brought

us to Mahîn; and on the fifth day from Damascus, a journey of three and a half hours brought us to Karyatên. Up to this point, although the country through which we had passed had been almost entirely bare, yet in several of the valleys there were springs, and wherever there was water there was a village with a patch of cultivation round it.

But at Karyatên the waterless desert begins, and extends to Palmyra, a distance of about fifty miles. Here we were detained for two days, owing to my wife being ill. The governor of the place came to call, and asked why we had not brought an escort of soldiers with us. He added that the night before we arrived, the Governor of Damascus with fifty soldiers was at Karyatên, having just returned from the desert with eighteen captive Beduins, who were charged with robbing the caravans going from Bagdad to Damascus (which pass through Palmyra) and with stealing cattle from Karyatên; and had marched off his prisoners chained together to Damascus. Fortunately we had not come the shortest way to Karyatên, and so we had missed the great man, or he would no doubt have stopped our further progress. The Governor of Karyatên said we must take four soldiers with us, as the desert was not safe from the predatory Beduins, and upon our asking whether the capture just made would not clear the route from danger, he replied that if we refused to take the escort, we must give him a paper to acknowledge that it had been offered and declined. So we accepted the offer, and the governor departed.

We determined to start from Karyatên in the evening, as George and the sheik wished to travel as far as possible at night in order to avoid the Beduins; and we were anxious to escape the heat of the sun, which was very oppressive in the daytime. The hour for leaving came, but the soldiers did not appear, notwithstanding the messages which we sent to the governor. In the East no one is punctual, or has any notion that promises are made to be kept; so we determined not to wait, not knowing when we should get away if we did, and we set off about an hour before sunset. We had engaged three camels to carry water for ourselves, our men, and our animals, and a man with a long fire-lock gun accompanied them as driver. Having read much about the cold at night in the desert we dressed warmly, but a Sirocco or Khampseen wind blew, and it was very hot and oppressive.

We passed through the village on the way out into the desert. Although it was near the close of the day, the heat radiated from the dry mud walls almost unbearably, and we had to cover our faces as we rode under them. We left the gardens and the cypress trees behind us, and then through the haze of the Sirocco we went out as it were into space, and lost sight of everything but our own men, and the ground beneath our feet. The animals stept as if they knew of the long journey before them—quietly, patiently—but as if determined to contend with and overcome the difficulties before them. The moon was at the full, but the dull, hot wind blew across our faces, and we breathed with difficulty. We went at a quiet walking pace or amble, the sheik leading with his fast-stepping horse, and we following him one by one, having to break into a trot now and then in order to keep up. No one said a word. Before us lay the desert.

Suddenly the sheik's horse stopped and pricked up his ears, and our horses followed his example; we all looked around us, but could see and hear nothing. The sheik brought his gun in front of him, and so did George; and after a little pause the horses went on again. Then we heard galloping behind us, and saw two horsemen emerge from the haze and ride up one on each side of us, carrying their guns as if ready for action. We thought, "Here are the Beduins," but no one spoke. There came into my mind these lines of Andrew Marvell:—

> "But at my back I always hear
> Time's wingèd chariot hurrying near,
> And yonder all before us lie
> Deserts of vast eternity."

I saw Sheik Nasr and George with their weapons grasped in their hands look furtively at these men, and dreamily I also laid my hand on my revolver. No one greeted them, nor did they say a word; and for some time we rode along wondering who they could be, when a little foal which followed the mare on which one of them rode caused the silence to be broken. Running in front of my wife's horse, it caused the latter to falter; and then the man who rode upon its mother —a dark handsome fellow—offered an excuse, and, greeting us, said that he and his companion were soldiers sent after us by the Governor of Karyatên. They were dressed much like Beduins, and except that they carried Remington rifles instead of flint-lock guns, there was very little to distinguish them from the Ishmaelites.

On and on we rode all through that long hot night. Occasionally a burning breath swept across us, leaving behind it a feeling of sickness and exhaustion, and making our hearts beat quickly. Then we seemed to be going on in a dream, and when a halt was called for a brief period of rest, we lay down on the warm sand and fell into a dreamless sleep, from which it was difficult to awake again.

That night of riding was the strangest which I ever passed. The thin dusty haze seemed to make every object unnatural, mysterious, and ghostly. All night long it appeared to me that we were riding up-hill, and yet I knew we were on a dead flat. Several times we thought we saw flashes of lights ahead of us, although it was probably only our imagination which " informed thus to our eyes," and I could not rid myself of the strong impression that was on me that we were approaching some great city ; although we were, as I knew, plunging deeper and deeper into the wilderness. As the day broke we could see more of the country. At last my wife was completely exhausted ; and, with the morning sunlight pouring in upon our tired eyes, the tents were pitched, and we were soon wrapt round with oblivion.

When we awoke we were enabled to look about us more carefully. There is a high range of hills on each side of the desert plain, which is, I think, about ten miles broad here ; and the Beduins live in these hills, especially I am told on the south side, where there are some springs of water. From thence they descend into the plains to plunder the caravans, or to seize cattle from the villages on the border of the desert.

A ride of six or seven hours through great heat brought us to El Bêda. The same sirocco haze lasted nearly all day, and the illusions of the desert continued. We had a mirage always in front of us of a lake of clear water, the shores of which we could never reach. Once we saw three islands on it, and the imposing buildings of a phantom city on the middle one. Then islands, buildings, and city, disappeared; and there was nothing left but the strange atmosphere, "the sea of air" which surrounded us.

About noon we saw some distant objects like giants walking towards us. We all halted, and Sheik Nasr said he thought it was a trading caravan. But the soldiers were not satisfied, and unslinging their rifles from their backs galloped forward; and George soon followed them. As we drew nearer the giants seemed to vanish entirely; then the figures appeared again, looking like cows, and finally as we closed with them, we found a flock of sheep and goats bound from Palmyra to Karyatên. Sheik Nasr jumped off from his horse, nimbly caught a she-goat by the leg, borrowed a metal cup from one of the men, and gave us each two cups of delicious fresh milk. We never tasted anything so pleasant in our lives.

El Bêda, which is not marked on any chart, is off the direct line from Karyatên to Palmyra, considerably to the north of that line, and near to the mountains on the north side of the desert. But there is at this spot a well of water, very brackish and nasty though it be, and here within the last three or four years the Turkish Government have established a small military station, consisting of a block house occupied by an officer and eight soldiers. There are no other buildings, nor are there any Beduin tents at this place, and these poor soldiers must lead a most desolate life in the desert. This station is about six hours' ride from Palmyra. It blew very hard during the night we spent there, and our tents were again in danger of coming down, and everything inside them was covered with sand.

The next morning just as we were going to start I met with a misfortune; the sheik's horse gave me a nasty bite on the leg which caused me a great deal of pain, and lamed me more or less for about ten days, so that I had to be lifted on and off my horse; and this accident hampered me very much in getting about the ruins.

As we approached the end of our journey, the visions of the desert faded away, and disclosed the southern hills curving sharply round to meet those on the north, leaving between them only a narrow gap, on the other side of which was the object of our desire. At last we reached the tall, round tower-tombs which stand just before the entrance to the ruined city, and saw the wide stretched solemn ruins before us, and beyond

> "Immense horizon-bounded plains succeed,
> Far as the eye discerns without an end."

After resting in one of the most sumptuous of these great monuments of human vanity and sheltering for a while from "the broad glare of the hot noon," we rode up the celebrated street of columns which leads towards the great Temple of the Sun, and found our tents pitched close to a stream of clear water.

SMALL TEMPLE, PALMYRA.

GATEWAY AND PART OF COLONNADE, PALMYRA.

CHAPTER VI.

TADMOR IN THE WILDERNESS.

> "Not Babylon
> Nor great Alcairo such magnificence
> Equal'd in all their glories."
> "PARADISE LOST."

> "Poor fragments of a broken world
> Whereon we pitch our tents."
> MATTHEW ARNOLD.

IT is mentioned in the Bible that Solomon built Tadmor in the wilderness.[1] Palmyra is called Tudmor by the Arabs, and it is generally believed that it is the place referred to in the Scriptures. But this is

[1] 1 Kings ix. 18; 2 Chronicles viii. 5.

doubted by some writers, who suppose the town built by Solomon to have been a place called Tamar in Judea.

At any rate Tudmor must have existed from a very early period, and have been used, as in historic times it always has been and still is used, namely, as a halting-place for caravans crossing the desert from the Euphrates to Syria; its site being an oasis with a copious supply of water in a dry and thirsty land. There appears to be no historical mention of the place other than that in the Bible until the time of Pliny.

The period of its greatest splendour began with the overthrow of the Nabatæans of Petra, A.D. 105, which left it without a rival. It passed under the protection of Rome under Hadrian, A.D. 130, and its influence and wealth rapidly increased. Though nominally subject to Rome, it was ruled by its own laws and governed by a Senate chosen by the citizens. It was at this time the great highway for all the luxuries of the east. West of Palmyra were Roman roads, on which no doubt there was fair protection to life and property, and the bales of goods were, it is said, conveyed in waggons by these roads to Palmyra. If so, there must have been some source or store of water on the latter part of the way which does not now exist. But east of the oasis there was no road, and life and property were very insecure. The trade was very profitable, but conducted at enormous risk, and to carry it to a satisfactory end was a distinguished service to the State. Public monuments were often erected by the Senate and people to the merchants of the caravan. These monuments were a conspicuous feature in Palmyrene architecture. They generally took the form

Part of Colonnade, Palmyra.

of statues placed on pedestals projecting from the upper part of the long rows of pillars which lined the principal streets, for every merchant was eager to see his name handed down to posterity, and to add to the colonnades a series of pillars. Thus arose the great central avenue which, starting from a triumphal arch near the great Temple of the Sun, formed the main axis of the city from south-east to north-west for thirteen hundred and forty yards, and at one time consisted of not less than seven hundred and fifty columns (or as one authority considers, fifteen hundred columns) of rosy white limestone, each fifty-five feet high. "In some parts the pillars seemed to have served to support a raised footway, from which loungers could look down at their ease on the waggons piled with bales of silk or purple wool, or with Greek bronzes designed to adorn some Eastern palace, the long strings of asses laden with skins or *alabustra* of precious unguents, the swinging camels charged with oil from Palestine or hides from the Arabian deserts, and the motley crew of divers nationalities which crowded the streets beneath; the slave-merchant with his human wares from Egypt or Asia Minor, the Roman legionary, and the half-naked Saracen, the Jewish, Persian, and Armenian merchants, the street-hawkers of old clothes, the petty hucksters at the corners offering roasted pine-cones, salt-fish, and other dainties; the tawdry slave-girls, whose shameful trade went to swell the State, and the noisy salt auction, presided over by an officer of customs." Pure salt was one of the chief local industries, and another was the manufacture of leather. The inscriptions also tell of a guild of workers in silver and gold.

All quarters of the town show signs of magnificent building. Still, wealth must have been confined to the few, and there must have been the usual Oriental picture of squalor and magnificence, mud-huts and palaces. The great families remained Oriental rather than Greek or Roman. The capable discharge of public functions ensured the public esteem, and the head of a great house was careful to add the glory of a splendid family tomb, consecrated as the "long home" of himself, his sons, and sons' sons for ever. These tombs which lie outside the city are very remarkable and interesting. Some are lofty, square towers with as many as five chambers occupying successive stories, and overlooking the town and its approaches; others are house-like buildings of one story, richly decorated inside and out with sculptured portraits of the dead. The scale of these monuments corresponds to the wide conception of an Eastern family, from which dependents and slaves were not excluded, and on one inscription a slave is named with the sons of the house. The style of all the ruins except these is late, classic, ornate, and without refinement.

Palmyra touched the highest point of all its greatness under Odenathus, and after his death under his widow, the renowned Zenobia, who assumed the government A.D. 267. Her policy was by playing off Rome and Persia against one another to increase the power of Palmyra, which she succeeded in doing until its empire included Egypt, as well as much of Syria and Asia Minor. This beautiful, brave, and intellectual warrior-queen reigned for five years; but "vaulting ambition o'erleaped itself," and in A.D. 271, the Emperor Aurelian turned his arms against her, and having defeated her in a pitched battle near Antioch, and another at Emesa (the modern Homs), he drove her back upon her desert home, and laid siege to Palmyra, which after a brief struggle capitulated. Zenobia, flying from Aurelian's troops, was captured on the banks of the Euphrates and taken to Rome; where, bound with fetters of gold, and almost fainting under the weight of the jewels which she was forced to wear, she graced the Emperor's triumph. She is said to have married again in Rome, and to have ended her life peacefully on the banks of the Tiber.

Aurelian took Palmyra in A.D. 272, and left in it a small garrison, but soon after his departure the people rose and massacred them. On hearing of this the Emperor returned, pillaged the city, and put to the sword those of the inhabitants who were not reserved for massacre in the amphitheatres at Antioch. The city was repaired and the Temple of the Sun was rebuilt, but the place never regained its former opulence.

Very little is known of Palmyra in the Middle Ages. Europeans were unaware of the existence of the ruins until in 1678 an English merchant of Aleppo visited them. In 1751, Messrs Wood and Dawkins made an expedition to Palmyra, and taking accurate drawings and measurements, and copying the inscriptions, published a folio volume upon the subject.[1]

[1] This sketch is compiled from various well-known sources. Any one interested in the romantic side of the subject should read "The Last Days and Fall of Palmyra" (Cassell and Co.).

The ruins now above ground stretch over a very large area, and no doubt there is much entirely hidden under the sand which during sixteen centuries has been blown in from the desert. The Temple of the Sun is

ARAB ENTRANCE TO THE GREAT TEMPLE OF THE SUN, PALMYRA.

of enormous size, about two hundred and fifty yards square, and encompassed by a wall seventy feet high. A great portion of it is standing, but the interior details are difficult of investigation, as it is filled up with the

GREAT TEMPLE OF THE SUN, PALMYRA.

hovels of the Arabs who inhabit Palmyra. The great colonnade is very striking. Only one hundred and fifty of the columns are still standing in their place, and long ranges lie prostrate.

All modern notices of Palmyra which I have read refer to the fact that no fresh water is to be found there, and some express wonder at the ancient prosperity of the place in the absence of this requisite. The guide books recommend the traveller to bring a supply of drinking water with him, as the stream of sulphurous water (which until 1888 was alone known in modern times as the source of supply there) is very disagreeable to the taste. We were therefore much surprised to find that the stream near to which our tents were pitched was fresh and pure. It appears that it was only discovered in the summer of 1888, and that we were the first European travellers to see it. It runs only a few feet under the surface of the ground, in an old flagged channel or conduit, which widens out at the spot where it comes to light, so as to admit of a landing on which people coming to fetch water, or to bathe, can stand; and it was a very interesting sight to see the hot and thirsty Arabs engaged in digging during the day in other parts of the ruins for water which they had not yet found, rush rejoicing at sunset to this spot. But the artificial channel ending here the water disappears shortly afterwards in a sandy hollow. The volume of the stream is about sixteen inches deep by twenty-two wide; the water is tepid, but when cooled in earthenware jars very pleasant and refreshing to the taste. I have no doubt that there are several similar streams conducted by similar channels in other parts of the ruins. The surface of the ground, presumably in consequence of the accumulation of sand blown in from the desert, has evidently risen since the erection of the chief buildings (as one may see from the proportions of the arches and columns in many places) and probably this is the cause of the disappearance of these streams. The finding of the one which we saw has stirred up the inhabitants to search for more fresh water, and pits were sinking in several places during our visit. If water is found in the abundance in which it must once have flowed, and probably still flows, underground, Palmyra may once more " blossom as the rose."

Soon after our arrival the Governor sent for our passport and *téskeré*, or permission to travel in the interior. He found fault with the latter for not having been properly countersigned at Damascus, and stated that he had just sent back a French lady for this very want. The poor lady in question had had the courage to come from Damascus attended only by a Dragoman, without tents, sleeping in the villages up to Karyatên, and afterwards on the ground. She reached Palmyra at eight in the evening, and at three the next morning was sent off on the weary ride of six days back to Damascus without having seen anything beyond what the moonlight showed her. With the exception of this lady, I believe we were the only travellers who succeeded in reaching Palmyra in 1889.

George put the matter right with the Governor, so far as we were concerned, by showing him the Turkish *visés* of many years' accumulation attached to my passport; the presence of Sheik Nasr, and the fact that we travelled with tents and as persons of consequence, no doubt helped to avoid difficulties; and I am afraid also that my importance was exaggerated. At any rate, the Governor paid us every attention.

He showed us a piece of sculpture, apparently of a sepulchral character, which had just been unearthed by some Arabs, and which was the only absolutely uninjured thing of the kind which we saw above ground at Palmyra. It was about five feet long by three feet

SCULPTURE, PALMYRA.

wide, and represented a man reclining, clothed in an embroidered dress, wearing a hat much resembling that worn by the present Shah of Persia, and holding a cup in his hand. A female figure, that no doubt of his wife, was seated at the opposite side, and behind stood three boys, who must have been his sons. It bore an inscription in the Palmyrene character, but I know no note of it, and could not decipher what was written.

The Governor had swooped down on the piece before the Arabs had had time to break off the heads for sale according to their usual custom.

In addition to the monuments mentioned in the guide books, we saw some more sepulchral sculptures, partly excavated, in a mound about one-third of a mile to the south of the Great Temple. Besides masses of these, there were here several columns without capitals standing *in situ*, and the appearance of the remains indicated an important family tomb. All the heads of the figures which could be reached from above had been knocked off, but there were some uninjured underneath and out of reach. There were many more mounds near which looked as if they contained similar remains. There must be a considerable trade in these stone heads, which are sold to passing caravans, and so reach Damascus, where they may be bought in the curiosity shops.

The Governor spoke to us of the enormity of this destruction, and we, entirely agreeing with what he said, refused to purchase some heads which were offered to me. We even declined one which was pressed upon us by an emissary, sent by himself at night, with a message that of course the governor would not expect any present in return; the meaning of which we took to be that the return present must be something valuable. But our virtue was not of much avail, as we afterwards found that our men (all except the faithful George, who obeyed orders) had provided themselves with busts of deceased citizens of Palmyra.

We took some photographs here, and at other places on our journey. But from want of experience, and from difficulties arising from accidents to the apparatus, some of those preserved did not turn out very well; whilst many were spoilt by the curiosity of an amiable little Turkish soldier who went about with us at Palmyra, and opened the box to see what was inside. As it contained a roll of Eastman's paper the result was disastrous.

COLUMN, PALMYRA.

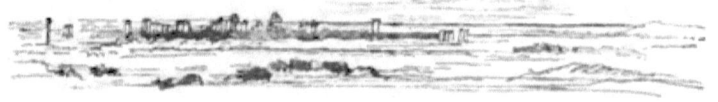

LAST VIEW OF PALMYRA.

CHAPTER VII.

THE RETURN JOURNEY.

"Be thy intents wicked or charitable,
Thou com'st in such a questionable shape
That I will speak to thee."
"HAMLET."

AFTER three days' stay in Palmyra the heat drove us away. It was most exhausting and overpowering, the Khampseen wind still prevailing; and although we had intended to remain for a week, we felt that we could not bear it longer. It was, however, with a sad heart that we paused at the gorge in the hills to take one last look back upon Palmyra. But nature is as beautiful as art, and when the great ruins were lost to sight we saw a different sight which compensated us for what was gone. At that moment a very large troop of camels, said to number with their little ones seven hundred, were coming into the place from the desert. They belonged to Sheik Nasr's tribe, and he rode off to see them, and to fall upon the necks of his brethren and kiss them before he returned with us.

We determined to go back to Damascus by another route *viâ* Homs (the ancient Emesa) where Zenobia was defeated by the Romans, and near to which the

Orontes rises. The first day we only rode as far as El Bêda, where we had halted before. The journey was most trying. A strong west wind arose, bearing great quantities of sand, and burning like the blast of a furnace. Eyes, nose, and lips became intensely irritated, and for hour after hour we had to struggle on with faces muffled up, and eyes almost closed against the wind. The wind increasing, we had to hurry forward as hard as we could for the last half hour through the sheets of flying sand, leaving our horses to find their own way, for we dared not uncover our eyes, and feared lest the animals should be overwhelmed. After six and a half hours of struggle we reached the little block house, where we were glad to lie down in a room, the shutters of which were closed (there were of course no glass windows) to keep out the terrible blast; and to be able to rest amidst the patter of the sand against the wooden shutters, and the rattling of the latter in their frames, until our tents were, with many efforts, put up and made fast.

On the way from Palmyra to El Bêda, passing near to the hills which bound the desert plain to the north, we kept for some miles along a line of old wells or pits, in some of which our men found a little water. I suppose that these were used in ancient times for the irrigation of the district to the west of Palmyra, and I imagine that they are connected with conduits running underground from the hills to the north of the gap through which the entrance to the city lies, and from which hills no doubt much of the water supply for the use of the inhabitants within the walls proceeded.

We presented the officer at El Bêda (a very hairy,

fierce-looking man, whom George christened the Hyena) with a Turkish dollar and a sheep, and in return he sent with us two soldiers as a guard (in addition to the two whom we had brought from Karyatên, and who were still with us) telling us that we should not be safe without at least four until the first day's journey from El Bêda was finished; by which time we should be clear of the desert, and well amongst the northern hills, where there were villages with peaceable inhabitants. We had a very fatiguing ride of nine hours before we reached the first spring, and here we encamped. As we ascended these northern hills the wind became very cold; it seemed to cut through the few extra wraps which we could put on by the way, and I felt very ill. By the evening of this day the temperature had fallen about thirty-five to forty degrees from what it had been at Palmyra. The four soldiers left us next morning, as we were now clear of the waterless desert, although we were still in the wilderness.

But we had not been riding for more than two or three hours when we witnessed a striking illustration of the insecure state of the country. George pointed out to Sheik Nasr and to us a hill, on the top of which were three horsemen standing. We knew enough of the Beduins to be aware that these were an outpost, and that there would be more men behind the hill. We stopped to enable our men, who were straggling behind, to come up with us. While they were assembling, and George, Nasr, and I were getting our revolvers ready, we noticed a sheik on a white horse, bearing a long lance in his hand, riding towards us from the plain below the hill. Sheik Nasr fired off his revolver in the direction of this man, to show him that we were armed, and the ball went unpleasantly near to him.

George advised me in case we were attacked to fire at the horses of the Beduins, not at the riders; for, while the Ishmaelites value their horses so highly that they might retreat rather than risk the loss of them, the death of one of the tribe must by their code of honour be avenged by the blood of the slayer; and George and Nasr rode off to meet the warrior on the white horse. It then appeared that the latter was connected with Sheik Nasr by marriage, so all was well; and the man with the lance explained that he thought we were coming to plunder his tribe. He said that the day before the Beduins from the desert had come and seized all their camels, which they had only recovered by bringing all their force out at once; and that seeing us coming from the same direction, whence none but marauders came, he thought we were on a similar errand. He was still rather suspicious, especially as we did not accept his invitation to eat with him (for we were anxious to get on), and he told George and Nasr that if we touched him, or made any movement towards the camels, the men on the hill who could see us clearly enough, would signal to the men behind it, and the latter would sweep round upon us. When we got past the hill we saw some seventy-five or eighty horsemen, all sitting as still as death, waiting for a signal from the summit; and as long as we were in sight they stood watching, evidently distrusting us. We had the last sight of them as we crossed over a high ridge to the northwards.

After a ride of eight and a half hours against a cutting wind, which got colder and colder as we advanced over the hills, we reached a miserable little village where the people received us kindly into one of their hovels, and made a fire of cow dung to warm us. We were glad to get even into this wretched place out of the furious and bitter blast, while our men struggled to put up the tents under the shelter of a wall. But there being no chimney to the hovel, the smoke soon drove us out again. By this time I was in a miserable state through illness. But the next day we reached Homs, where I got some medical assistance. It was a long time, however, before I recovered from the effects of the horse bite and of the chill which I caught in these cold winds after the intense heat of Palmyra.

At Homs we encamped on an open space near the town by the wall of a lovely garden containing flowing waters and beautiful trees and shrubs, and beyond which was a field where were tethered some fine Arab mares and foals which grazed in the shade, for here it was hot again. Near to this place Sheik Nasr pointed out to us the little property that the late Lady Ellenborough bought for Sheik Midjwell, her husband, when he was ill. It contained an arcaded garden with shaded walks, and a house with latticed windows, fit only for summer use. Sheik Nasr said that the air of Homs was accounted passing good for weak people, and that Sheik Midjwell was delicate in the chest. Sheik Nasr was his cousin or nephew, and was brought up in the house with him and his wife, and looked at the garden and ground with great interest.

Sheik Nasr seemed to be the perfect type of a high-bred sheik, equally accustomed to life in the desert and life in Damascus. His manners were admirable; and his polite, quiet way never changed even on the longest and most trying journeys. He was tall, slight, and handsome; an incomparable horseman, and a great smoker of the narghilé. He had two wives, one in the tents at Tudmor, and the other a Turkish lady who lived in Damascus.

At Homs we were much troubled by the curiosity of the women. We could not keep them out of the tents, or if we did they stared in at all the openings.[1] My wife was quite mobbed by them, although all in the pleasantest way. The people are mostly Christians here.

On leaving Homs we desired to look on El-Àsy[2] (the Orontes) which issues from the lake of Homs, a few miles south of the town. So deviating for a mile from our course, we rode through richly-cultivated fields and past strings of laden camels bound for Aleppo and and Diarbekir, till we came to a wide open country. How brilliant and fresh was the early morning, and how our horses enjoyed the keen air! Soon we came in sight of an old paved bridge amongst the trees, and met a drove of sheep and goats returning from their morning's drink, and the thick green foliage told of the approach to the gracious river. Then through the thick

---

[1] "A sensible person in this city is like a man tied up among a drove of mules in a stable, I once heard from a respectable stranger in the Syrian town of Homs, a locality proverbial for the sullen stupidity of its denizens" (Palgrave's "Central and Eastern Arabia").

[2] El Àsy, or the Rebellious, so called because it flows in an opposite direction to all the rivers in the country.

foliage we reached it, and looked upon it with eager eyes, stirred by the great name it bore. Swift and strong it ran away towards Aleppo, and we longed to follow it as we rested on the bridge, and looked far away to the northward where it wound through the fertile plain. And yet it had a homely English look, for it reminded us a good deal of the Thames at Streatley and Goring. Then knowing that a long journey was before us, and that we had to overtake the mules, we cantered back to Homs, and passed out of the town on the other side.

Four days' journey from Homs *viâ* Nebk and El Kutifyeh (where we purchased from the villagers some beautiful old embroideries and silver ornaments), brought us back to Damascus on the twenty-seventh of April, the nineteenth day after we had left it for Palmyra.

From Damascus we returned to Jerusalem, *viâ* Râsheiya and Hâsbeiya, keeping to the west of Mount Hermon. We had passed this mountain on the east side when going to Damascus from the south in the earlier part of our journey; and in 1887 we had crossed over its shoulder whilst proceeding in the same direction. From Hâsbeiya we journeyed to Tell-el-Kadi (the Judge's hill, the ancient Dan), and to Banias (the ancient Cæsarea Philippi), at both of which places branches of the Jordan rise; to Khan-Yubb-Yusef on the top of the hills to the north-west of the Sea of Galilee, from whence the whole of the lake can be seen; down to the town of Tiberias; up to the hills to the westward of the lake, across the high tableland, to the foot of Mount Tabor, which we had ascended in 1888; across the low spur or neck of land which connects the north-west slope of Tabor, to the hills which lead to Nazareth (which place we had visited both in 1887 and in 1888); to the village of Debûrieh; across the plain of Esdraelon to Jenîn, and by the ordinary route to Nablous and Jerusalem. From thence on the thirteenth of May, we took our last ride, passing through the corn lands of Philistia by the light of the full moon, and arriving in Jaffa after nearly eleven hours in the saddle at four o'clock in the morning; and so ended a journey in which we had spent sixty-two days under canvas, and ridden about twelve hundred miles.

I will conclude the account of this journey with an anecdote of canine sagacity. One of the town dogs of Jerusalem attached herself to us on our arrival there from the south, and accompanied us when we left that city. She slept in our tent, and took our defence under her peculiar care. After leaving El Bêda on our return from Palmyra we missed her, and learned that she had been seen to go away with some Beduins who fed her. We thought she had wandered off to a desert life, and I ventured to make to my wife some philosophical reflections about the inconstancy of the female sex, as exemplified even in the life of the lower animals, for had we not made a friend of this four-footed creature, and treated her with every kindness? But when we entered the streets of Damascus on our return seven days afterwards we suddenly became aware of "Werdie"[1] (for so our men had called the dog) jumping up at our horses' legs, and expressing her delight at

[1] In English, "Rose."

finding us again, with many waggings of her tail. In a moment later the dogs of Damascus had set upon her, rolled her over and over, and bitten her severely. One of our men rescued her, and placed her on his horse; but she jumped down again, and snarled, and fought, and bit her way victoriously through her foes. This intelligent creature must have returned to Damascus alone by the way by which we had gone there, a distance of one hundred and fifty miles of which fifty was across the waterless desert.[1]

At Debûrieh hearing some men walking in the night through the standing corn of the plain of Esdraelon, "Werdie" aroused George by pulling his dress, and led him to the place where they were passing. This action made him admire a dog for the first time in his life. We wanted to attach her permanently to us, and arranged with George to take care of her in Jaffa till we should come again. But we had not consulted Miss Werdie in our arrangements,[2] and when we reached Jerusalem on our return journey she departed on her travels again with our baggage mules which were hired for new work.

---

[1] "Strange to me was the daily sight of some half-score of Syrian street dogs that followed with the pilgrimage; every year some Syrian hounds go down thus to Mecca with the city of tents, and return from thence. The pious Eastern people charitably regard those poor pilgrim creatures, that are in their beast's wit, they think, among God's witnesses of the true religion. Eswad, if he saw any fainting hound, in the next halt he lured him, and poured out a little precious water to the unclean animal in the heel of his shoe" (Doughty's "Arabia Deserta").

[2] "The camel driver has his projects, and the camel his projects" (Burckhardt's "Arabic Proverbs").

In 1890 almost our first inquiry on landing at Jaffa was whether Werdie was alive and well, for we hoped to take her with us again. But we learnt with great regret that the Dragoman of the party with which she had gone after she left us had killed the poor creature in a particularly barbarous way because of her much barking. We were told also, and I hope truly, that the English people who were conducted by this man had refused to give him any backsheesh in consequence of his cruel conduct.

WERDIE CROSSING THE DESERT.

PART III.

1890.

Adventures South and East of the Dead Sea.

KERAKI DISCUSSING THE DIVISION OF THE SPOIL. MOUNTAINS OF WÂDY KERÂK AT THE BACK.

PART III.

1890.

Adventures South and East of the Dead Sea.

CHAPTER I.

OUR JOURNEY TOWARDS PETRA.   ARAR'S MESSENGER.

> "Thou com'st to use thy tongue; thy story quickly.
> *   *   *   *   *
> I doubt some danger does approach you nearly:
> Be not found here."
>
>   "MACBETH."

HALF way between the Dead Sea and Mount Sinai, hidden in a deep winding gorge below the shoulder of Mount Hor lies Petra, the rock city of Edom, the great stronghold of those Edomites who refused to let Moses and the Beni Israel pass through their country, and in later times the seat of the power and civilization of the Nabatæans. We had in 1889 visited Palmyra, whose greatness grew upon the overthrow of the Nabatæan kingdom in the second century of our era. We were now bent on getting to Petra.

This strange place has often been found very difficult of access. Burckhardt and Laborde had to go through many dangers to reach it. Since their days it has been visited by many travellers journeying from the southward, from Sinai, or by the Gulf of Akaba to the north

PETRA (AFTER ROBERTS).

of the Red Sea. But we had not met with any account of a successful attempt to approach it from the northward as we intended to do, except that of Irby and Mangles in 1815, and that of Mr. Doughty who travelled alone, and in a manner impossible for us who cannot speak Arabic. And for some years past, as we were informed since 1885, no European traveller had visited the place at all.

Mr. Moore, the British Consul at Jerusalem, and our good and trusty friend and dragoman, George Mabbedy (who now accompanied us on our travels in Syria for the fourth time) strongly advised us against the journey as being much too dangerous. But we had come from England to make the attempt, and were not to be dissuaded from it. Mr. Moore, finding us resolved, kindly did all he could to assist us in regard to measures for our safety: and George Mabbedy said that he was ready to go wherever we chose to take him. So on the seventeenth of March, 1890, my wife and I started from the Holy City, and turned our faces towards the south.

We were accompanied by Sheik Selim Abou Dahook, of the Jehalîn tribe, who made a formal contract with us before the Consul, to conduct us safely to Wâdy Mûsa, as the Arabs call Petra, with a sufficient escort, for the sum of twenty-five napoleons, of which one half was paid down before starting. He at first demanded one hundred pounds sterling, and it took us two days of wrangling to reduce his demand to a reasonable sum. He was a restless, grasping, wild-looking man, and we felt some hesitation in trusting ourselves to his care. The men from his tribe who joined us when we left the camp of the Jehalîn, which lies to the south of Hebron, were fifteen in number, of whom three were armed with Remington rifles, and the rest with flint-lock guns. All of these but Sheik Selim, who rode a fine mare, travelled on foot. They impressed us more favourably than their sheik.

We had the usual provision of tents, men, and baggage mules, and rode on horses in preference to camels; but we hired two camels from the Jehalîn to carry water for the horses and mules during the last part of the journey. Our servants consisted of dragoman, cook (an old soldier who had been through the Crimean War), waiter, five muleteers, the young man of all work called Nakhli who has accompanied us on all our expeditions, and a " Holy man," or kind of Dervish, belonging to the Adwan tribe whom we knew before, and happening to meet on our arrival at Jerusalem despatched to the Jehalîn camp, with instructions to bring in their sheik to the Consul, in order that he might make the contract. We found that this " Holy man " knew every one, and was acquainted with the route in every direction, and his character for sanctity seemed to give him a certain influence amongst the Beduins. Indeed Sheik Selim kissed his hand every morning.

We took with us gold and silver coin to the value of about seventy napoleons, but left the rest of our money and all our other valuables at Jerusalem, lest we should be robbed. We thought that the cash that we carried would be enough to pay our way to Petra and back again to Jerusalem, through Ma'an and Kerâk (places which lie to the east of the Dead Sea), by which route we intended to return.

Before we left Jerusalem the Consul discoursed to Sheik Selim upon the dire consequences to him of any failure on his part to provide for our safety; and

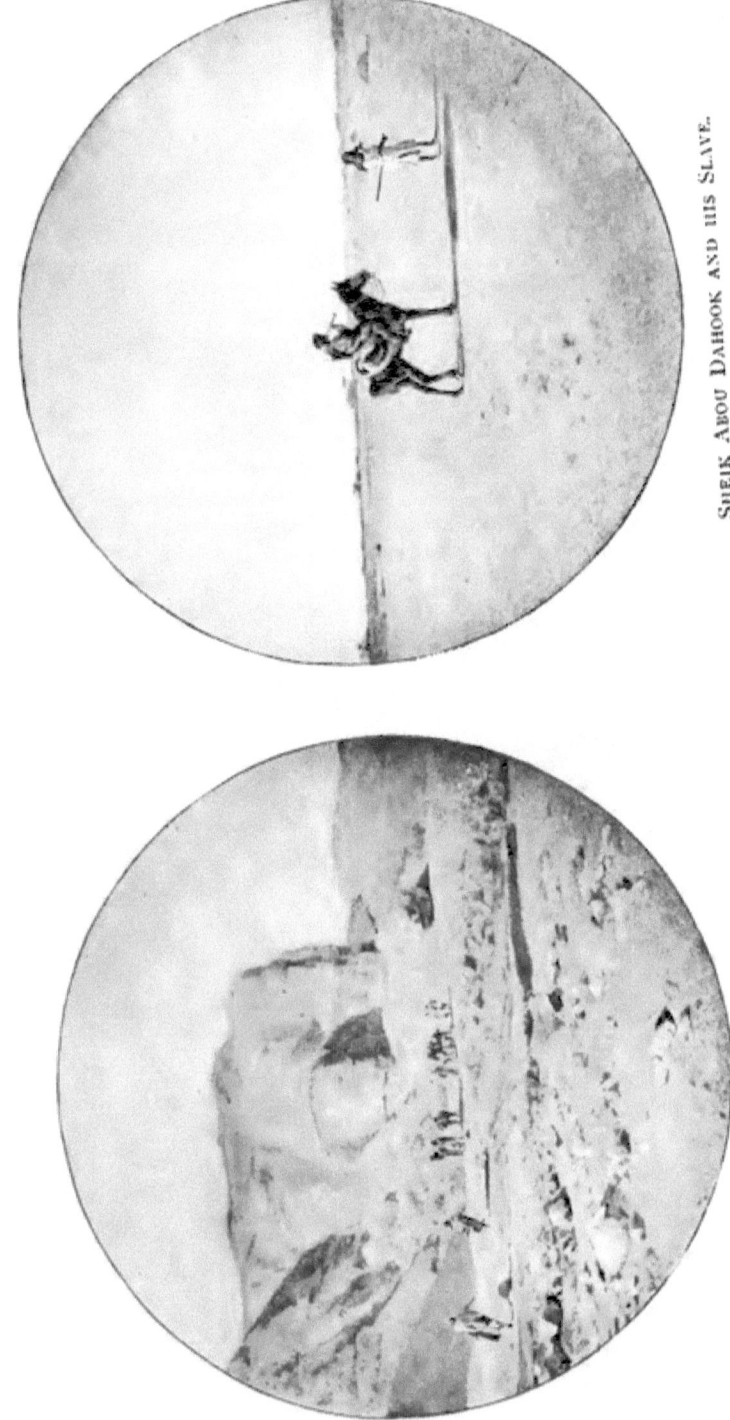

Sheik Abou Dahook and his Slave.

Passing Jebel Usdum (Mountain of Sodom).

furnished us with a letter of recommendation to Arar,[1] the Sheik of Petra. Having discovered that a foster-brother of the latter personage was a shopkeeper in Jerusalem, we bought from him some articles which we designed as presents for Arar, and for his wives and children. And the foster-brother gave us a letter to the latter requesting him to treat us well. We expected therefore to touch Arar's heart if it were capable of gentle emotions, and hoped that he would make us welcome. In answer to our inquiries we were informed that the Beduins to the south of the Dead Sea, through whose territories we had to pass, were according to the latest reports at peace with one another. Thus we considered that we had taken all the precautions in our power, and we began our journey with the full expectation that we should succeed in accomplishing our object. Indeed I quite believe that we should have done so, but that unknown to us war broke out amongst these quarrelsome tribes about the time we started.[2]

We had obtained from the Pasha of Jerusalem a letter of recommendation to the Kaimakâm or Governor

---

[1] Professor Hull in his "Mount Seir" calls this Sheik "Arari." I spell the name as I heard it pronounced.

[2] "The Beduin does not fight for his home, he has none : nor for his country, that is anywhere ; nor for his honour, he never heard of it ; nor for his religion, he owns and cares for none. His only object in war is the temporary occupation of some bit of miserable pasture-land, or the use of a brackish well ; perhaps the desire to get such a one's horse or camel into his own possession — all objects which imply little animosity, and if not attained in the campaign, can easily be made up for in other ways, nor entail the bitterness and cruelty that attend or follow civil and religious strife " (Palgrave's " Central and Eastern Arabia ").

of Hebron, which we presented to that functionary on our arrival at the latter place. After perusing it the Kaimakâm summoned Sheik Selim, and calmly informed him that if he did not bring back to him a letter from us reporting our satisfaction with his conduct, he would put him in prison on the first convenient opportunity. This was somewhat arbitrary, but made us feel more comfortable.

We journeyed past the pools of Solomon, through Hebron, and down the bare, wild, and rugged passes leading from the high land on which that most ancient of hill towns stands, to the Dead Sea, four thousand three hundred feet below. We kept along the desolate west shore of its blue waters under Jebel Usdum (the mountain of Sodom) which rose high above our path; and leaving the south end of the lake behind us, succeeded in getting at the end of the sixth day after leaving Jerusalem to a place called El Eskrib, which is within two long days' journey of Petra, and of Jebel Haroun (Mount Hor). We had kept this mountain constantly in sight all day, longing to reach its summit, and knowing that hidden in a deep valley near it lay Petra, the dearest object of our hopes.

We had not travelled far on the seventh day, and had been riding for a long time up rising ground, which we then supposed to be the "Ascent of Akrabbim," but which must have been a considerable way to the south of the part so marked on the map, when a commotion arose in front and all grasped their arms ready to meet an attack. We saw a man issue forth from behind a rock, as from a hiding-place, and run hurriedly towards us. We did not know if any

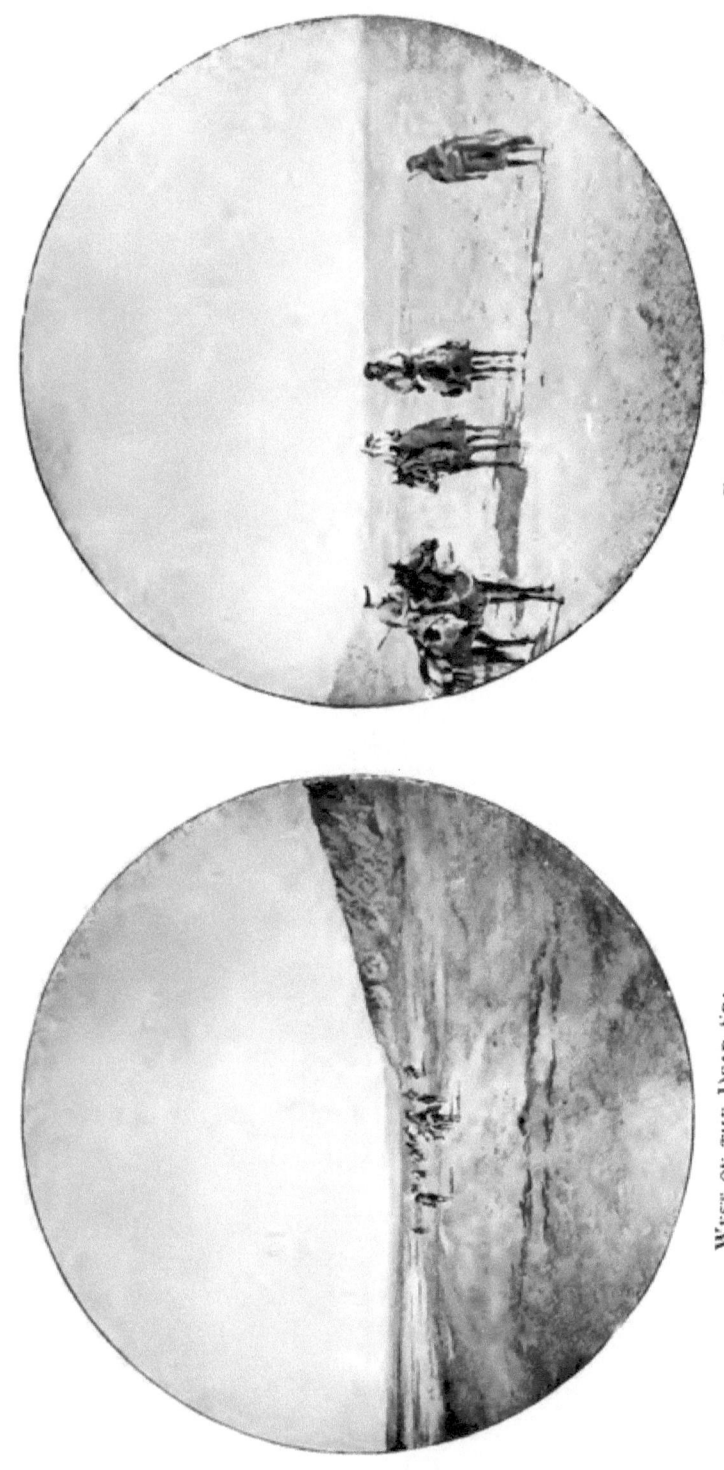

EAST OF THE DEAD SEA.

WEST OF THE DEAD SEA.

more might be behind. But he motioned to us that it was peace, made his salaam, sat down on the sand, and took a paper out of his breast which he handed to our sheik. This paper the latter passed on to us, explaining that it bore the impression of Arar's seal, and was evidence that the man came with his authority. We brought up our horses close to the messenger, who remained sitting on the sand while his credentials were examined, the Jehalîn crowded round to hear, and he began his tale. It was a strange scene, the man sitting cross-legged on the bare yellow sand, the wild Jehalîn men pressing forward to gaze and listen, Sheik Selim sitting on his mare indifferent, and George and we with straining eyes and ears full of anxious curiosity.

The messenger said he had been sent by Arar to tell us that the Beduins were fighting in Petra, and in the country between us and that place; that Arar and his followers had come out from Petra six days before, and were encamped to the south-east of us, and were at war with the tribe of the Howeytàt, whose camp lay to the east of us on the other side of the Ghôr, as the great hollow or depression which lies round the Dead Sea is called. The messenger added very emphatically that under these circumstances Arar could not be in any way answerable for our safety, for which he had not the power to provide; and that he strongly advised us to go back—in fact, that we could not go forward without the greatest danger; and were in risk of attack even where we were.

It was only by a lucky accident that Arar had known of our coming, and thus it happened. In a wild gorge at a place called Zuweireh el Tahta, where we had encamped with the Jehalîn before we reached the Dead Sea, we had found two Petra men. We shall never forget the scene. The Jehalîn men had gone lower down the ravine and found a dead tree, which they carried back upon their shoulders singing as they came. When the evening light had faded out on the tops of the tall cliffs of crumbling white stone which reared their fantastic shapes above us, the night had set in very dark, and fire being put to the dry trunk, the flames had leaped high into the air, and made such flickering lights and shadows on the wild faces of the men sitting and lying round, as they talked and gesticulated, and upon the towering peaks and deep crevices of the overhanging hills, as we never before saw the like of. It was the *beau idéal* of the witches' cavern of "Macbeth." Even the stage of the Lyceum Theatre never made such a "counterfeit presentment" of it.

Amongst this group the Petra men had been pointed out to us, and we had been told that they and some others of their tribe, who journeyed with camels to Hebron, had been robbed by the Jehalîn; that Arar, having sent to complain, they (either, as we supposed, out of fear of him, or for some other reason which we did not learn) had restored the camels and articles stolen; that they had sent on all the Petra men to Hebron except these two, only detaining them to feast and make much of them, which they were this evening doing; and that these men were now about to return to Petra. By them, therefore, we had sent on the Consul's letter; they had found that Arar had come out of Petra, and was encamped to the north of

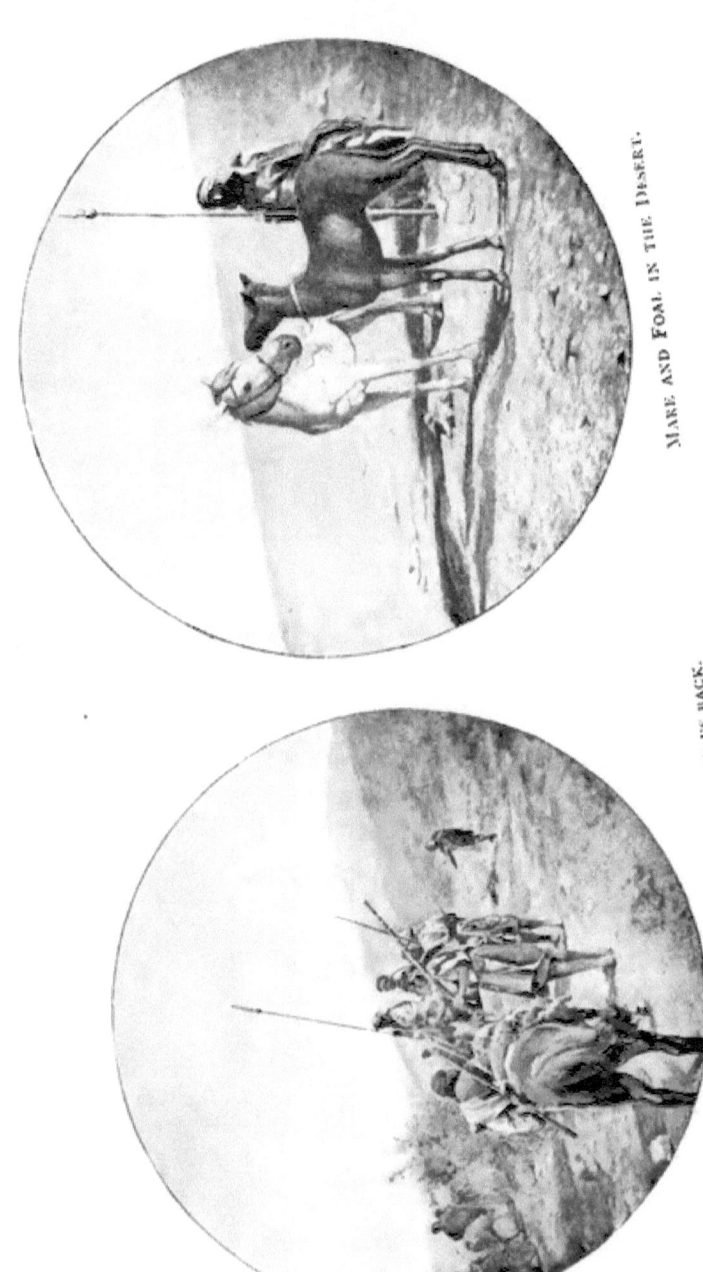

MARE AND FOAL IN THE DESERT.

ON THE MARCH, NEAR WHERE ARAR'S MESSENGER TURNED US BACK.

it; and thus he having received the letter had been enabled to give us warning of our danger.

There was no help for it. Three thousand Beduins were said to be on the war-path. The messenger told us that in making his way to us he had been pursued and nearly overtaken by some of the Howeytát men, and that they would certainly rob us if we went on, or even if we stayed where we were. It was a bitter disappointment, but we had to submit, and not being quite certain what to do, we retraced our steps to a place called 'Ain el Bêda, there to rest for the night. George advised us to return to Jerusalem, and plan a new trip from that place in another direction. But we could not make up our minds to retreat ingloriously without having accomplished anything, and against his advice determined to proceed to Kerâk (Kir of Moab), which is in the mountainous country on the east side of the south end of the Dead Sea.

ZUWEIREH EL TAHTA.

CHAPTER II.

THE HOWEYTÁT. A VERY ANXIOUS NIGHT.

> "Your eyes do menace me. Why look you pale?
> Who sent you hither? Wherefore do you come?"
> "RICHARD III."

> "In that desert dwell many of the Arabians who are called Beduins, ... who are people full of all evil conditions, ... and they are strong and warlike men, ... and they are right felonious and foul, and of a cursed nature."—SIR JOHN MANDEVILLE, A.D. 1322.

WE turned back again then to the sandy hillocks partly covered with scrub from which we had emerged but the day before, when journeying hopefully towards Wâdy Musa. How glad we had been to get past this country and to begin the ascent! Now it seemed more desolate than ever. After riding for some time along a deep hollow in the burnt-up sandy hills, we again caught sight of the wide open plain of the Ghôr. To the east rose the bare mountains, and all around us spread the desolate sands. Not a trace of a living thing was to be seen. But journeying northwards we passed along a depression full of immense reeds with plume-like tops; an opening appeared, and we again found the spring ('Ain el Bêda), bubbling up in the midst of a dense vegetation. The

'AIN EL BÉDA. BEDUINS OF THE HOWEYTÁT TRIBE COME OUT OF THE REEDS.

A HALT. LOOKING OUT FOR BEDUINS.

thicket of reeds was wide, as well as long, extending to the east, as well as the south.

Here we set up the tents. The horses, camels, and mules drank their fill, and wandered away after the juicy leaves of the tall rushes; the whole camp was composing itself to coffee and narghilés, and we were gazing dreamily out of the tent-door upon the red glow of sunset falling upon the eastern mountains, when three horsemen, coming from the eastward across the valley, pushed through the reeds, dismounted, tethered their mares to the tall stems, and walked up to our tents. These were the head sheik of the Howeytát, whose name I understood to be Ibn Jèsy, and two of his brother sheiks. They pointed out the direction of their camp, which accorded with the description given by Arar's messenger, and boasted that they had killed four of Arar's men that day. These sheiks, who were armed with Remington rifles, flint-lock pistols, swords and daggers, were very surly in manner. They had evidently come to spy out the land, and their behaviour was such as to make us extremely suspicious of their intentions. Nor did what followed remove our apprehensions; for soon afterwards another Howeytát came out of the reeds, then another, and again another appeared. The reeds were too high for us to see them until they actually dismounted and got clear of the foliage.

All these horsemen were well armed, most of them with Remington rifles; each as he arrived sat down by his companions, until they formed a formidable row; and all whispered together. By eight o'clock there were ten of these wild-looking men; by ten o'clock there were seventeen, and later in the night their number was made up to twenty-two. From the time when darkness set in we could see the huge red flames of the camp-fires of the Howeytát shooting high up into the air six or eight miles to the east of us on the other side of the valley; and we knew that there must be plenty of the Howeytát there. Would more follow? The late comers, like the first, had tethered their horses amongst the reeds, upon which we could hear them feeding, crunching the luscious sprays in their mouths as they eat. Our men had lighted a fire, and the arms of the Beduins glistened in the light of it as they sat each with his gun in front of him and his sword and pistol ready, watching us with greedy eyes.

The situation was a most anxious one. We could not tell how many more might come, or how many might even then be crouching in the reeds; and we felt perfectly satisfied from the way in which they looked at us and held whispered conversations together, that they were discussing amongst themselves whether they should attack us. We considered that they could not conveniently *capture* us, as while fighting with Arar they would probably not be able to keep us under restraint. The only question must then be whether they would rob us. Robbery, according to Beduin custom, involves stripping, and in case of unsuccessful resistance would no doubt be followed by murder. Everything depended upon our escort. Could we rely upon them?

George spoke to the Jehalîn men, who promised to stand firm, and he and I saw that our weapons were distributed to the best advantage. We had with us two double-barrelled sporting guns, four revolvers, and two flint-lock pistols. Those for whom there were no fire-arms provided themselves with the best substitutes, such as an axe, the iron bar from which the kettle hung, and thick sticks, and it was arranged that every one should watch during the whole of the night. George was careful to let the Howeytát see two of our revolvers, one of twelve and the other of ten chambers, which seemed to make an impression on their minds. And he told them some fables about the extraordinary skill with which both my wife and I managed similar weapons, which he cunningly feigned that we possessed.

We let them see clearly that we would defend ourselves. Our servants and the Jehalîn formed a circle round our sleeping tent,[1] and we, being very tired, lay down in our clothes. So, with a revolver by my side, I got what troubled sleep I could, but with the expectation of being awakened with the firing of the first shot. I do not think my wife slept at all. But she was very quiet, kept an anxious watch, and waited for the first flush of dawn. Until it came there sat our men and the Howeytát watching one another gun in hand.

The latter could not make up their minds to act, at any rate without a greater force on their side; for no more came. We had been most afraid of some one firing off his piece, as men sometimes do, out of mere excitability; for in the strained state of nerves in which all were, one shot would have led to a general firing, in which some loss of life must have occurred, even without any evil intention. But when the blessed

[1] Our servants said, "This is the tent from which we eat (*i.e.*, have our living), shall we not defend it?"

dawn appeared, and lifting up the tent door, we saw our good little "Holy Man" spreading his carpet to say his morning prayer, and heard the horses whinnying in the rushes, we felt a new hope arise in our hearts, and something told us that the danger was passed.

While the baggage was being placed upon the mules the Howeytát began to ask for backsheesh; and our Jehalîn sheik, much to our annoyance, urged their claims. We would give no answer until we were starting, and then gave the sheiks of the Howeytát a Turkish pound and departed, leaving them and their men grumbling and threatening. But they did not follow us.

That day we steered a most circuitous course, round the low hills on the west side of the Ghôr, bending first to the west, then to the north, until we got within about a mile of the south end of the Dead Sea, when we turned to the east, and then to the south-east, and picked our way across the wet salt sand. This detour was necessary, partly because of the winding of the white stony wâdy, which we followed in order to keep out of sight of the wandering Beduins, and partly to enable us to pass safely across the sands which contain dangerous places in which both man and beast might be lost. After proceeding in this manner for some hours, we crossed a small stream, in which, although the water was only a few inches deep, several of the animals sank up to their bellies.

As we rested on the east side of this brook to see the baggage mules safely across, a horseman came out of the scrub. All our men pointed their guns at him. Were more men coming, and who were they? Only

WE ENTER THE GHÔR ES SAFIYEH. 185

one more   They were men of the Howeytât, but not the same individuals as before. They put themselves at the head of our procession and led the way. First one and then another appeared out of the bushes, which grew thicker as we advanced, until about twenty horsemen of this tribe had joined us. Then other horsemen arrived belonging to the Ghawàrineh tribe, whose territory (Ghôr es Safiyeh) we were now entering.

A WÂDY SOUTH OF THE DEAD SEA.

THE DEAD SEA FROM NIMEIRAH.

CHAPTER III.

THE GHAWÀRINEH. WE ARE THREATENED AGAIN.
ARAR ASSISTS US.

> "Hold your hands,
> Both you of my inclining, and the rest."
> "OTHELLO."

THE way wound in and out of a thick growth of scrub with a few timber trees, so that we could not see either the head or the tail of the procession. But some men of each tribe rode near to us.

Presently one of the strange sheiks, who was mounted on a splendid gray mare, began a violent quarrel with our Sheik Selim, threatening him with a heavy club, which he carried, in addition to his Remington rifle and other arms. This man was a cousin of Arar, who had joined the Howeytát against his relative. He was disputing the right of the Jehalîn men to undertake to conduct us to Petra. He

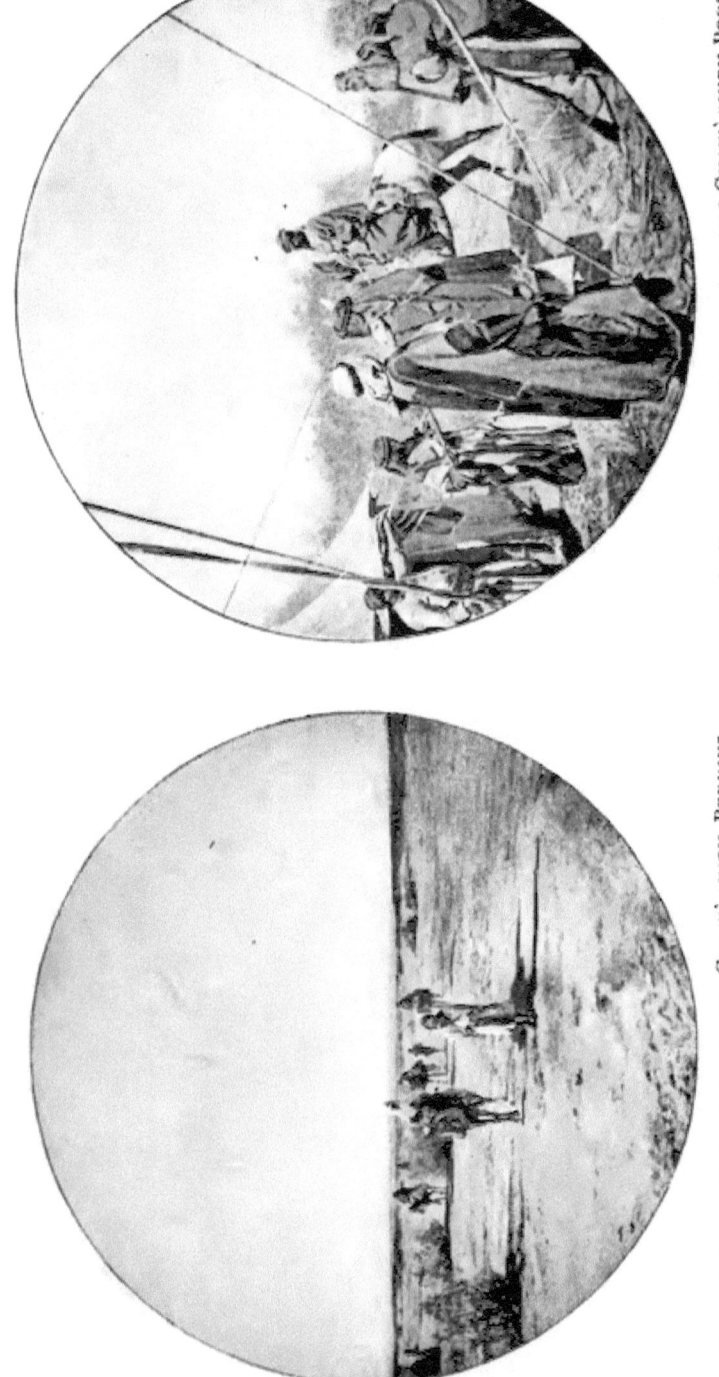

ARAR'S BROTHER ASSISTS US AGAINST THE GHAWÀRINEH BEDUINS.

WE ENTER THE TERRITORY OF THE GHAWÀRINEH BEDUINS.

ATTEMPT TO LEVY BLACK MAIL.

offered to take us there himself in spite of Arar, whom he would destroy, and whose camp the Howeytát would attack that very night.

We declined the offer, and after much more shouting and threatening of Selim this sheik rode away. Then accompanied by men of both tribes, who gathered around our escort, as if to hem them in, and feeling that we were again getting into a dangerous situation, we came to the encampment of the Ghawàrineh, near to which we pitched our tents.

No sooner had we done so than the very villainous looking old sheik of that tribe demanded from us a sum of one hundred medjidiés (about sixteen pounds), and this being refused, said we should not leave the place until we paid it. After a long discussion George told him he should have the money if he would put his seal to a paper acknowledging that he had extorted it under threats of violence, and that then we should take the paper to the Turkish Government, who would send soldiers to punish him. And he ran after the sheik with the ink-pot, in which he begged the latter to dip his finger, that he might seal in the most primitive of Beduin ways. The old rascal declined the condition, but insisted on his hundred medjidiés. We, however, told him we would pay nothing, and would go on the next day in spite of him.

Presently the brother of Arar, with seven or eight of Arar's men came up, and they afterwards informed us that their chief had sent them to assist us, as he had seen Beduins following in our direction. By this time about a hundred Beduins were sitting round our tents, and soon began shouting and squabbling with our

Jehalîn men, who sat watchful with their guns. Selim now told us that he and his men would not take us beyond Nimeirah (the ancient Nimrin [1]), which is near to the Dead Sea, in the bay south of the promontory which stretches out from the eastern shore. No doubt the threats of the Howeytát and of the Ghawàrineh had had their effect, and Selim was afraid of going much further out of his own territory.

Selim also recommended us to pay the Ghawàrineh what they asked, so that we felt that we could not rely upon him personally, although we had more confidence in his men. Under these circumstances, feeling somewhat anxious about the position of affairs, we thought it best to send to Kerâk for an escort to conduct us when the Jehalîn should have left us. We accordingly dispatched Selim's negro slave, and another Jehalîn man, with a letter from me to Mr. Lethaby (an English missionary residing at that place), requesting him to get one of the Sheiks of Kerâk to meet us at Nimeirah, where we promised to wait for him. In this letter was enclosed one from the British Consul, addressed to Sheik Saleh, the Ruler of the Keraki, and the head of the Mejelli (the governing family of Kerâk) recommending us to his protection. We calculated that it would take nearly twenty-four hours to get a reply from Kerâk, and sat down to look about us. We were now on the eastern side of the Ghôr, under some high, bare, red-coloured mountains, but with all else cut off from view by the vegetation around us.

Just before sunset a great brawl arose between the Ghawàrineh and our Jehalîn escort, and for a time it

---

[1] Not to be confounded with Tel Nimrin referred to p. 40.

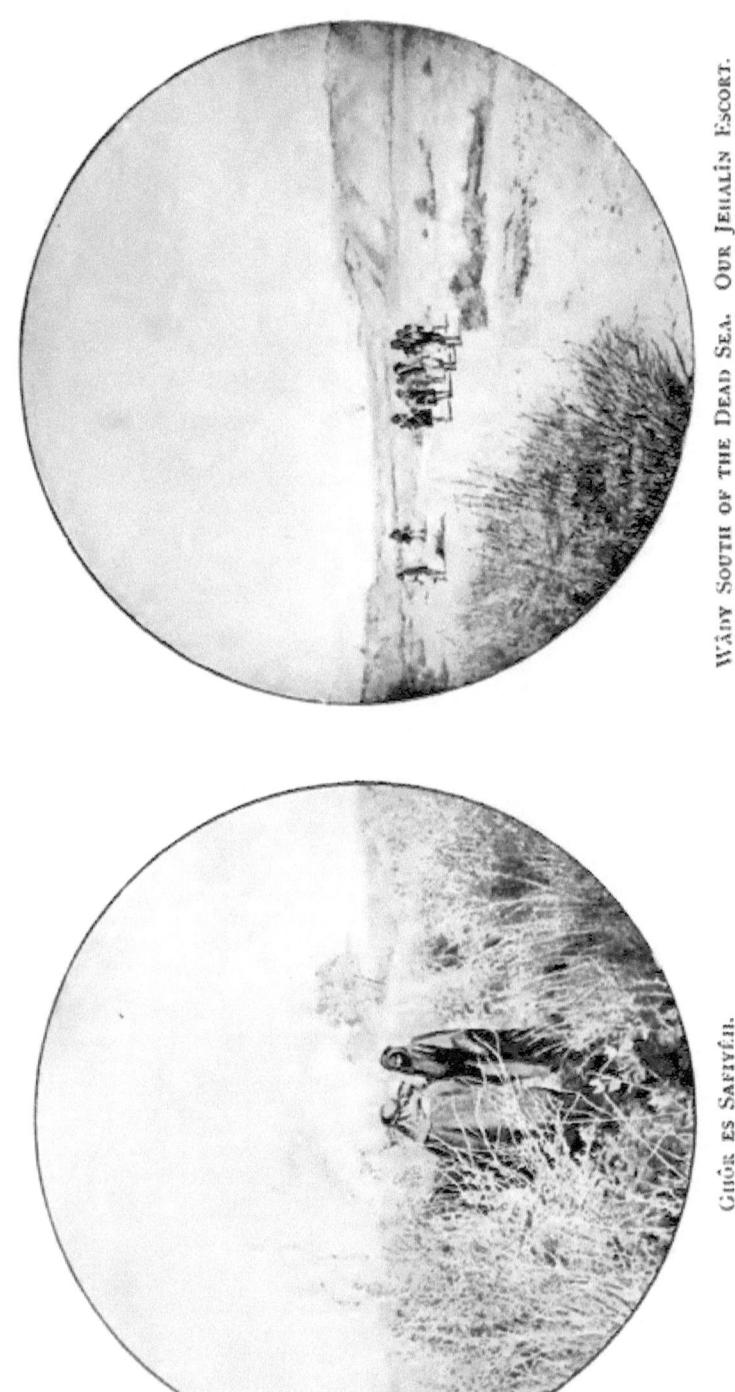

WÂDY SOUTH OF THE DEAD SEA. OUR JEHALÍN ESCORT.

GHÔR ES SAFIÉH.

looked as if it would become very serious. One of the Jehalîn was beaten with a stick, and his gun was taken from him; one of our own servants was struck, several stones were thrown, and the yelling became deafening. We all stood on guard ready to defend ourselves in case of necessity, but did our best to quiet the disturbance. If it had not been for Arar's brother, there would in all probability have been a fight. But he riding about on his horse exerted himself most energetically to keep the peace, threatening the Sheik of the Ghawàrineh if he did not call off his men.

After about an hour of great excitement all were calmed down, and the Ghawàrineh invited our Jehalîn men to eat with them; and as the latter feasted, stole one of their guns.[1] That night we had a splendid sunset, the eastern mountains turning a deep crimson in the evening light. So ended a most un-sabbath-like Sunday. But it was almost worth while to run the risks which we were encountering to see such a glorious sight. We slept as well as the mosquitoes would allow, but they were very troublesome at this place. Indeed poor George carried the marks of them on his legs for many weeks afterwards.

We heard no more of Arar or of his people. But I may pause here to say that his conduct in regard to us made us believe that we had nothing to fear from him; and that if his authority be firmly re-established in Petra, we need not have any great hesitation in again endeavouring to get there, although we should not

[1] An Egyptian proverb illustrates the converse case. "Entertain the Beduin, he will steal thy clothes" (Burckhardt's "Arabic Proverbs").

renew the attempt from the north, but make it *viâ* Sinai or Akaba.

The next morning we rose before dawn, and our camp was in motion before the first rays of the sun had touched the summits of the western mountains. The Sheik of the Ghawàrineh now improved on his demand of the evening before, asking for one hundred and fifty medjidiés instead of a hundred, and when we again refused to pay anything threatened to make me prisoner. However we were firm, only offering to pay him what we thought right for guiding us to Nimeirah if he accompanied us alone. When it came to the point he was afraid to attempt to detain us by force notwithstanding his loud talk, and he came with us as a guide, attended however by three of his followers. At Nimeirah we gave them a Turkish pound, and sent them away cursing and threatening to return. That old sheik had the most evil countenance that I ever saw, and had he not been a coward would no doubt have robbed us. He was probably afraid of the Keraki for whom he knew that we had sent, as well as of Arar's people.

Part of our journey lay along the beach of the south-east side of the Dead Sea, which is here of shingle, and shelves rapidly down below its surface. Beyond it the western hills rose precipitously from the water, the clefts and deep recesses in their scarred fronts lit up by the rays of the morning sun. The clear deep blue water was most inviting for a bath, but I could not be sure whether the Howeytát or Ghawàrineh Beduins might not follow us, and did not, therefore, stay behind for a dip. At Nimeirah there were no Arab tents (of course of houses or fixed dwellings there are none in this part of Syria); only a clear pure stream of water flowing from a deep gorge in the red mountains on the eastward down into the "Salt Sea." We walked up to this gorge, which is a most striking place, where the stream in the course of countless ages has cut a narrow cleft for itself on each side of which the red rock rises bare and precipitous, and towers high above. But the night fell before we could see much of it. There was, however, light enough to show us the footprints of a leopard-like [1] foot upon the sand. These animals are said to haunt the gorges on the east side of the Dead Sea.

The next day was very hot (ninety-two degrees in the shade), and we rested in our tents until four in the afternoon, when one of our messengers returned from Kerâk bringing a letter from Mr. Lethaby, which was carefully tied up in the man's shirt. From this we learnt that that gentleman had arranged for an escort for us, but that Sheik Saleh having been absent when my letter arrived, he had not been able to give him the letter from the Consul, which was enclosed in it; and had not dared to give it to any one else to deliver to him, lest the letter should be detained for a ransom. This did not give us a very favourable opinion of the Keraki. Soon afterwards there came nine horsemen of this tribe—tall, handsome, dark, dignified men, mounted on fine horses. With them arrived our second messenger Sheik Selim's negro slave, who was grinning from ear to ear at the success of his

---

[1] The leopard is called "Nimmr" in Arabic, so that the name "Nimeirah" or "Nimrin" may be connected with this animal.

long journey, and in joyful anticipation of back-sheesh and food. The two men had made the journey to Kerâk and back in twenty hours. They told us they had had nothing to eat but two small Arab loaves, and to judge from the appetite which they displayed they spoke truly.

SOME OF OUR FAITHFUL SERVANTS.

ISA SENAH, OF KERÂK.

CHAPTER IV.

THE KERAKI. TRAP NO. I. SHEIK SALEH.

"He (the late Sheik of Kerâk) is strong-handed, ambitious, a bird of prey, and they barbarous subjects who will not be guided by reason are ruled by strength, and that is ofttime plain violence. . . . The smooth Christian homicide whispered in my ear, 'Have thou a care of them, for these fear not Allah.'"—DOUGHTY'S "ARABIA DESERTA."

"They speak pleasantly until they get his head in a bag."—ARAB PROVERB.

THE Keraki were most polite; lamented that they had not the Sheik of the Ghawàrineh in their power that they might punish him; and, at a false alarm which was raised to the effect that the men of that tribe were coming to attack us, they galloped up the hill which hid the Ghôr es Safiyeh from our view, waving their swords back at us, as if to assure us that they would sweep our enemies off the face of the earth.

The next morning being anxious to get to Kerâk that day we arose at three, and getting the camp in motion by half-past four had two hours' riding before the sun became hot. The Jehalîn left us at Nimeirah, and we paid Sheik Selim the second half of the twenty napoleons with a backsheesh for his men. We gave him at his request a written certificate that he had safely delivered us to the Keraki, and letters to the same effect addressed to the Governor of Hebron, and to the British Consul, adding to the latter a short account of what had happened to us so far. We also handed to the sheik some letters to be posted to England. These and the letter to the Consul did not reach Jerusalem (as we afterwards heard) until about three weeks later.

Our way from Nimeirah lay at first over very rough and stony ground, but the views were very impressive. To our left lay the Dead Sea, still and desolate, but taking all kinds of opalescent hues in the morning light. Across it to the west were the deeply scarred mountains, and to our right the still nearer forms of the eastern hills. As we rode on we were often in a labyrinth of tamarisk trees, which hid the water from us. The pathway led in and out, now and again doubling back, and occasionally opening out into patches of lovely large yellow daisies. Then we would come upon the shore, and notice the countless small shells and the drift wood washed up by the water, and lying amongst the stone boulders of the beach. Then we began to mount the higher land of the peninsula which juts so far out from the eastern shore. As we ascended the views of the Dead Sea became more and more beautiful, and as the northern part of it opened out to the view, and the haze caused by the warmth of the morning sun arose from its surface, it seemed like a lake of silver receding into the distance.

After three hours' riding we reached a place called El Draa or Deraah (the stream), where there is a hollow, down which pours a rushing little brook, and near to which a little grass and wild barley were growing. Although it was still very early, the Keraki said that their horses were too tired to go on to Kerâk (six hours further) that day, and that there was no water between El Draa (or Deraah) and that place; so that we must pitch our tents here for the night. As they represented that they had come to us at great speed the previous day, and we were not at that time aware that there was plenty of water further on, we could only acquiesce. About an hour afterwards one of Sheik Saleh's sons arrived, and a little later the Mejelli himself with two more horsemen appeared.

Sheik Saleh is a fine looking man of about forty-five years of age, and like all his family has strongly marked Jewish features of the handsomest type. He wears a black beard and moustache, and has the air of being a very great man. All were invited into our dining tent, and coffee and cigarettes were handed round. A raised seat was made for the sheik with carpets, and his nearest relatives sat next to him.

Etiquette required us to sit silent until Mejelli spoke, which he was slow in doing. We had consulted his followers as to the possibility of getting to Petra from Kerâk *viâ* Ma'an. But they said that, independently of the fighting now going on in and near Petra, the route was too dangerous. They had also told us in answer to our inquiries that no European except Mr. Lethaby and his wife, and a young lady who just joined them had visited Kerâk for fourteen years, but that native merchants travelled occasionally between that place and Hebron *viâ* the south end of the Dead Sea, or between Kerâk and Jerusalem *viâ* the north end. I believe, however, that an English officer interested in Mr. Lethaby's mission recently made a flying visit to Kir of Moab travelling alone. Mr. Doughty seems to have been some time at the place in 1876.

Others of the Keraki arrived later in the day, until we had fifteen of them. In the evening we took a walk following the course of the stream up to a ravine with precipitous sides of red rock more striking even than that at Nimeirah. We got up through the thick vegetation as far as we could, but were stopped by a high steep rocky shelf, which must form the bed of a fine cascade in the rainy season, and up or past which we could not climb. Above it was a very beautiful date-palm tree, and on the south side of the gorge we noticed some old masonry lying along the face of the cliff, which looked as if it might once have carried an aqueduct. Walking back to our tents at sunset we looked down upon the Dead Sea, lying like a sapphire under the purple hills, and, above all, was the sweet

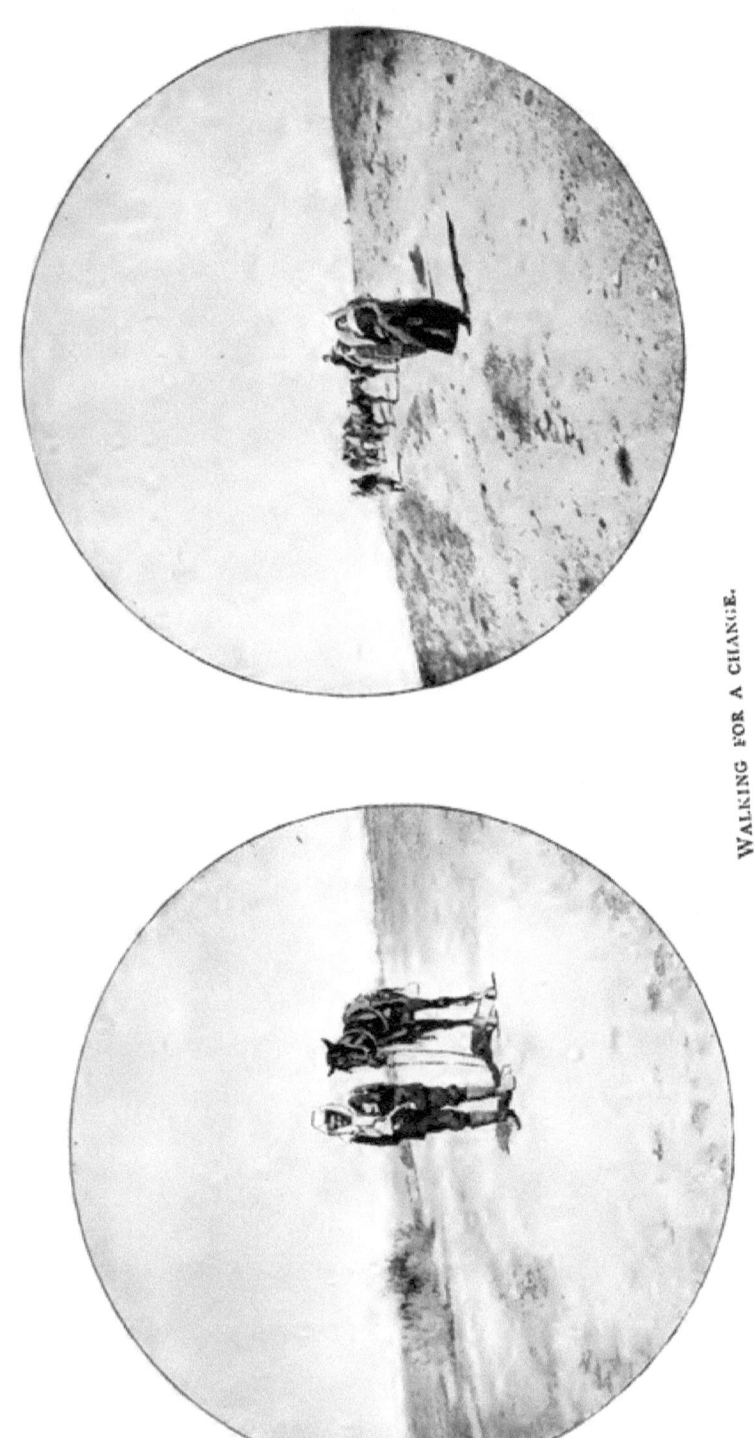

WALKING FOR A CHANGE.

daffodil sky in which star after star appeared in perfect beauty. The silence was only broken now and then by the cry of a solitary bird, and so deep a hush was on the scene that it seemed scarcely real.

But our troubles were now to recommence. Later in the evening Sheik Saleh and one of his principal followers, a Christian of the Greek Church, named Isa Senah, asked to see me. The latter is a tall handsome man with a pleasing countenance, but

> "There's no art
> To find the man's construction in the face."

He turned out to be an enemy, although he was full of protestations of friendship on the ground of our common Christianity. After beating about the bush for a while in regard to his ailments (for which we had given him some medicine) the sheik asked what we intended to present to him, and suggested that what we did desire to bestow upon him might be conveniently paid at once as "when we got to Kerâk he might be a little busy." The idea of his being busy was amusing, but just then we felt too anxious to see the humorous side of it.

We thought we had better begin at a low figure, and said therefore that a hundred francs seemed to us an appropriate sum. The sheik consulted with the other for a little while, and then asked for a hundred pounds, adding that the Pasha of Jerusalem had written to him last year requesting him not to allow us to enter Kerâk; that the Governor of Damascus had recommended him to rob any travellers who might come into his territory; and that Mr. Lethaby had promised him that every one of the party should receive six pounds. We knew of course that all these statements were false, but as he referred to Mr. Lethaby, we suggested that the amount of remuneration might be left until we could see that gentleman. "No," he said, "it must be settled now." The sheik, however, soon began to get sleepy with the chlorodyne which he had taken, and after some wrangling he reduced the amount of his demand to forty napoleons. But the Christian objected to this, and seeing that nothing could be arranged that night we went to bed, leaving some of the Keraki discussing the matter at the top of their voices with George, who was quite exhausted with watching and anxiety during the two previous nights, and had again very little sleep this night.

In the morning Sheik Saleh said that sixty napoleons was the smallest sum that he would accept. The advice of the Christian, and the clearing away of the quieting influence of the chlorodyne had added the twenty during the night. Refusal, indignation, remonstrance, were tried in vain. We should not go to Kerâk unless we paid sixty napoleons. At this point a letter in Arabic was handed to us, which being translated, was found to come from Sheik Khalîl, of Kerâk, and to state that we could not be permitted to enter that place unless we paid what Saleh demanded, but that whatever we settled with Saleh would be binding upon him, Khalîl.

This was the first that we had heard of Sheik Khalîl, and we knew nothing of the politics of Kerâk. We afterwards learnt that Saleh had only become Sheik on the death of the last ruler two years previous, and that although his claims by the Arabic law of succession were preferable, yet that Sheik Khalîl was more popular, and thought to be the fitter for the post.[1] However, Khalîl's letter if it was of importance, was satisfactory; if it raised a doubt of other interference, it seemed to dispel it.

We hoped that the question of amount was still unsettled. Saleh, however, insisting on the sixty napoleons, we determined that rather than pay that amount we would go back, and try our luck again with Ghawàrineh and Howeytát, and so informed him. It was of no use. He assumed a very threatening attitude, and said that we should not stir north, south, east, or west, unless we paid him sixty napoleons; and he despatched some of his men down the hill to prevent our retreat. We tried appeals to his honour. We had come to him as a guest with a letter from the British Consul (although it had not yet reached him): he had met as a friend, bidden us welcome, and eaten with us. Did he now want to rob us? He made a deprecatory motion, but said he must have the sixty napoleons. What could we do? He and his men were all armed to the teeth and carried Remington rifles. It was useless to think of resisting such a force. After a very long attempt to better the terms we found that there was nothing for it but to yield.

We arranged, however, that for this sum we should

---

[1] Some time ago the Keraki attempted a raid upon the Aenezeh, but the latter hearing of their coming, assembled a large force and overpowered them, taking from them horses and weapons, Sheik Khalîl alone of the whole party managing to escape on his mare. Notwithstanding his age, he is reputed the best rider amongst them.

be safely conducted not only to Kerâk, but through the territory of the Keraki, down the great pass of Mojeb, at the bottom of which the river Arnon flows, and to within one day's journey of Madeba, where we knew that we should be safe. But Saleh made it a condition that thirty napoleons (afterwards reduced to twenty-six) should be paid down immediately, and the remainder at Kerâk, and not at the northern limit of his territory as we urged. Then ensued a counting of money, which was mostly in silver, and a recounting, the sheik not being clever at computation, and being minded to look upon English sovereigns and Turkish pounds (which are worth twenty-five and twenty-three francs respectively) as of the same value as napoleons —worth only twenty.[1]

At last we started for Kerâk, scrambling down the steep bank to the south of the stream, and up the wild gorge on the other side, called Wâdy Kerâk, which is as steep as a staircase, and rises between three and four thousand feet above the Dead Sea. Only Syrian horses could climb up such a break-neck place. After ascending for about three hours, the ravine landed us on a long plateau, where the path lay for some way

[1] "The difficulty lies in the paying; for not only our friend is by no means over-ready to part with his cash, but he is, moreover, quite ignorant respecting the specific value of its component pieces. Accordingly a council of the wisest heads in the tribe has to be called to decide on the value of each separate coin, and, after that, to sum-totalize, which is, for the Beduins, a yet more Herculean effort of intellect, and the account must be cast up item by item full a dozen times before he knows whether he had twenty or thirty piastres in his dirty hand" (Palgrave's "Central and Eastern Arabia").

along the edge of a precipice, and past numerous small caverns apparently roughly fashioned by nature, and made more convenient for human habitation by man: many of which formed cavities in single rocks from which all but the outer shell was scooped out. From this tableland we again had splendid views of the Dead Sea. On the way the Keraki repeatedly quarrelled amongst themselves about the division of the spoil, and we thought, I am afraid we hoped, several times that they would come to blows: but they quieted down as we approached Kerâk.

The natural situation of Kir of Moab is extremely strong. It stands on the top of a very steep stony hill which is surrounded on all sides by deep valleys. A huge old castle built by the Crusaders and partly in ruins stands on the highest point, and the only entrances to the town were formerly by long winding tunnels cut through the rock, of which only one now remains complete. The town stands nearly three thousand feet above the Mediterranean and consequently nearly four thousand three hundred feet above the Dead Sea.[1] The territory of the Keraki is pro-

---

[1] "In going eastward from the Dead Sea, out of the borders of the Holy Land is a strong and faire castle on a hill which is called Carak in Sarmoyx, that is to say, Royal. That castle was made by King Baldwin when he had conquered that land, who put it into the hands of Christians to keep that part of the country, and for that cause it was called the Mount" (Sir John Mandeville, A.D. 1322).

It was on the walls of Kerâk that the King of Moab sacrificed his eldest son to Chemosh (2 Kings). As Mr. Lethaby pointed out to us, the inscription on the Moabite stone would seem to show that this was the Holy City of Chemosh. "And I have built this sanctuary for Chamos in Qarha (sanctuary of salvation). . . . It is

tected to the north and south by the mountains. These are only passable in the former direction by descending Mojéb, the great gorge of the Arnon, which runs east and west; and are ascended on the south side by the steep pass up which we had come. To the west there is the Dead Sea, whose waters are not navigated by any vessel: and to the east, the desert. The Keraki can muster from sixteen hundred to two thousand well-armed horsemen; and being thus protected by nature, and having long enjoyed independence, have come to believe themselves invincible, and express contempt for the Turkish Government, who hitherto have let them alone.

It is hard to say what the population may be, as some dwell in the town, and others in tents tending their flocks and herds; and the sheiks have their separate encampments in the country, in which they spend a great part of the year. But I understood Mr. Lethaby to estimate the whole number of the Keraki at from seven to eight thousand. There are amongst them a good many Christians belonging to the Greek Church, but these are in a decided minority, and are subject to considerable oppression; tempered however by the power which better means gives, the

---

I who have built Qarha, the wall of the forests and the wall of the hill. I have built its gates, and I have built its towers. . . . And there were no wells in the interior of the city in Qarha; and I said to all the people, 'Make you every man a well in his house,' and I dug cisterns for Qarha" (Translation quoted from M. Clermont Gauneau in "Twenty-one Years' Work in the Holy Land"). Mr. Lethaby says that there are no wells in Kerâk, and that every home has a cistern attached.

small trade and capital of the district being chiefly in their hands.

We knew that the place had an evil repute, that here Burckhardt had been plundered, De Saulcy and his companions held to ransom, and Canon Tristram much harassed; that the commander of the American naval party which explored the Dead Sea many years ago had also been troubled by the Keraki, whose sheik they took prisoner and carried to the Dead Sea as a hostage; and that Mr. Doughty had spoken of the dangerous character of the Mejelli. The British Consul at Jerusalem had also told us that it was a most dangerous place. But we thought that as an English missionary had actually lived there for the last three years there might be an improvement, and that we should not be likely to meet with any serious misfortune in entering the territory of the Keraki. We did not at that time, however, know of the conditions under which Mr. and Mrs. Lethaby were content to exist, and to conduct their work.

SHEIK FARIS, OF KERÂK, AND HIS BRETHREN.

CHAPTER V.

THE ENGLISH MISSIONARIES.

"The king's wrath is as the roaring of a lion."—PROVERBS.
"Now Mr. Great Heart was a strong man, so he was not afraid of a lion."—"PILGRIM'S PROGRESS."

AS our horses scrambled up the steep side of the hill on the summit of which Kerâk stands, we saw a little man in European dress, worn to the

MR. LETHABY, MISSIONARY AT KERÂK.

extreme of tenuity and shabbiness, climbing down on foot, and knew that it must be good Mr. Lethaby come to welcome us. He walked by our side, as wondering we passed through the dark tunnel into the wretched collection of one-storied hovels which constitute the town. As we threaded the dirty lanes from which ill-looking faces stared out upon us, it was a pleasure to see a female figure clothed in a neat clean simple English dress and apron, crowned by an honest smiling friendly English face. This was Mrs. Lethaby, and here in this one poor room lighted only by the door, is the residence and schoolroom of the missionaries and the mission.

That evening Mr. Lethaby told me his history. He was a compositor, had been apprenticed in London, and afterwards worked in a printing-office in a town in the West of England. On week days he worked at his trade, and on Sundays preached in a little Wesleyan Chapel. In 1872 he had tramped across Italy and got to Palestine, and walked about there; and some one in that country had told him of Kerâk as a benighted place, where the people were of the wickedest, and no missionary had ever been: and he had often thought of going to live there. Meanwhile he returned to England and preached away in a quiet country place. But his health troubling him, seven years ago he went again to Palestine; and his mind always turning to Kir of Moab he made his way thither from Jerusalem, with one man only as guide, proceeding round the south end of the Dead Sea. When within six hours of Kerâk the Mejelli knocked him off his horse and robbed him, and he had to return to

Jerusalem. Then he came back again, bearing a letter written by himself to the late sheik, in which he stated that he and his wife were ready to go to Kerâk, and to live there with a view of doing good to the people, and would pay for all they wanted, and seek no advantage for themselves; but that they could not give any backsheesh. The old sheik answered that there was plenty of room in Kerâk, and that there were plenty of stones with which to build a house. So Mr. Lethaby came, and afterwards returning with his wife they had established themselves in this den of thieves. For four years have this little hero and heroine lived and laboured on amongst the Keraki, being subject to continual insults, threats, and robberies. And three or four weeks before our visit Miss Arnold had joined them.

The poverty in which they live, their careful attention to the bodily ailments of the people, and the fact that the Moslems of the place are little more than Mussulman in name, having the Beduin laxity and indifference in religious matters,[1] account for their being allowed to live at all. Indeed Sheik Saleh mentioned

[1] "'What will you do on coming into God's presence for judgment after so graceless a life?' said I, one day, to a spirited young Shererat, whose long matted lovelocks, and some pretension to dandihood—for the desert has its dandies too—and all his ragged accoutrements, accorded very well with his conversation, which was nowise of the most edifying description. 'What will we do?' was his unhesitating answer; 'why, we will go up to God, and salute Him, and if He proves hospitable (gives us meat and tobacco) we will stay with Him; if otherwise, we will mount our horses and ride off.' This is a fair specimen of Beduin ideas touching another world, and were I not afraid of an indictment for profaneness I might relate fifty similar anecdotes at least" (Palgrave's "Central and Eastern Arabia").

to us in an indifferent tone that he intended to kill Mr. Lethaby some day. Mr. and Mrs. Lethaby are so patient, so simple, so earnest, so averse from manufacturing hypocrites, so free from cant of any kind, so careless of small doctrinal and ceremonial points, so brave and determined, that we were lost in admiration of their zeal and devotion.

The daily perils and annoyances to which they are subjected would be enough to drive away all but those of lion heart. One little instance made an impression upon us. Mrs. Lethaby told us that the walls of their room being old (for they did not build a house but only rented a room) were infested by snakes and scorpions, and that she often lay awake at night listening to a peculiar crackling noise made by these creatures in breaking out of the crumbling mortar. Four lean cats who had found a refuge in the mission room from the storms of Kerâk life rewarded their benefactors by hunting the crawling things. The only pleasant time the missionaries have is when work being over and the door locked, they can read aloud some interesting book, and endeavour to forget their surroundings. But even then some of the Mejelli will occasionally dance upon the roof over head, or rattle at the door, and threaten to break in and kill them. All Mr. Lethaby's little means having been exhausted in his mission, his efforts are only supported by friends in England.

So difficult and uncertain is the communication with the outside world, that although as the crow flies the distance from Jerusalem is not, I suppose, much more than seventy miles, yet they told us they were sometimes four months together without getting a letter, or being able to send one; and Mrs. Lethaby said, and probably with accuracy, that my wife was only the third Englishwoman who had visited Kerâk since the Crusades, she and Miss Arnold being the other two.

Whatever religious opinions the reader may hold, or even if he hold none, let him but see what we saw of the devotion of the missionaries of Kerâk, let him but witness as we did the effect which their gentle, true, and merciful lives, lived in the midst of savage, false, heartless, and ignorant people, have upon the children growing up under their influence, and unless his mind is warped by theological bigotry, or anti-religious fanaticism, he must recognize that here a noble work is being done, and he will not stay to inquire whether the doctrines taught are those which are in his opinion of the right colour. When the character and knowledge of the Kerâki are raised to something like the level attained by the average of that part of mankind which is called civilized, it will be time enough for the "subtle schoolmen . . . more studious to divide than to unite"—to quarrel over the nature of the education to be given.

I am glad, then, to have the opportunity of mentioning, for the information of any who care to assist the efforts of these devoted and courageous people, that the Rev. George Piercy, of 276, Burdett Road, London, E.C., receives subscriptions for their mission.

We pitched our tents in an open space at the edge of the town and of the summit of the hill. Then the wearisome business of the money began again. Sheik Saleh wanted us to pay him the rest of the sixty napoleons in the absence of his followers. We were determined not to pay without witnesses, and the presence of some of the escort. A Greek Priest promised at the request of the Lethabys to witness the payment. First we got the Priest, but the Sheik did not come; then we got the Sheik, but the Priest did not come. When both were present and the money had been counted out, Saleh would not take it because some of his own men were present. In the meantime we had obtained the Consul's letter from Mr. Lethaby, and had it translated to Saleh, and we asked him for a receipt for the sixty napoleons " to show to the British Consul, the Queen of England, and the Sultan of Turkey, that they might know how he had treated us." We hoped that this might have an effect, but he said that he was the King of Kerâk, and cared neither for Consul, Queen, nor Sultan.

The men of the escort remained watching until Saleh had departed, so nothing was finished that evening, and wearied and dispirited we went to bed. Saleh lay in the dining-tent to see that we did not escape, and kept poor George awake again with continual talk about the money until the morning. We felt that unless George could sleep he must soon become seriously ill, and then what could we do? In all our difficulties on this and previous journeys he had been our mainstay, and we had learnt from experience to place the fullest confidence in him.

In the middle of the night there came a messenger from Sheik Khalîl, from whom we had received the letter at El Draa, telling us that we must not leave Kerâk until we had seen that personage. In the morning Khalîl's two fierce looking sons, Ibrahim and Derweesh, came with a repetition of the same message. We asked Mejelli what this meant. His reply was that Sheik Khalîl was no one, that he (Saleh) was Mejelli and King of Kerâk, and that he would take us safely according to his word. He added that he wanted in addition to the money a new suit of Beduin clothes, consisting of silk shirt, embroidered woollen cloak, and red boots, which we had brought as a present to Arar, the Sheik of Petra, and which he had seen in our possession. He then insisted on the rest of the money being paid down, and we had to give him (but in the presence of some of the escort and of the Priest), all but twelve napoleons, which we managed to retain for the present.

At last Sheik Saleh was ready to take us from Kerâk on the road towards the gorge of Mojéb, and we began to walk down the hill in the charge of Mejelli and his horsemen, Mr. and Mrs. Lethaby kindly accompanying us. Khalîl's two sons had joined the party, but where was Khalîl? We felt sure we were being led into another trap. It was a very hot morning, and by the time we had got to the bottom of the valley, what with the heat, the exertion of scrambling down on foot, and the anxiety, my wife felt her strength failing, and nearly fainted. She was greatly comforted by Mrs. Lethaby with her husband's consent generously offering to ride with her for the first day's journey; and although the brave little woman was quite unprepared for travelling, she mounted a donkey and rode on. Mr. Lethaby said that he must not say "Good-bye," as there was risk for him on the way back even during the transit of that short distance, if he was observed to be returning to the town; but that he would *vanish*. So he lagged a little behind, ducked behind a stone, and disappeared.

When we got to the top of the hill we saw some horsemen armed with spears and rifles, and found Sheik Khalîl seated amongst them awaiting our arrival. We had to salute him, and then proceeded surrounded by the whole array.[1] Sheik Khalîl is an older man than Saleh, with a grey beard, tall, strong, and determined looking; but has the reputation of being less treacherous and grasping than his relative.

---

[1] " Threescore valiant men are about it; . . . they all hold swords being expert in war; every man hath his sword upon his thigh" (Song of Solomon).

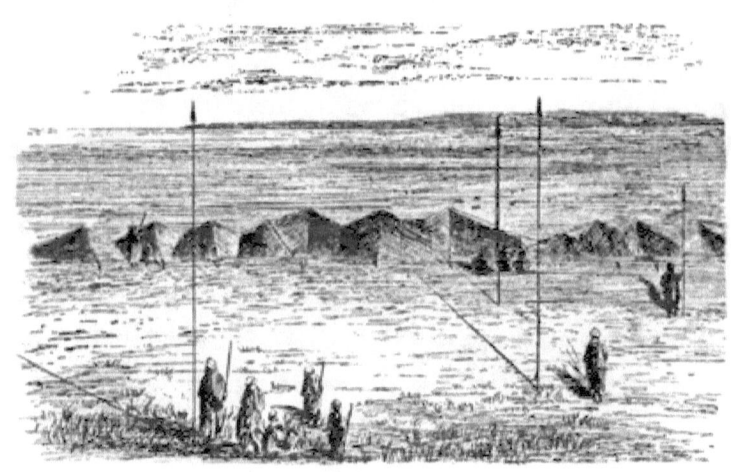

ENCAMPMENT OF SHEIK KHALÎL, WHERE WE WERE DETAINED.

CHAPTER VI.

THE KERAKI. TRAP NO. 2. SHEIK KHALÎL.

"I will run after him, and take somewhat of him,
. . . a talent of silver and two changes of raiment."
2 KINGS.

"It's an honorable kind of thievery."
"TWO GENTLEMEN OF VERONA."

TWO hours' riding over grassy uplands bare of trees, brought us to the ruins of Ar of Moab through which we passed, regretting that we had no opportunity of inspecting them properly; but at that time we still hoped that we should get across the Arnon, and within easy reach of Madeba that day.

Further on we came to the ruins of an ancient temple or castle built with large hewn stones, and containing above ground portions of a very large fallen column.

Passing these, and still journeying through the same kind of country, we arrived early in the afternoon at the encampment of Sheik Khalîl, which is about five hours' ride north of Kerâk. Here we were invited to descend. We declined, saying that we wished to go on towards Madeba; but the Mejelli insisted, and we continuing to object, Khalîl's sons put their pistols to George's head, and forced us to stop and pitch our tents.

As it was important that Mrs. Lethaby should be kept as free from the affair as possible, she went to visit some Christian children, old pupils of hers who were in Khalîl's camp, and we thought it best to accept an invitation from that sheik to eat with him. With the best grace therefore which we could summon out of very indignant hearts we sat down in his tent, ate various unpalatable messes,[1] drank coffee, and administered pills to various applicants.[2] Then we retired to our tents, but were speedily followed by a crowd, who sat down in front of them, and gazed at their contents with covetous looks.

Khalîl said he would send for some men of the Hamèydeh tribe (whose territory extends from the

[1] "When thou sittest to eat with a ruler consider diligently what is before thee." "Be not desirous of his dainties, for they are deceitful meat" (Proverbs).

[2] In our journeys amongst the Beduins we have been very often called upon for medical assistance, and we have found a good stock of chlorodyne, liver pills, quinine, and mustard leaves very useful. For doubtful cases, when the patient will insist upon having something and you are afraid of doing harm, a glass of sugar and water, with a little colour in it, or a bread pill, is easily made up.

Kerâk country northward to within a short distance of Madeba), to conduct us after we left him. What will he demand first, and what troubles shall we have afterwards with the Hamèydeh! These were the pleasant subjects of contemplation which filled our minds. But we managed to get George to sleep for a little while lying on the ground in our bedroom tent, as the place least free from disturbance. We thought that we might want his best strength for the morrow.

Later in the day Khalîl put aside formalities and courteous shows, and came to the point. He must have sixty napoleons—the same as Saleh. He and thirty of his men crowded into our dining-tent to make the communication. Remonstrances were of course made by George, and by us, but it was useless. Khalîl must be put on an equality with Saleh. Then we asked to see Saleh. He came, and sat silent for long, thinking no doubt of the most plausible lies to tell us. He had said in private to George in answer to the complaints of the latter, "Why did you tell Khalîl you were to pay me sixty napoleons? Why did you not say thirty?"

We pressed for an answer to our demand that Saleh should carry out his agreement to conduct us through his territory, and should free us from this new claim. After keeping us waiting for an hour, he got up and went out without saying a word, apparently because Khalîl's sons had seated themselves in the tent and would not leave. Then both sheiks, and a certain Sheik Faris, of Khalîl's family, who appeared to be on an equality with him—a tall, powerfully-built, determined looking man—and the sons of all three sheiks,[1] and their other principal followers, sat down on the ground outside our tents in a circle, and had a long and angry parley.

This being concluded we asked all three sheiks to see us. We appealed both to Saleh and Khalîl. Why had Khalîl written that what we arranged with Saleh bound him, and now refused to be bound, and demanded payment a second time? Khalîl and Faris replied that Saleh would not give them their share; and that if he would give them half of what he received they would ask for nothing. Indeed we became satisfied by all that we saw and heard during our detention by Khalîl and Faris that their demand was more induced by political motives than by greed.

Saleh made excuses. He had given all but eight napoleons to his followers. He had spent all his share. We pressed him as hard as we could, and after a most wearisome discussion in which we introduced the Consul, the Queen, the Sultan, and the reputation of the Arabs for hospitality without the slightest effect, Khalîl rose angrily and withdrew with Faris. Saleh being left alone with us fell back on the same story. Why had we mentioned sixty napoleons to Khalîl? Why had we not said thirty? We must

---

[1] The important part which the sons of these sheiks played in this affair in supporting the interest of their respective families made us more fully understand the value put by the Beduins upon male offspring, and their reason for multiplying wives. In a small community a large number of sons well armed and accustomed to be obeyed would be of great importance for the protection of the family, and the advancement of its interest.

satisfy Khalîl. He (Saleh) had spent all that he had received.

It was getting quite clear that Khalîl meant to be satisfied and placed on a position of equality with Saleh ; that Saleh did not intend to satisfy him out of his own pocket ; and that the satisfaction must, therefore, in the end be extracted from us, as the weaker party. Still we struggled against the inevitable, and the discussion went on, sometimes with us, sometimes amongst themselves, all that afternoon and evening. In the intervals a sheep was forced upon us in the form of a present ; double its value was demanded as a counter present ; and the Keraki arrived in force as soon as it was cooked, and ate it all up themselves served with our rice and bread. Mrs. Lethaby slept with my wife in our bedroom tent, and I with our servants in the dining-tent, and poor George, when after many hours the wretches at last left him unmolested, lay on the ground outside the ladies' tent to watch for their safety.

The same kind of thing goes on the next day. At last they agree, or pretend to agree, that Saleh shall give up to Khalîl the twelve napoleons still remaining to be paid to the former, and return something more out of what he had already received ; and that we, paying something to make the shares of both equal, and settling with Saleh in Khalîl's presence, shall be allowed to go free. We pay the residue of the sixty napoleons accordingly, but Saleh's mare stands close by, and no sooner does he get the money into his hands, than he slips it into his saddle bag, leaps on her back, and is off at full gallop on the road to Kerâk, followed by his sons, and other adherents. He has got our money, and instead of conducting safely through his country, has left us to the tender mercies of Khalîl, with only about fifteen napoleons remaining in our purses.

There is immediately a great uproar in Khalîl's camp, and soon from cursing Saleh, Khalîl's men turn to crowd round our tents and to threaten us. The door of the sleeping tent into which we have retired is lifted up, and dark angry faces fill up the whole entrance. Others raise the lower part of the roof and peer savagely in upon us over the sides. Especially threatening are the greedy eyes of Ibrahim, the son of Khalîl, which wander from object to object with the most covetous eagerness. It is a critical moment. One of the men at the door spits at my wife, and we fear every moment that there will be a general scramble for effects of all kinds, and that a mad fury will arise in which we may all lose our lives. But the cry is for the money.

We tell them again and again that we have not got it with us. The only answer is, "The money!" We can only get it by sending to Jerusalem. They reply that we shall not send there (no doubt they fear Government interference). "The money!" We offer to leave the tents and mules as security to be afterwards redeemed. "No! no! the money!" George offers his horse, his gun, his revolver. "No, the money—the money!" Again they put their pistols to his head. They threaten to kill the muleteers. "The money! You have it in your boxes." "Examine the boxes, and you will see that we have not got it." The only answer is, "The money, the money!" It is like Othello calling for the handkerchief.

The day is wearing on, and Mrs. Lethaby, who at our request, has kept away from these scenes, lest the position of herself and her husband at Kerâk should be injuriously affected, feels that she must now return to him, and mounts her donkey. Khalîl's sons will not let her go unless she promises to endeavour to raise the money at Kerâk. She tells us that the whole place could not furnish sixty napoleons, the few Keraki who had any money having sent it with some of their tribe to Damascus, to purchase the year's supply of necessities. Mr. Lethaby has very little cash, and must not appear to have any. But we have to go through the form of asking her to do what she can, and she through that of promising that she will; and then the brave little woman departs with the son of the Greek priest of Kerâk who had accompanied her. God's benison go with her. I can never forget her kindness to my wife. My wife is exhausted, the peering faces are withdrawn for another consultation, I give her some bromide, and she gets a little sleep.

Then again comes that insolent Ibrahim, who sits down with his pipe under her nose, and asks threateningly for a handsome new kofiyeh (head covering), which was amongst the presents intended for Arar. We decline to give it to him. I am not of a bloodthirsty turn of mind; but I inwardly resolve that if we are forced to make a despairing defence of ourselves against personal violence, I will take my first shot at Ibrahim. There is not much consolation in the thought, however, as most probably he would be quicker than I; for he has long lithe fingers, and his hand is always on the revolver or the dagger which he carries in his belt, the sheath of the latter sewn into his dress. At last they all again withdraw for awhile, and the good old cook sends up a capital dinner, and our spirits revive. But there again are those wicked eyes peering in, and Ibrahim says he has come for the silk Beduin dress that Saleh coveted, but in the hurry of his departure omitted to carry off. All these presents have been offered in *substitution* for the second sixty napoleons. Of course they will be taken in *addition*. Then comes more yelling for the money, and we go dispirited to bed, leaving poor George to be worried and threatened through half the night.

The next morning, Ibrahim forces himself into our sleeping tent while we are yet in bed, and it is with great difficulty that we turn him out. He wants some other article, and always the money, the money. We send to Khalîl to complain of Ibrahim's intrusion, and much to our satisfaction the old sheik administers a paternal blow of a substantial kind to his son of the greedy eyes. My wife is very poorly now, and we think (if matters do not mend soon) of painting red spots on her cheeks, and giving out that she has the plague, as a means of getting free from this continual harassing. We must try something. We cannot go on like this much longer. In the previous night the cook had been beaten, the food at the fire snatched away in spite of him, and half our bag of bread stolen.

The Keraki threaten to starve us into payment. They will sell us nothing. Our charcoal is failing. But now Mrs. Lethaby's kind offices with her little pupils (three shepherd boys of a Christian family) bear fruit. The boys come to see us. Thanks to the instruction given by the missionaries, they can speak English pretty well. They tell us that Mrs. Lethaby has instructed them to help us, and they bring hidden beneath their clothes loaves of Arab bread (pancake shaped), baked by their mother, hot from the oven, fresh goat's milk, and eggs, and assure us that we can have charcoal from their family. This assistance these good little fellows continue to render us during the whole of our detention.

We receive a letter from Mr. Lethaby, reporting, as we expected, that the money could not be obtained in Kerâk, and then after more consultations and discussions, they say that we may try to raise it from the Sheik of Madeba,[1] Khalîl Senah, who is a friend of George's. So Tanus the waiter, being the best caligraphist in the Arabic language present in our camp, puts on his spectacles and writes a letter to this sheik, and we arrange that our "Holy Man" shall take it. We also stipulate that if the money cannot be obtained at Madeba, he shall be at liberty to go on to Jerusalem; and I sit down to write to the Consul telling of our plight, and enclosing an order on Howard's Hotel, where our money is, for a hundred napoleons to be handed to the bearer, for we must have something to spare for emergencies over and above the sixty.

At last, in spite of continual interruption, Tanus and I finish our respective letters. But then a new scheme is proposed. A Christian shepherd belonging to Khalîl's camp, called Girius, has sixty sheep, all good wethers.

---

[1] Madeba is about fifteen hours' journey north of Kerâk.

He offers to sell us the flock for sixty napoleons, to hand the sheep to Sheik Khalîl instead of cash, and to go with us to Jerusalem to receive payment. We joyfully accept the proposal, and Sheik Khalîl agrees to take payment in sheep, but at the price of ten shillings only for each. We struggle against this Brennus-like condition, but have to yield ; and the eldest of the Christian boys writes out a little contract in Arabic for the sale, which is duly sealed with seals and fingers dipped in ink. But Khalîl's sons do not approve ; more consultations are held, the councillors all sitting on the ground in a circle as before. A new light breaks in upon them ; the sheep are theirs if and when they choose to take them. It is the money which they want. They fall on Girius, and beat him for making the offer ; and he escapes, leaving his belt in their hands, and his shoes on the ground. They seem to change their plans continually. What will come next?[1] We try again. Will they take the sheep alone, or with the tents and mules as *security* only, until we can send the money and redeem them? It is useless. They will listen to nothing. " The money, the money ! "

It is now dark, and we draw our " Holy Man " into our sleeping tent, give him the letter, with many injunctions if he cannot get the money at Madeba to place the missive in the Consul's hands immediately he reaches Jerusalem, whatever the hour, and to make all speed in going and returning. He mounts George's horse as the best we have at our command, and hurries off. Again there is a great disturbance, a rude incur-

---

[1] "The dream of the cat is all about the mice" (Burckhardt's "Arabic Proverbs").

sion into our tents, and a threatening appearance on the part of the impatient Keraki. Again the money is demanded, again George is menaced; and the old chief muleteer comes to us with tears in his eyes to say that the wretches are going to kill his two sons. His

SHEIK KHALÎL OF KERÂK AND ANOTHER OF HIS TRIBE.

mother and his two brothers were butchered before his eyes by the Druses in the massacre of 1862. If he now loses his sons, the joy of his heart, what is to become of him?

My wife comforts him; tells him that the threats are probably not serious and are only intended to force us to produce money which we have not got, but which they believe to be in our possession; that he and we are companions in misfortune, and must cheer one another. She bids him sit down and gives him something to eat. The faithful servant is ashamed. Was it ever known that he, Abou Faris, sat down and ate in the presence of a lady? But she prevails; and the good old man goes away comforted, and straightway offers himself and his two sons to the enemy as hostages for the ransom.[1] No, they want the money, the money.

Ibrahim comes again. He threatens to take our clothing, and tents, and all.[2] George tells us to be ready to make a rush for it in case of necessity, and the weather being cold and threatening, we are forced to wear double underclothing lest we should perish of exposure on the road, if we have to fly.

[1] "O good old man, how well in thee appears
   The constant service of the antique world!"
                                   ("As You Like it.")
[2] "If thou hast nothing to pay, why should he take away thy bed from under thee?" (Proverbs).

YOUNG CHRISTIANS AT SHEIK KHALÎL'S ENCAMPMENT.
(*Drawn from an imperfect photograph by Leslie I. Brooke.*)

CHAPTER VII.

WE AWAIT THE RETURN OF THE "HOLY MAN."

"She openeth her mouth with wisdom."
PROVERBS.
"There passed a weary time."
"THE ANCIENT MARINER."

AND now my wife says that as we must necessarily be here some days yet, she will try what she can do towards getting rid of the annoyances to which we are subjected, and placing ourselves on safer ground. My arguments, appeals, indignation, have been of no avail, but a woman's wit and spirit do better. She sends for Sheiks Khalîl and Faris, who come attended by their sons; and then she makes

George translate to them word for word the following little speech :

"We have travelled amongst Beduins before, and have been taught to believe, as those who went before us in our country have believed, that from the time of our father Abraham until now, if any one came as a guest into their tents their hospitality would be full and true. But we have lived to find ourselves mistaken. We have entered the tent of Sheik Khalîl, broken bread, and drunk coffee with him, and been treated outwardly like welcome guests ; but we find ourselves robbed and kept as prisoners. Is this well done?"

They listen with the utmost attention, and look, if they do not feel, ashamed. They cry out, "Clever! Clever!" They say, "Tell the Sitt (lady) she speaks well, and we swear by our heads (placing their hands on them) that she shall not be harmed. She and the gentleman shall go in peace, but we must have the money."

They then repeat several times to one another, "Clever, Beautiful, Sweet," and seem to be full of admiration. Pushing her advantage, my wife now asks that we may be protected from annoyance, and left alone in our tents, that nothing shall be demanded from us in the form of presents, and that what we require shall be sold to us at reasonable prices. They promise that all these requests shall be complied with, and Sheik Faris, waxing enthusiastic, expresses a desire to accompany us to England.

After this things went more smoothly. The promises were not kept with exactness ; Ibrahim in particular continuing to ask for everything which took his fancy, and making special inroads on our candles and coffee; food was taken repeatedly out of the cook's hands; the same exorbitant prices as before were asked for sheep, chickens, eggs, bread, milk, and charcoal; and we could not keep intruders out of the dining tent. But we were allowed to have our sleeping tent to ourselves, felt more confidence in refusing the demands for different articles which continued to be made, made successful appeals to Khalîl and Faris when they were pressed too urgently, and felt tolerably free from danger of personal violence. The little speech had produced an excellent effect, and the sheiks said to George, " Whoever speaks with the Sitt will break his head," meaning must submit to her.

We now remembered that—

" The robb'd that smiles, steals something from the thief.
He robs himself that spends a bootless grief,"

and, putting on a cheerful countenance, brought out our photographic machines, and began to take some portraits. It was fortunate that we did so, for as we afterwards learnt the Keraki had supposed the box which contained them to be full of gold. They now seemed at last to understand that they must await the return of our messenger before we could pay them. But they took precautions lest we should escape, not allowing us to ride or even to walk out alone, and keeping an especially strict watch upon George. They brought for our inspection an animal which they called a "white cow," a creature I believe unknown in Europe. It seems to be a kind of antelope. I wish we had taken a photograph of it, but some trouble arose at the time, and put the matter out of our minds. Khalîl sent his baby son, the child of his old age, to my wife to be doctored. She asked him whether he would trust her with the baby, seeing what motives we had to feel indignant at his conduct. Yes, he would trust her to treat the child as she liked. So she applied some little remedies and made it well.

The time passed wearily away. A great wind and rain arose, and we could not stir outside for twenty-four hours. The water fell in torrents. By the aid of trenches round the tents we prevented the flood from entering, and the double roof-covering kept out the rain bravely. But the driving wind caused the wet to soak through the sides, everything was very damp within, and that night I had to put the indiarubber bath over my wife's head to keep the drip off her face. The worst was that the bad weather must necessarily delay the messenger. We did not expect to get the money from Madeba, and felt sure that he would have to go on to Jerusalem. The streams would be swollen. Would he be able to ford them? At any rate he could not "bide the pelting of this pitiless storm." He must stop on the way until it was over. Then there was another serious risk. Would he be robbed on the road? Or would his virtue be too much for the temptation, and would he take the money for himself and leave us to our fate?

The little Christian boys came often to see us. They brought their Arabic Bibles, in which they evidently took great interest, and their whole behaviour and tone of mind were as different as possible from that of the grasping savage Mejelli. They appeared to us like little sheep amongst the wolves. They told us about the wild beasts that prowled about at night and threatened the flocks, although these were brought every evening close to the encampment for protection; of a kid that had been taken from their goats the night before; and of a shepherd who last year had been killed by a wolf. They lived entirely on bread and leben (sour milk) except on the occasion of a feast, when they got some mutton and rice. We were unable to keep the boys with us for long at a time, as the other Keraki soon followed them into our tent, or we should have been very glad to see more of them.

During our detention, news of the murder of a Christian at Kerâk and of the robbery of goods under under his care reached us, and it was whispered about that the Mejelli had had a hand in the deed.

The rain comes again. How it pours! The ground in front of us is like a marsh. How shall we get the baggage mules along when the money comes, and we are allowed to move. We borrow a chafing dish from Sheik Khalîl, and burn charcoal in it to keep things dry. What a wearisome waiting! George seems sickening for fever, above all things lacking "the season of all natures sleep," and when I guard the door of the tent, and dose him with bromide, he starts and tosses and shouts in his "slumbery agitation" without a moment's repose. We depend on him not only for all the arrangements, but even for our understanding of what passes, for he is the only one of our company who can speak English, or indeed anything but Arabic, except the cook, who knows about as much, or rather about as little Italian as we do.

Fortunately this sleep, broken as it is, enables him to avoid breaking down.

Khalîl's sons become so much more friendly that they suggest that we should build a house at Kerâk; and we not accepting the offer, they tell us they would like to go to England with us. Derweesh is appointed to attend to us, and both are much better behaved. Poor Girius, the Christian shepherd, has been so frightened that he sacrifices four sheep to make a propitiatory feast for Khalîl, Faris, and the rest. The Lethabys send us, by a chance messenger, some loaves of bread, with a welcome piece of boiled ham cunningly concealed within it, lest it offend Moslem noses. How we enjoy it!

We learn that the men of the Hamèydeh tribe, who have been waiting at Khalîl's camp for some days to take us on to Madeba, are preparing to ask us for a large amount. Of course they know all that is going on, and it would be contrary to Beduin, even to human nature, if they did not demand an exorbitant sum. But will they detain us? Well, they are the only tribe remaining after we leave the Keraki, and before we reach Madeba. What is the use of thinking of them while we are detained here? Will the messengers ever return?

At length the rain clears away, the evening of the seventh day of our captivity and of the fifth since our messenger left for Jerusalem closes in with a clear sky, and as the light begins to fail, we make out through our glasses a horseman coming down the shoulder of Jebel Shehan, a high hill near to us on the west side. Presently we recognize our little " Holy Man," and go out rejoicing to meet him. He comes on radiant with smiles,[1] enters with us into our sleeping-tent, opens his breast, and cuts a string that fastens a sealed packet beneath his shirt. It contains a letter from the Consul and the hundred napoleons.

[1] He was in a happy mood, for in passing through the Adwan camp at Hesbân he learnt that his wife had borne him twins, two boys. He had been known as Abou Seyr. Henceforth taking his name from that given to his first-born, he was also called Abou Nasr—the father of Nasr.

CHAPTER VIII.

WE GET FREE FROM THE KERAKI AND CROSS MOJÉB.

> "Come on, sir, here's the place. Stand still.
> How fearful
> And dizzy 'tis to cast one's eyes so low."
> "KING LEAR."

> "There was a deep ravine that lay
> Yet darkling in the Moslem's way,
> Fit spot to make invaders rue.
> .   .   .   .   .
> And on each side, aloft and wild,
> Huge cliffs and toppling crags were piled."
> "LALLA ROOKH."

THEN we summoned Sheik Khalîl, told him that we had got the money; and offered to pay half down, and the rest when he had taken us across Mojéb. To this he agreed, and we then struggled to arrange a route which would avoid the Hamèydeh. But about that point we could not get any definite answer; and then another council was called, and all sat in a circle again. They were still talking when we went to bed, and they afterwards turned to George and kept him up until long past midnight.

The next day, Good Friday, the 4th of April, we rose very early indeed, and as soon as we had sat down to breakfast the sheiks and their followers crowded into the tent, and the talk began again. They now said that the whole amount must be paid before starting. We remonstrated, suspecting some trick, although Khalîl assured us that he would not, like Saleh, "leave a stone in the well,"[1] but would carry out his agreement. However we knew that we had a long journey before us, and that we had no time to lose in fruitless discussion, so paid down the money, which seemed to take a vast time to count and recount.

Then they demanded with greedy and threatening insistence the articles which they had coveted, the silk dresses, kofiyehs, cloaks and boots; and then they asked for our bag of coffee, and grumbled much because it had been reduced in bulk by their own previous abstractions. And Ibrahim abandoning himself to his greedy disposition began to demand many things for his own private account. The tea tray which bore a pretty pattern especially attracted his cupidity, but my wife pushing it to him with one hand placed her other on the best dagger in his girdle (the beauties of which he had displayed to us before) and offered to make an exchange. At this the other Keraki broke out into an admiring laugh; Ibrahim looked sheepish and withdrew; and old Tanus the waiter was allowed to shut his box in peace.

At last—how long it seemed—we were off. We had to make a long detour to avoid the swampy ground, and went so far to the southward, that I began to fear,

---

[1] "A well from which thou drinkest throw not a stone into it" (Burckhardt's "Arabic Proverbs"). The same proverb is to be found in the Talmud.

lest like human shuttlecocks we should be tossed back again from Khalîl to Saleh, and be conducted to Kerâk.

Then we noticed that the men who were conducting us were not the headmen. Was Khalîl going to hand us over to Faris (who had kept away in his tents two miles away saying that he was ill), that the latter might extract more money from us? What was in the wind? We had not much time to speculate upon it all, for our horses after their week's idleness were very fresh and excited, and required our best attention. At last we saw horsemen galloping towards us, and found that Khalîl and his sons had made a short cut to save their precious mares and the little foals which trotted after them. They joined us, and we proceeded northwards with a large escort of the Keraki.

But who were these strange men with spears who had joined us on the march and were following the Keraki? They were the Hamèydeh. Ah yes, the Hamèydeh. For the moment we had forgotten them. Well at any rate they are the last, and we must keep up our courage, and remember that every step takes us nearer to Madeba and freedom. But would the Keraki really take us down to Mojéb, and across that Arnon which bounds their territory? That was the all-absorbing question.

After some hours of riding over undulating uplands, we came to the brink of the mighty pass of Mojéb, a chasm down which it made one almost dizzy to look. On the face of the cliff on the south side was a goat path as difficult of descent as rocks and precipice could make it. All here descended from their horses, the mares whinnied to their foals, of which we had eight altogether following us, and one after another the silent cavalcade of men and horses descended the deep ravine. The two-footed and the four-footed were intermixed, and if the animals had not been so sagacious, they must have trodden on some of the former.

Although we slipped often as we walked, and the Beduins stumbled several times, the tread of the horses' feet was perfectly sure, and it was a beautiful sight to see the care and wisdom with which they managed to descend the breakneck path. At the bottom one mare missed her foal, and whinnied and whinnied till the rocks resounded with her cries. The Beduin rider waited patiently, knowing that the little foal would soon appear, and presently he was seen peering down over the rocks and dancing along the path like a goat. Before long he was at the mother's side at the bottom of the valley to her intense joy, and she kept the little creature very close to her as we forded the Arnon. The river flowed rapidly, but notwithstanding the recent rain it was not deep; its course to the Dead Sea being so short, the accumulation of water coming down from the hills soon runs off.

On the other side we rested a little, and gazed up at the mountains both north and south, which looked even more inaccessible from the bottom than from the top, and we wondered how we were to get up and away on the road to Madeba. The Keraki had been very kind and pleasant on the way, helping my wife over all the difficult parts, and making polite little speeches. "Would the Sitt think of them kindly, and would we return and build a house at Kerâk?" No, after the way they had treated us, she was sorry that she could not think of doing so.

The Keraki bade us observe the steepness of the path by which we had come, and the great depth of the ravine. Did we think that Pasha or Sultan or Queen could ever enter their country against their will? Would not their guns sweep down any soldiers who attempted to climb the precipice? Could any horsemen stand against the Keraki on the plain at the top?[1]

The late Laurence Oliphant had a scheme for emigration to the country between the Jabbok and the Arnon, and although apparently the Jews who were to

---

[1] "We have heard of the pride of Moab: he is exceeding proud; his loftiness and his arrogancy and the haughtiness of his heart" (Jeremiah).

I believe that Kerâk could readily be subjected to the authority of the Turkish Government and be brought into a peaceful and orderly condition by a simple and comparatively inexpensive process. A steam launch, or even a row boat, plying at the narrow part of the Dead Sea between the peninsula and the western shore, with facilities for carrying animals as well as men across, would be enough. To protect the ferry a small stone fort on each side, garrisoned by a dozen soldiers, would be necessary. A light toll would pay most of the cost. The distance to Jerusalem would then be shortened very greatly, and those making the journey would be relieved of the risk of being robbed by the tribes to the south of the Dead Sea. Trade would spring up, for the Keraki have very large flocks and herds, and there are rich pastures for vast quantities of cattle and sheep, and the land yields bounteous harvests; and the Sheiks of Kerâk would be transformed from robbers into merchants.

"What war could ravish, commerce could bestow,
And he returned a friend, who came a foe" (Pope).

be the emigrants, are not the best people for an agricultural life, there is no kind of doubt of the extraordinary fertility of the soil; not only as far south as the Arnon, but all through the district of Kerâk, and even farther south. Some day this land will again support a large population.

We ascended to a low tableland on the north of the Arnon,[1] from which the mountains rose, and pausing there the Keraki handed us over to the Hamèydeh and descended again towards the river.

[1] "Arnon, which is in the wilderness that cometh out of the coast of the Amorites, for Arnon is the border of Moab, between Moab and the Amorites" (Numbers).

CHAPTER IX.

THE HAMÈYDEH. WE DECLINE TO BE STOPPED AGAIN.

> "Our indiscretion sometimes serves us well,
> When our deep plots do pall."
> "HAMLET."
>
> "Let's take the instant by the forward top."
> "ALL'S WELL THAT ENDS WELL."

WITH a sigh of relief, and yet with a feeling that a chapter in our lives was closed, we watched the Keraki ride slowly down to the stream, and turned to scan the Hamèydeh. More of the latter had joined us as we had proceeded, and there were now fifteen of them. Looking carefully at their arms, I noticed with great satisfaction that there was not a rifle amongst them, and only one flint-lock gun. There were six or eight spears; every man had a sword, dagger, and flint-lock pistol; and the sheik carried a good six-chambered revolver. But these fellows did not look to me so redoubtable as the Keraki, and with easier minds we sat down after riding a short distance with them, by the side of a tributary of the Arnon to take our lunch. The stream ran through a channel worn in white rocks which lay in regular flat layers like broad steps rising above one another, over which the water fell in pretty little cascades. Here we reposed under an oleander bush, and watched fish which looked like trout working up-stream.

We looked too at the Keraki ascending the pass again on the south side of the Arnon, their guns, and pistols, and white dresses glistening in the sunlight as they crawled up the heights, until they were lost to view. Then we followed the Hamèydeh up the toilsome ascent to the northward. If the descent on the south side of the ravine of Mojéb had been difficult, the ascent on the north side was more laborious still, for the poor horses and the heavily-laden mules. It was a hard portion of a very hard day's work.

Two or three hours further on we entered a narrow grassy valley, where the Hamèydeh invited us to stay for the night. No, we wanted to get on to Madeba. They pressed us, urging various reasons, but we were firm; then they insisted and began to threaten. We had paid each sheik of the Mejelli sixty napoleons, and we should pay them as much. We answered them that we would pay them what we thought proper and no more. While we discussed, our baggage mules were going on in front, seeing which the brother of the sheik and several of his spearmen pushed forward and stopped them. George and I shouted to the muleteers to go on. The sheik and his spearmen got in front, and placed their spears across the narrow path, and pushed the end of one within an inch of old Tanus' breast. I called to my wife that we must run the risk of resistance whatever came of it, for the thought of being detained again was insupportable. She recognized the necessity and consented. Then agreeing with

George that we would fight if necessary, I galloped forward with him. He beat on the mules and pointed his gun at the sheik's brother, and I covered the same man with my revolver across the mule that separated me from him; and with our blood up, for the adventure had become wonderfully exciting, we told him that we would shoot him if he did not let us pass..

The way was so confined that the rest of the Hamèydeh could not pass us, and they came pressing on behind, bearing on my wife and her horse with them, close to whom kept the faithful cook with his revolver and gun ready for action. And so we all passed up the valley—the brother of the sheik and the Beduins gesticulating and yelling out threats, our men urging on their mules, and those that had arms holding them ready for use. The sheik's brother was, or appeared to be, in a terrible passion, his eyes starting from his head, and called on his men to assist him. I felt that we were casting our lives upon a die, and for a time it was impossible to know what would happen. But the spearmen had given way and were only threatening, and the men behind hesitated and consulted together. The sheik's brother still keeping on the other side of our mules and gesticulating at us madly, George shouted to him through the hubbub, enlarging upon the number of shots we could fire from our revolvers, and telling him that the Turkish authorities, the British Consul, and the Sheik of Madeba were all expecting us, and that he and his followers would be severely punished if they persisted.

Probably this consideration had more influence than all our warlike demeanour, for we learnt afterwards that the year before the Hamèydeh had been well beaten by the men of Madeba assisted by some Turkish troops. At any rate after the tumult had lasted about half an hour it died away into grumblings and mutterings, the spearmen dropped behind, and we were allowed to proceed unmolested. We were again urged to stop, but threats were not renewed; and we continued to push on as fast as we could for several hours, until we had passed over a range of hills, and come down a long descent to a water-course (dry except for a few pools left in it) which made a deep horse-shoe curve under a high cliff to the northward, that seemed to cut us off from Madeba and help. This must have been the bed of the Zerka Main. We could not get to know how far we really were from Madeba, the accounts given varying from two to seven hours; the sun had set, there was said to be no water between this place and Madeba, and my wife was completely exhausted; we had been kept in a state of tension through anxiety and excitement ever since three o'clock that morning, and had by this time passed nearly eleven hours in the saddle: so we were forced to rest here for the night. So ended Good Friday, 1890.

We only set up two of our tents, so as to be free to move the more rapidly in case of any further trouble. The Hamèydeh bivouacked on the south side of the water-course opposite to us who were under the cliff on the north side: the fires were lighted and we gazed out into the short twilight. So much had happened in this eventful day that we could hardly believe that we had descended Mojeb that very morning: it seemed so far off, the dangers with the Hamèydeh having almost wiped away for the time "from the tablet of our memory" the impression made upon us by the Keraki.

We were afraid that the Hamèydeh would send for more men in the night, and renew their attempt in the morning. But only one more man arrived, and although they asked again for payment on the same scale as the Keraki, and refused to take us further, we told them we would pay nothing till we saw Madeba in the distance, as we did not know the way there, and declined to discuss the amount of their remuneration. So we started up the hill to the north as soon as it was light, they grumbling and consulting with one another as they followed. At length they stopped in a deep valley and insisted upon payment then and there, alleging that on the hill beyond was an encampment of Christians with whom they had a blood feud, and that they would not therefore take us further. We kept them discussing the matter until we had passed on the baggage animals and my wife up the side of the hill, and then gave them thirty medjidiés (a sum which we had offered to pay and they had refused to accept as the price of their service when we were in Khalîl's camp) and cantered off to join our party.

The Sheik of the Hamèydeh had had the impudence that morning to ask me for a certificate, and with the money I gave him one which I had written out the night before in anticipation of such a request, which will I trust prove a sufficient warning to any traveller to whom he may hereafter offer his services.

On reaching the top of the hill we saw the Christian encampment lying in a hollow to the south east of us, and passed a shepherd with his flock belonging to it, who stared at us with the greatest astonishment. His Christianity was not however very perfect, for he seized the last of our mules which was somewhat in the rear of a long procession, and called to his fellows in the camp below to come to help him. But George galloping back soon knocked him over, and we pushed on without any further trouble.

A DRINK IN THE DESERT.

CHAPTER X.

MADEBA AND MOUNT NEBO ONCE MORE.

"Which of us, like Moses, has not his promised land, his day of ecstasy, and his death in exile? What a pale counterfeit is real life of the life we see in glimpses, and how these lightnings make the twilight of our fate more dark and dreary."—"AMIEL's JOURNAL."

"From that height he came down no more."—STANLEY's "JEWISH CHURCH."

IN three hours' time we came in sight of Madeba. The land all around was well cultivated. The country lay stretched out before us in many coloured patches (as George said, with a sudden remembrance of his geographical studies in Bishop Gobat's school at Jerusalem: "this look like map of Europe: one country green, another red, another yellow"). The larks were singing in the sky; the air was "as virginal and sweet as ours"; and we sat down peacefully to lunch and rest while the baggage animals pushed on, that the tents might be prepared for us in the little town.

On entering the place we were received by Khalîl Senah the Sheik (a very fine and benevolent looking man of about fifty-five years of age), and all the principal inhabitants, and welcomed as Christians escaped from the Moslem tyranny of the Mejelli. Senah had been absent when our messenger passed through Madeba on the way to Jerusalem, but on his return had been found ready with the money for us.

How delightful it was to have a mighty wash, and a quiet sleep, to put on clean clothes, and to feel that all anxiety was over.

Madeba was a place of no importance until a few years ago, when this same Senah, having withdrawn from Kerâk, bought a large quantity of land here, and attracted a number of Christians of the Greek Church to the neighbourhood. He has re-sold plots to such as settled here, and lent them money wherewith to buy oxen, sheep, and goats, and there has been a considerable migration to this place from Kerâk. The inhabitants can now muster four hundred horsemen, and are able to hold their own against Beduin attacks. And families are continually flying from Kerâk to this little City of Refuge. The quantity of land under cultivation and the flocks and herds are rapidly increasing; and we noticed a very decided growth since our first visit to the place in 1888. It is built upon an eminence, the dwellings being constructed of hewn stones found in the ground in great abundance in the shape of walls of houses, churches, and other buildings, of which nearly all the parts above ground have disappeared, although a few Roman remains are still standing above the surface. There is here a large, old, open cistern or pool something like that at Hebron, or one of the pools of Solomon; and a remarkably fine Roman pavement in a perfect state is to be seen in one of the houses.

With our arrival at Madeba all our troubles ended; our thirteen days of anxiety, danger, and ceaseless harassing with Howeytát, Ghawàrineh, Keraki, and Hamèydeh were over, and we were awakened at dawn on Easter Sunday, the sixth of April, by the peaceful tinkle of the bell belonging to the little Greek Church calling worshippers to prayer. We were here within an hour and a half of the summit of Mount Nebo; and that evening taking our kettle and teapot with us, and gathering some dry scrub on the way, while the sheiks of the Adwan tribe who had come to meet us at Madeba, and whom we greeted as old friends, deftly milked some of the goats which we passed, we drank our dish of tea in the most perfect bliss, enjoying at the same time the celebrated "Pisgah View" of Palestine by the evening light.

Our good old cook as a devout Moslem was much impressed with the thought that Moses had been here; the great Hebrew being a mighty prophet in Moslem as well as in Christian and Jewish belief. He rubbed his bad eye with a little water which he found in the hollow of a fallen column of the old Christian Church which once adorned the summit, being under the impression that Moses had built it, and having before him the hope of a miraculous cure; and offered up a loud and energetic thanksgiving for our escape, and prayer for our future safety, health, and happiness.

CHAPTER XI.

ABOU SEYNE. THE KAIMAKÂM OF ES SALT AGAIN.

> "On active steed with lance and blade,
> The light-arm'd pricker plied his trade;
> Their gain, their glory, their delight
> To sleep the day, maraud the night."
> "MARMION."

> "Well, you must now speak, Sir John Falstaff, fair."
> "HENRY IV.," Part 2.

KHALÎL SENAH was greatly interested in our adventures with the Keraki. Just before we were released he had learnt of our detention by the letter which our "Holy Man" had left for him on his way to Jerusalem, and no sooner did he know of it than he despatched letters to the Governor of Damascus (in whose district Madeba is) and to Zatam el Faiz, the head of the Beni Sokr Beduins, whose country lies east of Madeba and of the territory of the Adwan tribe, informing them of the affair. He urged us to apply to the Turkish Government, and ask them to obtain compensation for us. He looked at the matter as one of great importance for the safety of the Christians in this part of the country, believing that if the Mejelli were not punished for what they had done there would be no restraint upon their rapacity ; and he told us that it was impossible for us to understand the importance to the Christian population of our taking energetic steps with this object.[1]

[1] Several travellers in Syria, whom we afterwards met, urged us, as Khalîl Senah had done, to obtain redress for the acts of the Keraki, if only for the sake of travellers generally ; and, as will be seen, we visited the Kaimakâm of Es Salt and the Governor of the Hauran with this object. A difficulty, however, arose which has prevented our making any progress in the matter. When we returned to Jerusalem we found that Sir W. White, the British Ambassador at Constantinople, seeing a paragraph in *The Times* about our capture by Beduins, had at once telegraphed to the British Consul at Jerusalem for particulars, which had been immediately supplied. Sir W. White was prepared to make a claim upon the Turkish Government, or to urge them to obtain redress from the Keraki. It so happened also that the moment was, owing to other causes, propitious for so acting. Before our adventure happened some of the principal citizens of Jerusalem had petitioned the Porte to send a garrison to Kerâk to establish a Kaimakâm there, and to put the place under the Pasha of Jerusalem instead of the Governor of Damascus, which is at an inconvenient distance from Kerâk. It seemed as if the Turkish Government were willing to grant the request, and only wanted a little urging to induce them to give effect to it ; and it was said that Sir W. White had been requested to support the petition. It appeared also that Sheik Saleh, being in some apprehension of the coming of the troops, had sent a message to Es Salt to say that he would submit to the Government, although I cannot say if he meant this honestly or not. But Sir W. White, knowing that the English missionaries were at Kerâk, and thinking that an attempt to take possession of the place would probably be attended with bloodshed, in which case their safety might be imperilled, desired Mr. Kyat, the acting Consul at Jerusalem (for the Consul had by this time left for England), to send a messenger to Mr. Lethaby to advise that he, Mrs. Lethaby, and Miss Arnold, should leave Kerâk and come to Jerusalem, there to remain until the storm should be past. It was

From Madeba we sent our man Nakhli to Jerusalem with a written account of our doings for the British Consul, with letters to be posted for home, and with instructions to bring any letters which had arrived in Jerusalem for us, and to purchase various articles which we required for our camp. These things he was to

some weeks before an answer could be obtained, and then one was received from Mr. Lethaby absolutely declining to do as advised, on the ground that his duty to his little flock required him to stick to his post. Of course under these circumstances we told the acting Consul that we should not urge our personal claims, and must leave the matter to the discretion of the Ambassador. The latter, as naturally, was as unwilling as we to put the lives of the missionaries in peril. We cannot but admire Mr. Lethaby's courage and constancy, and could not weigh the pecuniary consideration against his feeling of duty. But the question is whether he took sufficient account of the protection which would be afforded to the numerous Christians of the Greek Church at Kerâk by the establishment there of a settled government. Khalîl Senah's point of view is worthy of consideration. So far as regards European travellers who desire to visit the country occupied by the Beduins, I very much fear that the result of the whole affair is that they will run considerably more risk than heretofore. For if the Beduins find that travellers can be stopped and held to ransom with impunity by the Keraki, they will surely be tempted to try whether they also cannot act in like manner. From all that I can learn about the matter, however, I think it quite possible that the Turkish Government will, for its own purposes, and without being requested by any one, take possession of Kerâk; and if they should do so, the risk to the missionaries being then over, I suppose that we ought to ask the Foreign Office to take up our case. The amount of the loss suffered by us is not very material, but it is important that the Sheiks of Kerâk should be punished for their conduct. Here again, however, a difficulty occurs. Will not the Turkish Government merely recover an indemnity which will be extracted by these powerful sheiks from some of their innocent subordinates? Will they really lay hands on the Mejelli? I doubt it.

bring with him to the encampment of the Adwan at Hesbân, where we intended to go next. At night the moon was at the full, and rose on the horizon of a deep rich orange colour; and when it had risen high in the heavens our messenger and a man of Madeba, also bound to the Holy City, rode off together, and we watched them disappear in the ghostly light.

That evening came a messenger from the Beni Sokr with a letter to Khalîl Senah, reporting that their sheik, Zatam el Faiz was dead; poisoned, the rumour was, whether true or not, I know not. We had heard much talk of this sheik, and had often wished to see him, but that was not to be.

From Madeba we revisited the ruined palace of Mashita, taking with us two Adwan sheiks (Fellàch and Ali Abdul Aziz), who had come for us from Hesbân, and four men of Madeba. But, although a careful lookout was kept, we did not see any Beduins. On the way our escort treated us to a display of their skill in horsemanship—"for give pleasure to the lady," as George expressed it—tearing about on their mares, waving their swords, firing off their guns, flourishing their spears, and conducting sham pursuits, retreats, and hand-to-hand fights with one another, with the utmost skill and grace.

We then revisited Hesbân, where we received a hearty welcome from Ali Diab and the Adwan, and where two Turkish soldiers, despatched by the Kaimakâm of Es Salt to look for us, ran us to earth. They had been as far as Umm Rosàs (about north-east of Kerâk, on the Hadj road to Mecca) to look for us, and had coursed us to Hesbân. They said they must take us to Es Salt, as the Kaimakâm wished to see us; and we promised to go there with them, although not by the shortest route. After staying two days at Hesbân we proceeded to Ammân (Rabbath Ammon). Here we met our old friend Abou Seyne, of the Adwan tribe, who seemed very pleased to see us. He had recently married a wife, but at once said that he would accompany us. So he took his spear in his hand, and, leaning upon it, leaped into his saddle at one spring, and rode forth with us in his usual easy way, without stirrup, girth, or bit.

The Turkish soldiers and Abou Seyne danced along on their horses, executing rival feats of horsemanship; but admirably as the former rode he was their superior. Indeed, he seemed like the gentleman of Normandy, praised by Claudius, for

> "he grew into his seat,
> And to such wondrous doings brought his horse,
> As he had been incorpsed and demi-natured
> With the brave beast."

And then, when we passed a flock of sheep or goats, it was a rare sight to see the dexterity with which Abou Seyne would single out a good wether, or great she-goat, with udder distended, catch her, draw off the warm milk into an empty biscuit-can, with which we provided him for the purpose, and bring us a delicious draught. When we could see a shepherd we paid for our milk, but this greatly annoyed Abou Seyne, who much preferred stealing it, or taking it by open force. Abou Seyne would sing too—always the same tune (I never heard the Adwan Beduins sing more than one), but with infinite gusto, as if it were the rarest and sweetest of melodies.

With these men we passed through a pleasant, undulating, grassy, woody country of hill and dale in two days of rambling to Es Salt, and as we neared that place we were rejoiced to see some spearmen in the distance. There was no danger here, and a sight of Beduins is always pleasant when there is none. Who could these be winding up the side of the high hill on which we stood? We drew rein, and waited by the path.

Presently they came up to us, and we learnt with great interest that they were the sheiks of the Beni Sokr tribe, led by a Turkish soldier, and going to the Kaimakâm of Es Salt to make friends with the Government.

The Kaimakâm had wisely chosen the occasion of the death of their ruler to invite the sons and near relatives of the deceased to see him. The two sons were young—about fourteen and sixteen respectively, but married already—dark, and good-looking young fellows. With them came their uncles and attendants —eight altogether—every man carrying his spear, sword, and pistol: a very picturesque little procession. We rejoiced to think that we now had an opportunity of making acquaintance with the Beni Sokr, which we had never yet had a chance of doing. They are indeed very rarely to be seen out of their own territory—that is to the westward. So we asked George to make our compliments, and present our condolences on the death of their celebrated chief, Zatam el Faiz, and to tell them that we hoped some day to visit them if they would receive us.

They stopped, a circle of horsemen was made, and they asked who we were. George told of our adventures with the Keraki. Why had we not sent for the Beni Sokr to help us? The Keraki were not true Beduins; only peasant bred.[1] They would get the money back again for us for the honour of the Beduins. We asked if they had received a letter from Khalîl Senah informing them of our situation.

"Yes," said the youngest son. "It came the day our father died, so it was not opened till the next day, and then we had much people with us." We told them that we hoped to visit them next year, and they answered that we should be welcome. Then making them a farewell salute we made way for them to pass first down the very steep and difficult hill-path, which leads from the eastward, we following at a respectful distance; for these were very great people, the head of eight thousand horsemen.

The head soldier, or "choweesh," who accompanied us had galloped forward through the town to announce our arrival at Es Salt, and we went straight to the house of the Kaimakâm. As we passed through the narrow, crowded, dirty streets, under the gaze of the inhabitants of the town who crowded the house roofs, we wondered if he was the man who ordered us so abruptly to our tents in 1888. We passed from the crowd under a gateway into a

---

[1] Speaking of the former Sheik of Kerâk, Mr. Doughty says, "His father or else his grandsire was an incoming rich peasant body from Jebel el Khalîl, the mountain of Hebron: for which cause any who are less his friends disdain him as a sheik fellàh; 'a peasant lord,' they say, 'to rule them!'" ("Arabia Deserta.")

courtyard, and, dismounting, followed the soldier up a steep outside staircase, and found ourselves in a large reception or business room. Two men in European clothes sat at a desk, and all around were divans, except where an armchair and footstool were placed for the Kaimakâm. We were very tired with our hot ride and the long, rugged descent into the valley of Es Salt, which we had accomplished on foot. But here we had to sit patiently and be stared at by many coming and going, who wished to see the "Franghi" who had been seized by the fierce men of Kerâk. Outside the room was a little gallery, and face after face rising out of robes of varying colours appeared and disappeared —one friend beckoning on another to the "coin of vantage." Every now and then a soldier flicked the faithful away with the kurbash, but no one was hurt. They only grinned, ran away, and immediately afterwards returned.

At last the Kaimakâm entered, and we all rose. We knew him at once, and he evidently recognized us; but he did not refer to the previous affair, and it was not our cue to do so. He knew all the details of our adventure, of which he had heard from Jerusalem, and he told us that the Governor of Damascus had sent to him to say that "the measure of the Mejelli was full," and that it was intended to send soldiers to Kerâk and appoint a Kaimakâm to keep order there. He wished, however, to have a statement taken down about the business. So a clerk, writing with a reed pen upon paper held in the palm of his hand, wrote the whole history of it at great length from the narration of George. As he wrote, the Kaimakâm asked questions, made sympathetic remarks, abused the Keraki, and referred to the friendship of England and Turkey. Had he not sent his own servant, his invaluable "choweesh," to find us and guide us to him?

The Kaimakâm treated us with the greatest politeness and consideration, offered to receive us as guests in his house, gave us lemonade and coffee, and insisted on sending a soldier with us as far as Jerash, where we were now bound.

When the Kaimakâm had finished our business, and disposed of two law cases (he seemed to do it all although the Kadi sat by) we rose to go, and, descending the flight of steps into the courtyard, mounted our horses amidst a crowd of soldiers and staring men, women and children, who seemed to know all about what had happened to us, for they repeated the word "Mejelli" many times as they pointed at us.

Abou Seyne took very good care not to go into Es Salt. It appears that when recently travelling as one of this same Kaimakâm's guides in the Adwan territory, he disappeared in the night on his mare, and came back in the morning with a flock of five hundred goats. The Kaimakâm told him to take them back to the owner. Abou Seyne declined. The Kaimakâm threatened to shoot him. Abou Seyne replied that his hands were not bound, that he had his gun, and that he would defend himself. Ultimately, he was allowed to keep twenty of the goats upon condition of returning the rest. It is useless to be angry with him. He was brought up to look upon the camels, cattle, horses, sheep, and goats of others as lawful prize. He confided to George how hard it was that we were so particular. His wife expected him to bring home something, and he wished to please her. Was he to return empty-handed? What would she say to him?

CHAPTER XII.

GEORGE'S PATRON SAINT. THE GOVERNOR OF THE HAURAN.

"Miracles are required of all who aspire to this dignity, because they say an hypocrite may imitate a saint in all other particulars."—ADDISON.

"One of the company spoke him fair and would have stopped his mouth with a crust."—L'ESTRANGE.

FROM Es Salt we wandered over the hills to El Bukeia, a depressed plain, supposed once to have been a lake, and which is surrounded on all sides by hills; it contains a considerable number of ruins of large buildings, constructed for the most part without mortar.

As we journeyed on, some Beduins of the tribe of Beni Hassan joined our party, and, seeing our Adwan guides, railed most bitterly against them, and against Ali Diab and the Adwan generally, who, they declared, robbed the Beni Hassan of all they had. Our guides kept a discreet silence, and these unhappy men continued to pour out their upbraidings until they separated from us to take a different path. Another old Beduin, belonging to a different tribe, who knew our story, which seems to have spread far and wide, with many additions, sang a song of praise for our escape, which was as loud as the bitter cry from the others. Fortunately, the Beni Hassan were in front and the other man was behind, or the conflicting sounds would have been even more confusing to us than they actually were.

Then we crossed the river Zerka or Jabbok, which formed the boundary between the respective dominions of those familiar kings of the Old Testament, Og, King of Basan (to the north), and Sihon, King of the Amorites (to the south); and on the second day after leaving Es Salt, we pushed through the dense growth of oleanders in full bloom, which grow on each side of the stream, and encamped in the valley on the north bank. In this place George and I had the following little conversation, a specimen of many which threw light upon his ideas:—

George. Did you know that I write these tents and baggage (which are his property) for St. George? [1]

Myself. What do you mean?

George. My father made vow that if he have son he will write him for St. George—that is, make him for service of St. George. So when my mother *borned* me I was for St. George. And once every year before the day of St. George I clean church of Copts in Jerusalem, and I wash steps outside. I put oil of my own money in lamps. So I write those tents and baggage for St. George, and he help me.

Myself. Do you think that St. George helped us to get away from the Keraki?

---

[1] Mr. Doughty mentions that the Moslems believe that St. George, since his death, has become a Moslem, and lately appeared in Montenegro, chasing with his spear the Christian *hounds*. ("Arabia Deserta.")

George. Yes, I think so.

Myself. Did the priest write it?

George. No, Sir, the Bishop.

Myself. What did he write?

George. He wrote one paper that tents and baggage are for me while I live, but if I die they go for Church.

Myself. What, your mother, wife, and children are to have nothing! If you die they will have no provision?

George. Nothing. But I shall not die before I am sixty-three. When I am sixty-three I die. I have English hymn-book. I buy it from Jew. I pay him sixpence.

Myself. Do you read in the hymn-book?

George. Yes; but I read more in *Graphic* what you send me. Did you read in *Graphic* about young negro what have little lion, and then take five cows and marry girl? That was good.

At sunset, Abou Seyne, as had been his wont, notwithstanding all his misdeeds, made his evening prayer with the little "Holy Man," who still accompanied us, and the season of Ramadan having come, he kept his fast as absolutely as the other.[1] He is the kindest, pleasantest, most amiable man that ever stole a sheep, or slew a foe in border fray.

From the banks of the Zerka we journeyed to Jerash, and explored its ruins again. While here a soldier brought a letter to us, written in Turkish, from the Governor of the Hauran, who happened to be at a place called Tekitty, about an hour's journey from

[1] "What is it to fast? It is a universal Eastern usage. Hindoos, Hebrews, Mahommedans, all fast" ("The Oriental Christ").

Jerash. No one amongst our servants could read Turkish, and we had to get the letters translated to us by a learned Circassian of Jerash. It contained a request that we should go to see the Governor, who was on a tax-collecting expedition.

Our road lay along the side of the hill amongst olive trees and past corn-land. The sides of our path were luxuriant with poppies and cyclamen, radiant in the bright sunlight, and yet fresh after the rains, so that the colour of every flower was heightened. As we approached the mud village of Tekitty we could see horsemen in the distance, and a stir about the place betokening the presence of the Governor. On reaching the village we saw a bell-shaped soldier's tent, and beyond it, under some beautiful trees, a long black Beduin booth, inside of which, seated on gay Persian carpets, were some men with dark handsome faces, smoking the pipe of peace.

We dismounted at a little distance and were received by the secretary and aide-de-camp of the Governor. Every one rose and received us with grave politeness, and places were arranged for us on carpets next to the Governor's vacant seat, which was piled higher than the rest. What was our joy to find that the dark handsome faces belonged to the Beni Sokr sheiks, for here was an opportunity to improve our acquaintance with them, and to pave the way for our intended visit to their country. They had come to see the Governor of the Hauran, after concluding their visit to the Kaimakâm of Es Salt. We were glad of a few minutes' quiet to take in the scene, for the sheiks, although most courteous, were not talkative. Their beautiful mares were tethered in front of the tent, and were enjoying the fresh grass in the dappled light under the trees. The sun poured in upon us from the open front, and one of the soldiers hung a kind of carpet from the roof, so as to shelter us.

Then the Governor of the Hauran arrived. He was most polite and attentive; but as he only spoke Turkish, and George who alone spoke English did not understand the former language, everything that the Governor said had to be translated first by his

BUSRÂH-ESKI-SHÂM.

secretary into Arabic, and then by George into English, and our replies went through the converse process. Again a long statement of our affair with the Keraki had to be taken down. The Governor told us, as the Kaimakâm of Es Salt had done, that soldiers would be sent to Kerâk and a Kaimakâm established there. We were careful to impress upon him, as upon the Kaimakâm of Es Salt, the necessity of avoiding any risk to the English missionaries. After many polite speeches on both sides, and such extra attentions as we could throw in to the Beni Sokr sheiks, whose striking faces had quite won our hearts, we left Tekitty, and turning to the east passed by Jerash and made for Busrâh-Eski-Shâm in the Hauran.

CHAPTER XIII.

THE HAURAN.   THE DRUSES.

> " Some old volcanic upset must
> Have rent the crust and blackened the crust,
> Wrenched and ribbed it beneath the dust,
> Above earth's molten central seethe,
> Heaved and heaped it by huge upthrust
> Of fire beneath."
>
> SWINBURNE.

WE were accompanied by a soldier of Kurd birth, who had been sent with us by the Governor, and by two Circassians from Jerash. We had now rather a mixture of nationalities in our camp. Our road lay over hill and dale, and along grassy valleys well wooded in some parts, and with solitary oaks in others. The country looked as if it had once been the site of a great forest, but the destruction of trees is apparently going on at a great rate, and of course no one thinks of planting any young ones. If the Beduins want to cook something they often set a tree on fire to do it, and it is common to see large quantities of dead trees standing together all destroyed by flames which have spread from one to another. This wooded country was succeeded by a rich tableland perfectly bare of trees, but well cultivated, and here

Abou Seyne and the Circassians were moved to display their skill in horsemanship, greatly to our delight.

We passed a heap of stones which marked the place where two men had recently been killed in some cattle-lifting fray, and after a delightful ride of eight and a half hours reached the village of Rantha or Er Rentheh, very much to the surprise of the whole of the inhabitants, who turned out to stare at us. Abou Seyne tells my wife that her voice is like almonds, raisins, and figs, and that she must have been fed upon sweets ever since she left her mother's breast. He certainly has a pretty way of turning a compliment. She tries to teach him a few English words, but he objects that she wants to teach him Turkish. His idea is that all foreign language is Turkish; just as ignorant English people suppose any language which they do not understand must necessarily be French.

We journeyed on from this place to the eastward, and soon reached the beginning of those loose basaltic stones which are so plentiful in the Hauran, where the decay of other volcanic matter makes such a fruitful soil. For a long way we followed the old Roman road, the pavement of which was however so much deranged, so as to make travelling on it very difficult. We passed through Edrei or Ed Der'ah the capital of Og, king of Bashan, and after two days reached the celebrated ruined city of Busrâh-Eski-Shâm, the Bozrâh of Moab, mentioned by Jeremiah in his prophecy against the Moabites

From Edrei onwards to the eastward, the country is a very strange one. The surface of the ground is covered in every direction with loose basaltic stones, shot forth in past ages from volcanos now extinct, and as nothing is done to clear the road or track in any direction, travelling is slow, difficult, and disagreeable. You are always in sight of one or more ruined towns. If you ascend any eminence you can see a large number on all sides. In some there is a small human population; portions of others are used as habitations by shepherds, cows, sheep, or goats; and some are quite unoccupied either by man or beast.

The ruins are all built of basaltic stone which is of a dark melancholy grey colour, and the country is quite bare of trees. The general aspect is therefore extremely gloomy. It is in this country that are found the strange stone dwellings with great stone doors, moving on stone hinges, and the underground houses and towns which have so often been described in the accounts of the Hauran. At Busrâh the Roman remains in the form of gateways, columns, and other portions of buildings, are extensive, and there is an enormous castle with immensely thick walls and deep vaulted passages, in which I was allowed to enter, upon depositing my revolver at the frowning gateway. In the middle of the castle rise the proscenium and several of the upper rows of the seats of a great Roman theatre. The lower seats are built into the castle, and are thus hidden from view.

At every place the people crowded round our tents and stared at us. At one village on the way we disposed of some empty wine and ginger-ale bottles to advantage, by bartering them with the women and children for eggs; seven eggs for one bottle being the average rate.

At Busrâh we had a great deal of rain and wind, which threatened to blow away the tents. But we ploughed on through the wet ground towards Salkad, after dismissing our Circassians, who having brought us to the country of the Druses were of no further use to us, and who returned to Jerash with their pay.

We had followed the straight, uncompromising Roman road for many hours before we reached Bosrah, and it led away due east to Salkad, up and down the undulations. It seemed as if it had been ruffled by some swell on the surface of the earth, so that the stones which once formed its pavement were all jostled together, set on end, and disarranged as far as possible. It was bordered on each side by a wall of loose stones, and sometimes we tried one side or other of the walls to endeavour to find an easier path. But the road bad as it had become was better than the land on each side of it, and we had always to return to the disorganized pavement. But we kept at it, for Salkad is a purely Druse town, and we had come to the Hauran to see the Druses.

Never before had we ridden over a more difficult country. The stones were tumbled about everywhere —for the most part great round ones, making the task for horses and mules of carrying their burdens safely over them, most painful. It was a journey of six hours, but there was not one yard of the way free from stones, except where the heavy rains had swollen the streams and formed morasses, into which our frightened animals stepped with much caution and anxiety. Sometimes they went in up to their knees, and sometimes deeper, but the uncertainty of every footstep told upon them, and even upon their riders.

It was a beautiful sight to see how the head mule led the way for the baggage animals, sometimes diverging completely from the track, but nearly always with a fine instinct and intelligence, doing the best. Towards the end of the journey the rain came down in torrents, and Salkad, which up to this point had been before our eyes on a great eminence, was blotted out from view. We thought as the rain swept over us how wet our camping ground would be and wondered how we were to dry our clothes. It was now decided that we should ascend the steep mound on which the castle stands, and inspect the ruin whilst the tents were being set. What walls of slippery basalt we had to climb over, and how carefully the good beasts carried us!

At last we came to the foot of the hill whereon the castle sat. There was no path; only a vast pile of loose slippery stones, like a hill of coal thrown up from a coal mine. Up this we had to go. The poor horses strained every nerve and muscle, and it required some courage to remain on their backs, instead of dismounting, which we should have done had not our men found it impossible to get foothold when they tried. At the top we were in the sweeping mists. But, with Abou Seyne and the cook, I scrambled down into the dry moat, and up through a hole in the wall opposite, into the huge building, and with them explored its dark passages as far as practicable.

Far down below us in the wet ground, we saw the mules casting their burdens. In the pouring rain we descended the precipitous side of the hill and passed down through the filthy streets, in which were the dead bodies of camels, oxen, and horses left to putrify. It seemed harder for the horses to wade through this slough than even to step over the slippery rock. What a stony place! stone walls, stone buildings, stone paths; and what terrible gusts of wind and rain—as dispiriting a land as weary travellers could look upon.

We were at once surrounded by a staring crowd of men, women, and children, who gave us no peace. They were intensely inquisitive, and were quite wanting in that grace of bearing and courtesy displayed by the Druses of Mount Carmel. The crowd was, however, soon called away from us by a quarrel in the town. We could see the people in the terraced streets above us running to and fro, and hear their shouting. Two families who had a blood feud were inveighing against one another, and an old man had his head cut open with a sword. The next day the quarrel was renewed, and the assailant of the day before shot dead. His blood must now be avenged, according to the prevalent code of honour, and so the feud goes on from one generation to another.[1]

We were kept here two days owing to the rain, and began to think that it was useless to struggle against such tempestuous weather and such detestable roads. But what absolutely determined us to turn back was that the Druses told George to inform us that if we went on they would kill Abou Seyne. His speech betrayed him as one of the Adwan tribe, and

[1] Shortly after our visit there was some fighting between the Druses and the Turkish troops in this district, in which many Druses were killed.

the depredations of the Adwan are well known even so far from their territory as this. So we hired a Druse sheik of Salkad whose authority would be respected to protect us on the way back to Busrâh, and turned again to the westward.

Abou Seyne, although quite aware that his life had been threatened, held his peace at Salkad. But in the night at Busrâh, he came to George, and waking him, asked if there would be any objection to his killing the Druse sheik and escaping on his mare to his own country. He had nothing against the sheik but that he was a Druse, and that the Druses had threatened to kill him, and he did not seem to recognize that this man had been brought specially to protect him. George told him that although he might escape on his mare, we, his friends, would be left, and should get into trouble if he carried out his plan, and when the matter was put before him in this light he readily gave up the project.

At the next halting-place while we were eating lunch in a barley-field, the horses belonging to Abou Seyne and the soldier sent with us from Edrei, had a great fight, and tearing and rushing at one another in a mad fury nearly trampled us both under foot. Abou Seyne and the soldier espousing the cause of their respective animals, immediately fell to quarrelling themselves, and we had much difficulty to restrain them from an encounter with their weapons. They were white with rage—one with pistol, the other with sword in hand—and their eyes were starting out of their heads.[1] This kind of rest was more fatiguing

[1] "As herdsmen and wolves, soldiers and Beduins may never agree together" (Doughty's "Arabia Deserta").

than a long day's ride, and we were glad to mount again and go on in peace.

Two days' more journey to the westward, through a very pleasant undulating country, which became better and better cultivated as we advanced, brought us across the great Hadj Road by which the pilgrims go from Damascus to Mecca, and to the village of El Husn which we had visited in 1888. Here, on the hill to which we had removed our camp in that year after the night of my wife's illness, we pitched our tents, and enjoyed the splendid view of Mount Hermon and the wide plain of waving green corn and broad ploughed lands of the Western Hauran. Indeed, by the light of the evening sun we even saw, or thought we saw, as far as the castle hill of Salkad, fifty or sixty miles off.

At sunset, the cattle from all the country round and goats innumerable came to drink at the pool by the little town, and to lie under the protection of its houses until dawn, when after drinking their full again, they went forth once more to graze. Every path leading over the plains to the east or up into the hills which, beginning at El Husn, rise into the Jebel Ajilûn to the west was marked by long lines of these animals, preceded by their shepherds, armed with their long flint-lock guns. The scene reminded us of one of those widespread plains depicted by the Dutch master, Philip de Koening in which lines of figures of diminishing size lengthen out the distance. But the sky was not the humid sky of Holland; the brilliant cloudless heaven of Syria hung over all, for the rain was over and gone, and only the beautiful freshness which it left in herb and wild flower and

DRUSE SHEIK OF SALKAD AND HIS SERVANT.

waving crops of corn remained to tell of its having been.

A Greek priest (not the one whom we had seen here in 1888) came up the hill to our tents to ask for money. We had but very little with us, and a considerable journey was still to be made before we could reach Jerusalem again: so we only presented him with half a medjidié. He protested that this was no gift at all, and asked for more; offering to return our little present as beneath his notice. But George told him that we had been robbed and were very short of money, and that we had been thinking of borrowing somewhat for our necessities from him. Upon hearing this threatening intelligence the good man started up from his chair in great haste, crying out that he would pray for us, and taking the silver piece with him (as half a loaf is better than no bread) vanished with the utmost rapidity from the tent, not even staying to say good-bye, or to make us a salutation of any kind.

CHAPTER XIV.

THE JOURNEY BACK TO THE JORDAN VALLEY. THE OLD PRIEST OF AJILÛN.

> "O sir, you are old:
> Nature in you stands on the very verge
> Of his confine.
> . . . .
> He that will think to live till he be old
> Give me some help."—"KING LEAR."

THE dawn broke in perfect splendour, and George, opening the tent door, showed us the wide plain stretched out before us as far as Salkad and Mount Hermon, with its long crown of snow. Then descending the little hill to the westward, and mounting up a long winding valley, we reached in two hours the undulating summits of the hills of Gilead, and entered upon the beautiful woodland country which lies about the Jebel Ajilûn. A long descent brought us by a path coming from the north into the sweet little valley in which we had encamped in 1888, and here under the olive trees, and near to the clear rushing brook we set up our tents once more in Ajilûn.

Hardly had we washed and changed our clothes,

than we were surrounded by patients with ailments of all kinds, and we were called on to distribute medicines and plasters according to our lights. While so engaged we heard a noise without, and a poor old man was borne hurriedly into the tent upon the back of his son, and set down in our folding-chair. It was the old Greek priest of Ajilûn, whom we remembered from 1888; but, alas, how changed! Ague shook him, and old age bent him; but he raised his hands to heaven and cried that Allah had sent us to save his life. I thought with the Doctor in "Macbeth," "This disease is beyond my practice." But my wife, instead of making useless reflections, at once poured out a glass of wine, and made him swallow it. He was so weak that he looked as if he would have died on the spot, but the wine revived him. It was a most pathetic sight. The old man, with long white beard sweeping his naked breast, looked a very painter's model for a picture of "the last stage of all that ends this strange eventful history"; and yet he was so hopeful and cheered by the sight of us, and so confident that we could cure him, that we could not tell him of our ignorance. His family, too, all gathered round, seemed to look upon us as something more than mortal.

How little we knew, and how useless seemed our efforts! But we thought that hope and sympathy might do much, and made a pretence of helping him to a greater extent than it was possible for us to do, "most ignorant of what we most assumed." He departed much comforted; and the next day before leaving, we visited him in the room which formed the house of himself and his family. If he had lived through the worry of this crowded apartment, and the coming to and fro of the noisy restless talkers, there seemed some hope yet. So we turned out all but wife and son, gave what simple directions we thought most helpful, and left with them half our stock of quinine, for the ague wore the poor old man terribly; and a little money, for his poverty was apparent. We have often thought of him since. He was so grateful, the tears rolled down his cheeks so fast, and the whole family (evidently very much attached to him), sang such praises in our honour, that we left, saddened by the feeling of our inability to do real good. What an extensive practice a doctor would find in this part of the country! The fees would not come to much, but he would be able to relieve a great deal of distress. The medical missionaries scattered in various parts of Syria are very successful, but their number is but small.

From Ajilûn, our day's ride was, perhaps, the most delightful of all. Our course followed the stream which rushed down a lovely valley (the Wâdy Ajilûn) to fall into the Zerka before it joined the Jordan. The narrow bottom of this ravine was green with tall waving corn mixed with great masses of red poppies; the trees overhung the path for many a mile; the honey-suckle spread its perfume on the way; the wild flowers adorned the hill-sides; and the sweet young cattle were basking in the sunshine. After descending towards the west for two hours, a turn in the valley opened out to our view the plain of the Jordan, and the wide line of dark green foliage "that muffles its wet banks." As we descended still further the heat became greater, all the wild flowers but the hollyhocks had disappeared, and the grass was dried up.

We passed at last down a very steep and stony path, noticing on the way many of the small dolmens described in Major Conder's accounts of Syria, and which are to be met with in many places east of the Jordan; and then coming down upon the plain in which that river flows, pitched our tents near to a little mosque or sacred tomb of the Holy Man Obêida, who is much revered by the Beduins, and to whom they are said to pay special devotion before they go on a predatory expedition. Close by is a little stream, margined by oleanders and a thick undergrowth of bushes, which falls into the Jordan; and near here is also a well of fresh spring water—a rare and welcome thing in this valley.

We had come down some four thousand feet from the high ground on which we had been, and it was so hot here that we were fain to lie down and gasp, in a square little chamber near to the mosque, from which openings to north, south, east, and west, gave us a view of the country in every direction. Here we rested until the tents were up, and the heat of the day had somewhat abated.

As we sat at dinner in the evening, the little son of the neighbouring sheik came with servants from his father's tent, bearing with them a present of a sheep, and a beautiful little gazelle; in return for which we presented them with a piece of money. The sheik himself came later in the night after we had gone to bed, and there was a great feasting and talkee-talkee; and after he had gone the dogs barked furiously at a roving hyena, so that it was hard to get any sleep. The sheik had heard of our adventures,[1] and the whole matter had to be recounted all over again, and commented upon from every point of view. Like all the others he abused the Mejelli, for whom none seem to have a good word. They are feared as strong and grasping, and despised as upstarts; men not of the true old aristocratic Beduin blood, but mere peasants from Hebron.

Near this place are several "tells," or small solitary hills rising in the plain, and there are similar hills in the plain south of the Dead Sea. They look as if they might contain ruins, but I could not see any sign of buildings on the two which I ascended.

---

[1] Of these very exaggerated reports were circulated. At Jerusalem the story went that George and I had been chained together in a cave, and that my wife had married Saleh the Sheik of Kerâk! And while we were still in Palestine we received a letter from home, telling us that some English newspaper had stated our ransom at thirty thousand pounds!

Jerusalem from the North End of the Mount of Olives.

CHAPTER XV.

WE FORD THE JORDAN.   A NIGHT MARCH.

"Until the day breaks and the shadows flee away."
                                    SONG OF SOLOMON.

"See how the morning opes his golden gate."
                                    "HENRY VI."

THE next morning we rose at four, and getting the camp in motion by daybreak, saw, as we began our march, the first light of the rising sun upon the tops of the Judæan and Samaritan hills which it turned to a deep red colour. Two jackals stole away as we pushed through the barley field to the west of us, and made our way in the direction of the fords of the Jordan which lie between Es Salt on the east, and Nablous (Shechem) on the west. As we descended the range of low hills which border the river during the whole of its passage from the Sea of Galilee to the Dead Sea, we passed the encampment of the sheik of the ford, whose business it was to conduct us safely across. He rode up accompanied by four of his men. We pushed through the wide margin of trees and thick undergrowth which lines the river, and soon came upon the brink. The width of the stream depends somewhat upon the season. It was then about forty yards across, and the yellow water came down with a great swirl round a wide curve which the river makes at this point.

All dismounted and made preparations for the fording. The packs on the mules' backs were carefully examined, and my wife was placed upon the top of the strongest who had been relieved of his other burdens. George sat on the same animal in front of her to see to her safety, and supported by two Beduins who walked in the stream on each side of her she got across safely, and without being wet. She was not comfortable, however, for the rushing and swirling of the water made her head go round (and indeed it had a similar effect upon mine); and the shouting of the men and the plunging of some of the animals caused the passage to be rather nervous work for her. By taking off my boots and stockings and turning up my knickerbockers above my knees, I was enabled to get over without getting my clothes wet, except for a little splashing. It was an extremely interesting and pretty sight to see the animals crossing, the Beduins in the water, and our men gathered on either bank.

Very sadly we started from the western bank; for the charmed land east of the ancient river was now left behind us. We encamped some hours further on in a south-westwardly direction from the ford, near to a little stream called the Fârah, which is one of the western tributaries of the Jordan, and where the oleanders were more splendid than ever. It was the twenty-third of April, and we drank to the memory of the immortal Shakespeare. What had he to do with this ancient Hebrew land? Nothing but that great spirits are "cabin'd, cribb'd, confin'd, bound in" to no land, and seem at home in every country.

It was so hot in this valley, and the flies and mosquitoes were so troublesome, that we determined to make a very early start the next morning, so as to get to Jericho if possible, before the noonday heat came on. And mistaking the time of rising, we found when we were dressed, that we had got up at half-an-hour after midnight. However it was useless to go to bed again, for the camp was roused, so after hesitating, and watching a dance with much clapping of hands, which our men performed by the camp fire to amuse us, we had our breakfast, and all the baggage being packed on the mules' backs, we started off in the dark, after a regretful parting from our friend, Abou Seyne, who left us here, recrossed the Jordan and made for his own country. The little "Holy Man" led the way on his horse, and the muleteers held lanterns in front of our horses, so that we might see our way, for it was extremely dark and the path was very irregular and uneven; meandering amongst land partially cultivated, but for the most part covered with thorns and scrub.

It was a strange experience journeying thus at night; very impressive, but not quite safe. After we had proceeded for a little time we heard a great barking of dogs, and found ourselves amongst a herd of cows close to a Beduin encampment. But we were allowed to pass without interference, and held on our course watching for the coming of the day. Very faint were the first indications of dawn, and very gradually did the morn "walk o'er the dew of yon high eastern hill." But as its pale light waxed we began little by little to see our friends in front, and the plain before us: anon the western mountains stood out in cold distinctness; and then suddenly they were lit up with the splendour of the coming day.

> "All the distance is white
> With the soundless feet of the sun;
> Night with the woes that it wove,
> Night is over and done."[1]

By Elisha's fountain we found a man of the Keraki, but who had had nothing to do with our affair. George began to abuse him. "Why!" I asked. "Well, if he answer I beat him." "But why?" "Well (apologetically) beat him a *little*." George is very bitter against the Keraki. He does not forget the pistols being held at his head.

On the twenty-fifth of April we made the long ascent from Jericho to the Mount of Olives, and, ending our eventful journey, pitched our camp at the northern end of the ridge, upon the highest point of the hills that stands about Jerusalem, a place where neither pilgrim nor tourist comes. Here stood a little piece of land and a cave therein, which we had bought and had "made sure unto us for a possession," that we might have a little spot to call our own in the land that we love. And here we remained for three weeks, riding about the country in the neighbourhood of Jerusalem.

When the time came for us to part from our faithful servants, many kind words were spoken by them;

[1] Swinburne.

of whom one said, "Why should you leave us? why not always live in this our country? May the ships break in pieces and the sea dry up, that you leave us not."

Why should we leave them? Why not always live in their country? Why not dwell upon this quiet, solitary spot; far enough from Jerusalem to be free from the bitterness of its religious animosities, and yet near enough to be able to drink in the spirit of its great past? Why not rest here, to watch, morning after morning, the dawn break in unclouded beauty over the mountains of Moab and the Dead Sea, and the first rays of the rising sun strike across the deep valley of the Kedron, light up the domes and minarets of the Holy City, and creep slowly down the mighty walls of the Haram?

ADIEU TO SYRIA.

PART IV.

The Stories of Abou Suleyman.

THE SUMMER PULPIT. DOME OF THE ROCK, JERUSALEM.

PART IV.

The Stories of Abou Suleyman.

THE following stories are selected from a large number which I wrote down as I heard them in the very words, so far as I could remember them, of the narrator. Some of the best I am unfortunately unable for various reasons to insert here.

"I will set down what falls from *him* to satisfy my remembrance the more strongly."—"MACBETH."

AN ILL-ASSORTED MARRIAGE.

IN Jerusalem there was old woman. She have eight sons, all grown up, and they go to Jaffa to work. They are carpenters, and they make boxes for oranges. They are strong men, and they take for their work each one five shillings for day. That is good. And their father was dead. Their mother was old, white hair, ugly. And there came man of thirty years, and want to marry her, and she tell him "All right." So her brother like not that she marry, and he write to her sons at Jaffa to tell them that she will marry. Then her sons come quick to Jerusalem, and when they come their mother and that man have just come from church; they have marry. And they ask their mother what she do, and she tell them she is marry. Then some of them say, "All right. We are glad; now we have one uncle, another father or so." But one tell her, "Why you do this thing. Your hair is white, and you are old. Why you marry this man? It is shame for you."

And she tell him, "Well, it is done. They cannot make this not marriage." They are Copts, and our church is hard for them. So this son come to bridal chamber, and he take knife and put bridegroom on his knee, and begin cut his throat. And my sister see it and she come to our house, and she cannot come in, but she cry, and then I run and save that man. He was cut little, not much. And we tell the Government it was scratch. We not say *knife*, because we are all Copts, and it is a shame for the Mahommedans to punish us. Our Bishop will punish that man what cut the other a little. Then they take their mother away to Jaffa, and on the way she die because her son beat her. Well, it is a shame for her. She have white hair, and shall she marry young man?

THE DAUGHTER OF THE SHEIK.

I will tell you story of Beduins. It is true but little long. There have been two tribes of Arabs, one stronger than other, and weak tribe pay tax to other. But Sheik of weak tribe very kind. When any one come to camp he kill sheep for him, till all his sheep finish. Then he take from his tribe, and when all their sheep are finish they tell one another, "If we stay with this fellow we all become poor. Better we go." So one family take their tent to another place, and then another, and so; till only remain that Sheik and his family.

And then that strong tribe come for their tax, and Sheik tell them, "I have no money, but perhaps in one month." And when they come after one month he tell them "In two months;" and afterwards "In three months." And then that strong tribe tell to him, "Make yourself ready, and in ten days we come to fight with you because you no pay tax." So that Sheik tell them, "All right." But he tell to his family, "Better we go away, or they will kill us all. Get camels ready."

So they bring out carpets, and put them on camels; and it was night. And they put that daughter of Sheik on camel; and camel rose up and began to walk fast. And he walk all night, but he do not know where he go. So in morning that girl see camp, and she do not know what camp it is, and she put her stick on neck of camel, and he kneel down.[1] But she is tired and sleep on back of camel. And it was the camp of their enemy, and Sheik of that tribe see her, and he tell to his wife, "Here is girl asleep on back of camel. Go see her." So that good lady come and make covering for girl and sit down, and wait till she wake. Then that girl awake and tell her, "Where am I? What is this tribe?" And wife of that Sheik tell her,

---

[1] The Beduins direct their camels and horses by touching them on the neck with a small stick.

"Never mind, you are my daughter." So she go to that camp, and she stay forty days.

And after that Sheik tell his wife, "Ask of her what she want. If she want to go back to her tribe I take her. If she will stay with us we keep her. If she want marry I find for her husband." So that wife tell to girl; and girl tell her, "After three days I make answer." Then she think, "If I go back with these men I fear from them. If I stay here what shall I do; it is not my tribe. If I marry perhaps this Sheik find for me shepherd or plougher, and I am daughter of Sheik: Better I marry." So she tell to that wife, and wife tell to that Sheik.

So Sheik make one hole in curtain of tent for girl to look, and he make all the men of tribe to walk past so she may see them. And those young men comb their hair, and put on clean dress, and make their horses to dance; for they say, "This is very nice girl; we like marry her." Then Sheik tell to girl, "You like this man?" She tell him "No." "That other?" "No." "And that other?" "No." Then when all have passed Sheik tell her, "These are all the young men what we have. Who will you marry?" She tell him, "I marry *you*." He tell her, "All right."

But she very clever. So she tell him, "You must tell me first what you give me, how many camels, how many cows. And when we make price, you put upon camels and cows the mark of the sign of my father." Because she think, "If the Sheik put the mark of *his* tribe then if he is tired of me and put me away,[1] I shall have no cattle, and shall be very poor." So he put the

---

[1] A Mussulman can divorce his wife at will.

mark of the sign of her father upon the camels and the cows; and he marry her, and he have by her one boy, and the name of the boy is called Hassan.[1]

THE CIRCASSIANS.

In Sheik Ali Diab's tent at Heshbon (Adwân tribe of Beduins) we noticed some Circassians, and I asked Abou Suleyman how they came to this part of the world. He told me the following story :—

They come from Russia. The Russians drive them away and they came to Heshbon. These people of Heshbon very fierce, and Circassians very proud. And one day one Circassian kiss wife of one of people of Heshbon. And that husband said, "Never mind; he is a stranger. If he will kill my wife it does not matter." But afterwards one Circassian went by wife of another—no it was not his wife, it was his daughter. Then brother of girl get six men to go with him, and they shoot at those Circassians and kill forty-two of them. Then those Circassians go away to Jerusalem, and there they steal from the people. Their wives go into houses, and take things, and hand them one to other what run away. So they are driven out of Jerusalem. Then Sheik Ali was very kind to them. He gave them land in Ammân (Rabbath Ammon) to make crops, and he say, "If you have money pay price of land, if not never mind."

One day Sheik Ali go on his horse to see that land

---

[1] The adventures of Hassan followed, but feeling that my memory could not preserve with anything like verbal accuracy more than the above I turned a deaf ear to the rest, which I hope to be able to hear again and record some day.

of those Circassians, to know if any one steal from them, or so. You know great man like that never walk, so he go on his horse. He pay £260 for that horse, but man what sold it to him gave back two ponies. And one of those ponies went with him. And this pony eat mouthful of corn of those Circassians, and one of them threw stones at that pony and break bone near eye, and eye came out. And Sheik Ali did not see this, but his slave that was with him see it, and he fire his gun at that Circassian and wound him. Then that Circassian killed that slave, and wanted to kill Sheik Ali, but he ran away on his horse. Then this Adwan tribe came and kill thirty-five or forty-five of those Circassians, and drove them all away. But afterwards the Circassians come and kiss hands and feet of Sheik Ali, and he take them under his protection. If they quarrel now they go to Sheik Ali like judge, instead of go to Government, because Government wants money.

THE REFUGEES.

You see that dark man what sit in corner on carpet in tent of Sheik Ali and smoke pipe. Well his brother killed man. He and his family belonged to tribe of Beni Sokr, and he killed man of that tribe. His name is called Faiz, and family of dead man wanted to kill him and he sent to Sheik Ali for protection; and Sheik Ali sent four hundred horsemen, and took him away and his wives and children and brothers and all that he have, and now they all live with Sheik Ali. They have become men of Adwan—no more Beni Sokr. Some men of Beni

Sokr followed them little way but they were afraid. They fear much from this tribe of Adwan, what are small, but very strong. This happened month ago.

THE BANDIT.

In 1888, we were standing in the ruins of the Castle at Ammân (Rabbath Ammon), and Abou Suleyman told us the following story :—

There was man, his name is called Daile Ali, who was robber and murderer. I knew him—he has eaten in my tent with me. He was good man sometimes, and sometimes bad man. There were two other men with him but the *name* was of him. And they killed many people near Damascus and Jerusalem. They did not go into town, but outside. And Government want to catch them, and they come here to Ammân, and they live in this little fortress (he pointed to a square tower with very thick walls, windows for shooting through, and a doorway). This was two years ago, and twenty soldiers come; and they kill two or three of those soldiers, and Government was afraid that Circassians would help robbers, because Circassians afraid of them. And they tell those Circassians, "If you help them, we take your women and give them to our soldiers." And those Circassians tell them, "All right, we not interfere."

But those soldiers were afraid, and this Government ask Ali Diab (the Adwan chief) to help. So Ali Diab send some Beduins, and amongst them was this man, what is here, and that other Beduin who has left us what you call "Ishmaelite." And Daile Ali put stones in door, and fire at soldiers and Beduins, and kill two more soldiers and one Beduin. And one robber ran away, and after some time other man killed. He was lying by door. You see his blood on lintel.

And Daile Ali only remain. And they fire many shots—you see marks of bullets on walls—and one shot came back from wall behind him and hit him. And this Beduin come in, and think at first that Daile Ali was dead. But he look and see him putting a cartridge, and so he fire at Daile Ali and kill him. And they take both men and cut off their heads just there where you see me roll down stone in valley, and they take those heads to Damascus and this Government give Ali Diab a good present. But Daile Ali was sometimes good man. He should be general in army—then he be all right.

SHEIK GOBLAN.

Turkish Government offer five hundred Turkish pounds to any one who bring the head of Sheik Goblan. He was old man, about eighty. His face was cut about with fighting. Then Governor of Jerusalem ask him to come to dinner to make peace. He come and with him four hundred horsemen. Governor say, "Who is this?" They say, "Sheik Goblan." So Sheik Goblan stopped his mare, and tied his bridle to a stone. And in his sleeve he had a dagger, and in tieing mare to stone that dagger cut his arm where he have old wound, and it began to swollow (swell) up. And Sheik Goblan had slave, tall man, fit for war, who had eight children, and this man like Sheik Goblan very much, and this slave understand Turkish. And the Governor said (in

Turkish), "You think I let Sheik Goblan go. No I cut off his head at once." And that slave said (in Arabic) to his lord, "Those Turkish dogs will kill us, better we go." And Sheik Goblan say, "Get my mare ready."

So that slave get her ready, and say, "She is ready." And Sheik Goblan take his pistol, and tell to the Governor, "Who say that?" And the Governor sware by God no one said it. And Sheik Goblan held his pistol like that, and go to door backwards, and jump on his mare, and tell to that Governor, "You are twenty men; we are four hundred. Will you fight? We will kill you all." And that Governor tell him, "Please not—go away." So he went away, and his men with him. And his arm swollow more and more, and in six days he die. Then his tribe tell another tribe, "You kill our Sheik; we make war on you;"[1] and they kill six men and twenty horses of other tribe, and they are not satisfied. They say they must kill twenty men more, then they be satisfied.

I remember this Sheik Goblan kill man once for dress of cotton. He ask that man for it, and the man tell him, "No." Then he say, "I was joking, I do not want it." And that man ride on with his donkey, and Sheik Goblan come behind him with his spear and strike him back of head and end of spear come out by his teeth. I tell to him, "Why you done this thing?" He tell me, "He is a peasant. He shall not wear such nice clothes."[2]

[1] Because the other tribe had given him the old wound.
[2] Sheik Goblan was celebrated amongst all the Beduins of the land of Moab, and was accustomed to accompany those few

A GOSPEL PRECEPT.

There was man and wife at Jerusalem; not poor, not rich; and they have son ten or twelve years, and he go to Bishop Gobat's school, and he was away from his mother one year. Schoolmaster tell his father, "Leave him here, do not take him away." And there come time of holiday, August—September, and father buy for son very nice suit of clothes—they were of cloth—that he should go home to his mother. And that son walk out in them first time, and he see poor boy what have no clothes on his legs. So he take off his trousers and give them to this poor boy, and poor boy tell him, "Thank you," and run away.

Then this boy what had the new clothes go home and his father tell him, "Where are your trousers?" And that boy is very happy and he tell his father, "The Bible say if a man have no cloak you give him yours." And that father begin to beat his son. And son tell him, "But look, father, here is place," and he show him place in Bible. But that father beat him again. And that boy tell his father, "God will beat you for beat me." And that father beat him still, and tell him, "Where are those trousers I bought for you?"

SNAKES.

I. THE MAN OF NABLOUS.

There was old man of Nablous and he have two daughters. And this government take husbands of

European travellers who visited the Adwan tribe. Many stories are told of his prowess in war and of his adventures. I do not give the above as correct in fact, so far as regards the cause of his death (which I believe it is not), but as interesting in itself.

his daughters for soldiers, and that poor fellow have to keep his daughters and their children. And he was poor man. So those daughters speak together, and they say, "Come let us get our gold and silver things (what you call jewels), and bring them to our father, and he can make some work, so that we all live till our husbands return from Constantinople, or such a place." And they bring these things to their father, and he sell them, and he go to Moab and buy cattle and sow corn, and afterwards he reap, and gain much. For one medjidié he make one hundred, and his cattle increase.

And after one year he go away from Moab with much corn and cattle. And he have with him some Beduins of Beni Sokr, and the camels of those Beni Sokr carry his corn. And when they were come to Jericho, those Beduins of Jericho said, "Come, we make a feast for our guest." So they kill three sheep and one kid. And the man of Nablous was old, with long beard, and he was weak. And he went by that old house what is near Roman building at Jericho, and sat down to rest upon stone. And under that stone was snake—very bad kind—and he bite that old man in leg. Then he fall back against wall—die—finish.

And those Beduins wait for their guest. And they say, "Our guest will come in few minutes—or in half hour." And afterwards they say, "He will come in hour," or, "He will come in two hours," or, "He will come in three hours." So when he do not come and they wait long, they go to look for him. And they find him lying against that wall, and under him is snake;

and that man is swollow (swollen) big like large barrel. So they kill that snake and they say, "What shall we do with this old man? Shall we bury him here?" And one of those Beni Sokr—he was old man and wise—tell them, "No, if we bury him in this place they will say that we murder him. Better we put him on mule and take him to his own house." So they take him to Jerusalem.

And when the Beduins see those girls his daughters, and that they weep and are very sad, they say, "We do not take any wages for our camels. Only give us some bread that we may eat as we go back to our country." And those daughters have no bread. But their neighbours give one little and another little, and those Beduins go to their own country. Then those girls sell that corn and cattle what their father brought to Jericho, and now they have much bread.

II. BY THE JORDAN.

You remember those slippery hills on that side of Jordan next to Jericho. Well there have been one fellow what come from Es Salt. He have with him his mother, his wife, and three children; eldest child three years, second two, and youngest one year,—like that—also his brother. That fellow was young, twenty-two or so, his wife twenty, and his brother much older, thirty-five or forty. It was in August. When they come to those slippery hills, his mother and wife very tired. His wife carry little baby in arm. Then he tell them, "Take your rest here." And they all lie down, mother, wife, children, and brother; and all sleep.

That fellow have good gun; he buy it at French store in Beyrout—very good French gun. When he see them all sleeping he tell to himself, "Better I take my gun, shoot pigeon, partridge, or so, then make little fire, and cook meat for them, so when they wake they eat something." So he go away and shoot four—five pigeon. When he come back he see two snakes lying between those children and that wife; one thick like my arm, and very long; another flying snake, thin and small, what you call viper. He jump, and if he bite you, doctors no use—all finish.

That big snake lift up his head half yard, and move it backwards and forwards. That fellow stand so, and look. What shall he do? He have no sword. If he shoot, he kill his wife or children. Then these two snakes begin quarrel. Thin one wind himself round thick one, and they begin to move away. Then his mother wake and see those snakes and that fellow. And he make like this to her to say nothing, and she watch quite quiet. And those snakes move little more away.

Then that fool of brother awake and begin to cry, "Here are snakes," and this fellow tell him, "Be quiet till those snakes move away; then I shoot them." But that brother cry more and run away. But now he can shoot without hit wife and children; and he hit big snake; but he is not killed, and that snake move straight at gun. He shoot again and kill him. Then that thin viper make jump to man, and make himself into little ball—like you see one in Lebanon. Then that fellow try to tread on it with his boot, but he do not hit it, and then he kneel on it hard with his knees and kill it, but little bone of viper come in his leg. He go to Jerusalem and they cut his leg open like dead sheep, and inside they find little bone.

III. THE PORTER OF JAFFA.

There was man in Jaffa—he was porter. He have six children, four girls, and two boys. Those boys were naughty; they were sons of his brother what die, so he take them. One day he eat nothing all day, and in evening he buy little cheese and bread for himself and children, and put it in his girdle, and he have bare feet, and he put his foot on small snake, black and white—very bad kind. He do not see the snake, and the snake bite his heel, and in minute he die.

IV. ABOU SULEYMAN.

"Abou Suleyman, were you ever bitten by a snake?"

"Yes, sir, once on hand.

"I was by Jordan. It was that time when I wait for my money for pay for wood which I brought for bridge over Jordan. I have three pieces of wood for bedstead, and slept on them, and I made fire close to me. It is always cold early in morning by Jordan. I awoke suddenly and felt my hand cooled. I jump up. I was close by Jordan. If I jump little further I fall in and never get out. I swim just like piece of lead. I jump up and see snake. I make shake with my hand so hard, and snake fall in fire. I cry out with very large voice. Then I ride off to Jerusalem as quick as I can. I had large donkey—very fine donkey—belong to Governor of Jerusalem. I get there in six hours. I could not move my hand."

"Did you go to a doctor?" "No, sir, they all stupid. I go to old Beduin woman. She put some bran in hot water—very hot. I put my arm in. I could not feel nothing. She rub my arm, so. Then I get better. But my head was swollowed (swollen) for two times right size when I get to Jerusalem. That governor give me one dollar each day for three days, because it was his fault I wait by Jordan."

V. THE SNAKE AND THE BABY.

My people in Jerusalem live in house—in upper part. Underneath is very old Roman. And one day there was baby asleep on floor, and mother of baby go out of room, and when she come back she see large snake coiled up and sitting on that child, and that snake's head was by that child's face. And that baby sleep quiet all the time. Then that mother she become dumb. She could not do nothing. She could not move. She try cry out, but she say nothing. And my wife came. And I was not in house. I was sitting in tobacco shop opposite with some others. That tobacconist want from me three hundred piastres for tobacco what I have had, and I give him two napoleons, and I say, "I pay the rest by and by." He tell me, "All right." And there was piece oak wood, and we try to lift it up by one arm-stretch, so. If one lift it up high, they give him good lunch, what he like. And all try, and could not. I lift it little way, then I try again, lift it half yard.

Then I see my wife. She look very frighten. I say, "What matter?" She tell me, "One snake is by that baby." Then I take my gun and go and see snake. But I can do nothing. If I shoot snake, I kill baby. All we men can do nothing. And that baby sleep quiet all the time. Then my wife take large spoon of wood and knock snake on head, and run away. And snake come off baby, and run round the room—so—make hissing. And that baby sleep quiet all the time. Then I shoot snake. He did not die first shot—not till second. Next day they find another, and day after three more. Week after they find very large one. One man kill it with sword. That snake ran at him. Those snakes come from hole. One filled it up.

CROSSING THE JORDAN.

There was company of Germans. They wish to cross Jordan. They were one hour half from Roman bridge. Then one of them tell rest, "We shall cross. I do a boat." So they cut three or four trees and put them together. Then he tell them, "See my ship." So he put rope to tree on bank and go across on his ship. Then he come back. Then he go again. But he fall down and go in water. They see his head long way off, but no body. Then he disappear. That rope make fast to his foot. If they pull that rope, they pull him up; but instead, they pull that ship. After four hours they find him, and bury him in rubbish at Jericho. The Moslems like not Christians buried in their place.

THE —— CONSUL.

One Sunday I have been walking in Jerusalem with my daughter, that big one (about seven years old). ——

Consul came on horseback with three ladies. They all gallop in street. I stand on one side and put my child on my shoulder, because I fear those horses run against her. So he struck me with his whip three times, and third time he hit my daughter. So then I take him off his horse. Then I am afraid, and I go at once to Governor of Jerusalem and tell him all. He say, "What your name?" I tell him, "Abou Suleyman." That Consul was there, and he look at me very fierce, and I look at him the same.

That Governor say, "Because he is Consul!"[1]

I say, "I do not care for any consul. Shall he kill the people because he is consul? I am under protection of Turkish Government."

That word make this Governor proud, so he tell me, "Never mind," and I go away.

Then that Consul send for me to go to him. I am afraid to go alone, because he have his Janissaries, so I ask two of my nephews to go with me. I choose them, and they come with me, and bring big sticks, and pretend to be lame. And I say to Janissary to tell to Consul I am come. That Consul come out and tell me, "Come in," but he do not ask my nephews. And they stand and look at us through window, and he say, "Who are these?" I tell him my nephews. Then he ask them come in; and he give us all lunch, and say, "Never mind," and he open beer and champagne, and we have chicken and coffee—very good lunch. He very nice man.

[1] Meaning a Consul is a privileged person. What can I do against him?

THE THIEVES AND THE DONKEY.

At Jenîn people all thieves. Uncle of Michael is muleteer, and he was with other men in Khan, and they had animals with them. All were sleeping, and those thieves could not get in at door, so they went to top, and got down and began to pull donkey up. And Michael's uncle woke up and saw that donkey going up, and he cried, "See my donkey going to heaven! Wake up—wake up!" And those thieves hear him cry, and they laugh so much that they could not pull up donkey, and they let him fall. Whenever Michael's uncle tell this story every one laugh.

THE SLAVE AND HIS LORD AT TIBERIAS.

There was Copt merchant. He was merchant of wool, butter, and so. He buy these things and take them to Damascus, where he sell them, and buy silks, and then bring them to Jerusalem; and then he buy boots and clothes and sell them in villages, and buy wool and butter and so. And he have slave, old man about sixty, what have been slave of his father, and have brought him up from his youth and married him. So he tell that slave, "You are no more slave; you have your liberty because you bring me up." And that slave tell him, "What can I do? Will you send me away?" And that merchant tell him, "Then you stay in our house, and do as you like, and keep all our money, and buy for us what you like." And that slave tell him, "All right." And they had made long journey—sixteen hours—and were very tired, and came near to Tiberias, and that slave tell his lord, "I go to this town to buy food." And it was evening, and he go, and all night his lord wait for him, but he do not return.

And very early in morning that lord go to town, and it was still dark, and as he walk in street he stumble and fall, and then he find that slave. His head was broken, and he have three cuts with knife in his breast. And when he can speak little, his lord ask him, "Who did this?" He say, "I do not know his name, but I know that man." And while that lord and his slave are in that street that slave see this man and say, "That is the man," and take him by his throat and throw him down, and that lord put his boot on this man's neck and draw his sword, and say, "If any one help him, I kill him," and he keep him till people of Government come.

Then they say to that man, "Is it true?" He tell them, "Yes." They say, "Where is the money?" He tell them, "In my belt;" and they find it all there. Then they tell him, "Who helped you?" And he tell them of three men what helped him, and all are taken to jail. Then Governor of Tiberias tell this merchant he want ten Turkish pounds from him, and merchant say, "Why I pay you money? Is it because people of your town kill my slave?" But he was obliged to pay him. And that merchant went to Damascus, and told all to Governor there. Tiberias is under Damascus, and because that merchant was rich Government helped him, and sent for Governor of Tiberias to Damascus, and made him pay back this ten pounds. And those men were also brought to Damascus, and they remained in jail three years. But that poor slave did not live. They take him to Jerusalem, and in four days after he die. The side of his head was broken.

GHOSTS.

I. THE BLACK DOG.

Other day Sitt (lady) asked me for ghosts. Yes, I have seen two.

When I was little boy I ride donkey, and I came to cemetery. It was noon—sun very hot—one cannot breathe. It is August. And I see black dog. He look at me, and his eyes very large, and he have brass on his neck. I tell him, "Go away." But he still look at me. And he begin to grow bigger and bigger till he is almost big as donkey. Then I cry against him with very large voice, and I come down from donkey, and I stand by him. But that black dog come to me, and I run fast down slope to English school, and that master take me and make so with my nose, and give me camphor, and put that bottle in my nose and eyes till my head is all of fire; and that night I have fever. But many people of that village by tombs of prophets see that dog, and they tell me that he come sometimes, and that no one can speak with him. And after this some boys of that village see him, and they cannot speak, but wrote; for they find not their tongues for thirty-six hours.

II. THE STRANGE KNOCK.

Other ghost was different. I was in schoolhouse and door was shut. It was strong door. Piece of iron go behind it up and down, and piece of wood across, and it have other pieces to fasten. When it is shut one cannot move it. And one make great knock at the door. I run to open, but there is no one there. Then again great knock, and again I open, but there is no one. And that master tell me, "Why you open?" I tell him that one knocks, but that I see not any man. Then he look through window, and again there is great knock. And he see man—black man; how tall he is I cannot tell. And master call to him, but that black man say nothing. Then this master fire gun at him, but it do not hurt that black man. No one can tell where he is. And no one see that black man any more.

III. ROYAL GHOSTS.

Once our master go to cemetery alone, and he see there one like king sitting on throne with long stick in hand. He think it is spirit of King Solomon or King David. And others have seen the same.

THE QUARRELSOME MAN.

Once there was very naughty man. He always quarrel. Then my uncle tell him, "You shall not do such things. You shall not quarrel. You shall not beat any one. You shall not everything." The man tell him, "All right." Then he have been going in street and one take his cap and throw it. This was joke, but this kind man like not joke. Then that man take one stone and throw it at other man and hit him on head, on temple. So they put him in jail for three months and my uncle get him out. Then my uncle tell him, "Why you do such things?" He say, "You tell me not to quarrel, not to beat any one, but you never tell me if man take off my cap and throw it, not to throw stone at him." Now he is very quiet man.

"Perhaps, Abou Suleyman, you will settle down into a quiet man."

"I am very quiet, no more naughty, all finish now."

CHOLERA.

I remember cholera when I was very little boy. I was very little, it is like one dream. There was man named Nasr. The Beduins owed him money and gave him two camels to pay. He came with those camels to Jerusalem, and after he have his dinner he lie down, and never speak any more. Then they said, "Nasr is dead; Nasr is dead." And they went to the funeral and I ran out after them. I had no cap, no shoes. And one of those men took me on his shoulders and brought me home to my mother. She was looking for me everywhere. There died in Jerusalem every day forty—fifty people—every day.

ABOU SULEYMAN'S GRANDMOTHER.

My grandmother was very old. She lived till one hundred and twenty-five.[1] She became deaf. When I was little boy I was very naughty. I pull her ears so she may hear. It was before I go to school, but I remember it. She died after I was marry. I was

[1] It is very common in Syria, especially amongst the Beduins, to find patriarchal years attributed to old people. But, as the exact age of young ones is often unknown, there is no reason to put faith in such statements.

marry when I was thirteen. She was always in bed. She have no teeth. When she eat she make like this. One day she have cup of coffee. Then she say, "Good-bye,"—all finish. No one weep. We put her in coffin — large box. Next morning take her to church, bury her.

THE LAST WORDS OF A BEDOUIN SHEIK.

There was old Bedouin Sheik. He was dying. He was groaning for death: his soul just going out of him. He tell his friends this. "Never light fire at night. Never sit under crooked building.[1] If you go before one governor put old man first what can speak well." Then he die. Finish.

[1] That is, lest it should fall. The Beduins, living in tents distrust buildings.

Religious Animosities in Jerusalem.

I. JEWS AND COPTS.

ONCE I pass Jews' quarter, and one man call out with large voice, "Abou Suleyman! Abou Suleyman!" I tell him, "What you want?" He say, "Not you." Then I go on, and again he say, "Abou Suleyman! Abou Suleyman!" And one Mahommedan pass, and he tell me, "He mock at you Christians!" Then I go back to that Jew, and tell him, "What you want? Why you mock?" And he he tell me, "If I mock, can you do anything? All Christians are dogs," and he push me.

When he do that, I put him on ground, and other Jews come up, and among them one old man with big stick, thin at one end, but thick at other. I take that stick, and then I see one Greek, and' he come to help me. But soldiers come and take me to Governor. He tell me, "What is this?" I tell him as it was. Then he put that Jew in prison fifteen days. When he come out, he come over to our house to kiss my hand and make peace, and he take from me ten francs for three teeth what I knocked from his mouth, two above and one below.

"Abou Suleyman, you are too quarrelsome!"
"No more, sir! All finish now!"

II. JEWS AND COPTS.

Once we have no rain two years in Jerusalem, and wheat grew very scarce. My mother tell me, "We have money, but there is no wheat." So I get for her of her money, and she go to buy of Jew fellow, and he sell to her not wheat, some other kind—very bad—when we make bread it fall to pieces. Then she cry, and tell me, "That Jew man cheat me." So I go to Jew man, and tell him, "What for you sell my mother this bad corn?" and he tell me, "Go away," and he throw at me little weight of brass in his shop, and it hit my head, and there come little blood.

Then I take that fellow by his girdle and lift him from his shop, and knock him on ground, and he lie there. Then there come other Jews to help him—many—two hundred—three hundred—but they cannot touch me. Those Jews have no heart; they fear. Then one Copt pass, and he see me, and he run to call our Copts, my uncles, cousins, and all. It was in Jews' quarter; there was one corner, and we put those Jews in corner and beat them. It was like slaughter. Then soldiers come, and Governor tell, "What is this?" I tell him all. Then he tell me, "You keep that bad corn, and you also take from that Jew good wheat." And we did so. I was in prison twenty-four hours.

III. MAHOMMEDANS AND COPTS.

There was Copt girl at Jerusalem. She was *girl—*

not married—about sixteen. She love one Mahommedan, and he love her. She run away from her father and mother, and go by him for six days, and afterwards she tell him, "Let us go to mosque and be marry." He tell her, "All right, but I will not go at Jerusalem, only at Hebron." It was Sunday, and some one tell our Copt priest that they go to Hebron to be marry that morning. Copts go to church very early—five o'clock. And about four hundred men were at church that morning, and our priest tell his people that this Mahommedan soldier and that Copt girl would go that morning to Hebron to be marry.

And all Copts went out of church, and took their swords and guns, and went on road to Hebron, not altogether, some here, some there, and some further off. About seven o'clock there came that bridegroom and that girl, and father and mother of that bridegroom, and his other relations; they were twenty-four the whole lot. After they pass some of Copts, those that were behind ran forward, and those that were before ran back, and all close round those Mahommedans. Do you know what happened that morning? No one was killed, but some wounded. That bridegroom had top of his shoulder cut off with sword, and his mother have hole in her head. The Copts take away that girl, and now she live with her father and mother, and is the best girl in the world.

IV. THE COPTS—A HOUSE DIVIDED AGAINST ITSELF.

At Jerash Abou Suleyman was sitting in the tent with his sleeves drawn up and his arms bare. We noticed a large scar on his right forearm, and asked him how he got it. "That was in quarrel. It happened at Jerusalem seven years ago. My cousin—old man—talk with another old man of another family of Copts, and they quarrel. Then one of the young men of that family hit one of my family, and the blood flow. When the blood flow the *word came*, and the men of both families run out of their houses. It was outside Jerusalem. It was on Sunday. And I run up, and one man of that other family take his pistol, and fire first shot, and it struck me here on my arm; you see it came very near bone. Then I run at him; he try to get out other pistol, but I take it from him and shoot him in leg; he go lame now. One of our people who had nothing in his hand ran to tree, and broke off large branch, and begin knock others down with it. They were forty-five. We were twenty-six, but we beat them well."

"Was any one put in prison for this?" "Yes, these two old men what began the quarrel. They were put above, not below, in nice room with carpets, very clean, and people to wait on them. But we got out our old man by force." "How by force?" "Well, one of my family go to Governor, and tell him, 'If you do not let our old man out of prison, we kill all that other family.' And he afraid, and tell him, 'Let him go.' But other old man was in prison for one week. They were forty-five and we twenty-six. But we beat them well."

V. THE COPTS—A RECONCILIATION.

You remember that I tell you of that fight between

those Copt families at Jerusalem. Well, the Government try to make them friends, and Greek Bishop he try also. And many were gathered together in one room and our old men speak, and then the Greek Bishop he speak much. He speak too much. He say that young men of each side shall kiss beards and heads of old men of other side; and that is good to make peace.

But he speak too much, and because he speak too much when he have finished, I that am younger than those elders and am ashamed to speak, I stand up in my place, and I say, "Yes, it is good that young men kiss beard and head of old, but who shall begin? Shall we begin? The other side began the fight. They shall begin the peace. They shall kiss our feet." Then there was much talk. All speak at once, but afterwards my word was taken for us not to kiss their feet, but that they shall begin. And so peace was made.

VI. THE CONVERSION OF THE JEWS.

I think English people have no minds to send clergymen here to Jews. English bought land for converted Jews at Jaffa, and built houses for them. If one was carpenter they gave him his tools, they gave these Jews horses, donkeys, and carriages (carts) and ploughs and gave each one one shilling for every day. Those Jews took all and when they were rich they ran away back to other Jews. I think only five or six remain.

Once when I was going from Jaffa to Jerusalem I found people beating one Jew. It was near Ramleh. He have been eating and drinking and he jump on his horse and run away without paying. They went after him and caught him. They beat him too much. I said, "How much is it?" They tell me "seven piastres." I pay it. He tell them he have no money. Then I want to know whether it was true that he have none. So I ask him. He say, "Yes, I have plenty money, but I did not want to give it. I thought I could run away on my horse." He paid me. He give me one medjidié and I take seven piastres and gave him the rest. He was converted Jew. I ask him, "Are you Protestant?" He tell me, "Oh no I go by them, and tell them I very poor, and they give me house and clothes and one shilling every day. When I have enough I leave them."

Never any Jew is converted. They only laugh at English. You know that court of Church of Holy Sepulchre at Jerusalem. No Jew can pass there. If he do they kill him. Christians have one firman from Sultan that if any Jew go there and they catch him they may kill him.

Fables.

I. ABOU SEYNE (The Father of Naughtiness).

ONE day Fox make walk in country and he see two Dervishes what sleep, and they have with them beads for make prayer. So while they sleep he steal the beads, and he put them round his neck, and he walk along and look very good. And as he pass by he came to house of the Cock, and his wife the Hen. And Hen tell him, "How you do, Mr. Fox? Where you going?" So that Fox tell her, "Do not speak with me, I am now Holy Man, I go to Mecca." So Hen tell him, "Is it true?" And Fox tell her, "Yes it is true, I will pray for you at Mecca." Then Hen tell him, "Wait till I call my husband." So she call that Cock and tell him what Fox tell her.

Then that Hen and that Cock tell Fox, "Shall we go with you?" And that Fox tell them, "It is good to go to Mecca. So they go with him. And as they pass by they see Duck, and Duck cry, "How you do, Mr. Fox, Mr. Cock, Mrs. Hen? Where you go?" And Fox tell him, "You must not speak with me. I Holy Man, I go to Mecca." And they all tell that

Duck, "We go Mecca, we pray for you there." And Duck tell them, "Shall I go with you?" And they make answer, "It is good you go Mecca." So that Duck go with them.

And as they go they see Owl on tree. And Owl tell them, "Mr. Fox, Mr. Cock, Mrs. Hen, Mrs. Duck! Where you all go?" And they tell him, "We go to Mecca. We pray for you there." And Owl tell them, "Shall I go with you?" And they tell him, "It is good to go Mecca." So Owl go with them. And as they journeyed night came on, and that Fox tell to Cock and Hen and Duck and Owl, "Better we look for some cave for shelter lest wild beasts eat us up." So they find one cave and all go in. And in night that Fox was hungry and he tell to Cock, "Come with me outside I have something to tell you."

So Cock go with him, and when they are outside Fox tell him, "My son, in morning when every one will sleep you wake all with the cry 'Cock o' doodle' that you make. This is great sin, and you must not do it any more." So Cock tell him, "All right, I not do this thing." But that Fox tell Cock, "I must prevent you from do this any more. You cannot go to Mecca." So he bite off his head and eat him up.

Then Hen hear little noise, and run out, and she tell to Fox, "Where is my husband?" And that Fox tell her, "He go for little walk. But, my daughter, I have something to tell you. When you make egg, you make great 'Cluck, cluck,' and little boys instead of go school run to look for egg. You are too proud because you make egg. This is sin." Then Hen tell him, "All right, I make cluck no more." But that Fox tell her, "I must prevent this. You cannot go Mecca." So he bite off her neck and eat her up.

And then Duck hear little noise, and run out of cave. And that Fox tell her, "My daughter, I have something to tell you. Why you make 'Quack, quack,' so all people look at you, and say what this Duck want? This sin. You must not do so." And Duck tell him, "All right, I make no more quack." But that Fox tell her, "I must prevent you make that proud noise. You cannot go Mecca." So he bite off her neck and eat her up also. Then Mr. Fox is happy, and make very proud because his belly is full of meat.

II. THE MOUSE'S VISIT.

I hear my mother tell this story to my children to make them sleep. There was mouse, and he ask other mouse to be guest. And other mouse come to first mouse and tell him, "How you do?" And other one tell him, "Thank you." Then first mouse tell other, "It is good you have come because the man what is landlord of this house he have good cheese and sugar from Damascus, and many good foods in his shop." So the mouses go round that shop, and eat little this and little that other, and that mouse what is guest is very please. And then they see little trap cage with door.

So first mouse run in and tell to other, "See what nice little room." And then other mouse come in and look. And then first mouse jump out again very quick, but guest mouse see one hook with bit bread, and he bite it and then door close. So guest mouse tell first mouse, "Come help me from this room, I am in prison." But first mouse tell him, "No, it is good you are there. My landlord made that trap for me. To-morrow he will find you, and he will not make it again." So he tell him "Good-bye," and finish. Then my mother tell my children, "If you do not shut your eyes that trap come catch you." So they shut their eyes very fast.

III. THE DONKEY AND THE SHEEP.

These Arabs make little hymn [1] (poem) about donkey. It is like this. One donkey and one sheep are friends one with other, and they go together far away to mountain, and there they live for three years, very nice. And one day they hear some people pass in valley. And sheep tell to donkey, "There are people there, perhaps they see us." And donkey tell to sheep, "What I care, we live here three years. See I must make little hymn." And then he say "He-haw, he-haw."

So those people hear him, and they look up. They say, "This is good. Here are donkey and sheep." And they go up mountain and they take them. And there are three people, and they all ride upon that donkey. And sheep tell donkey, "How you like your hymn now?" And then those people are hungry, and they go to kill sheep. And donkey tell them, "Well,

---

[1] Abou Suleyman is not aware that there are any poems in English which are not hymns, and therefore speaks of poems generally as hymns.

beg your pardon it is my fault. Do not hurt that poor sheep." But those people go still to kill that sheep. So donkey tell to sheep, " Now what say ; who is worst?" And sheep tell to donkey, " No, I finish my days. It is better. You have always labour."

VIEW FROM THE PALACE OF THE COPT BISHOP, JAFFA.

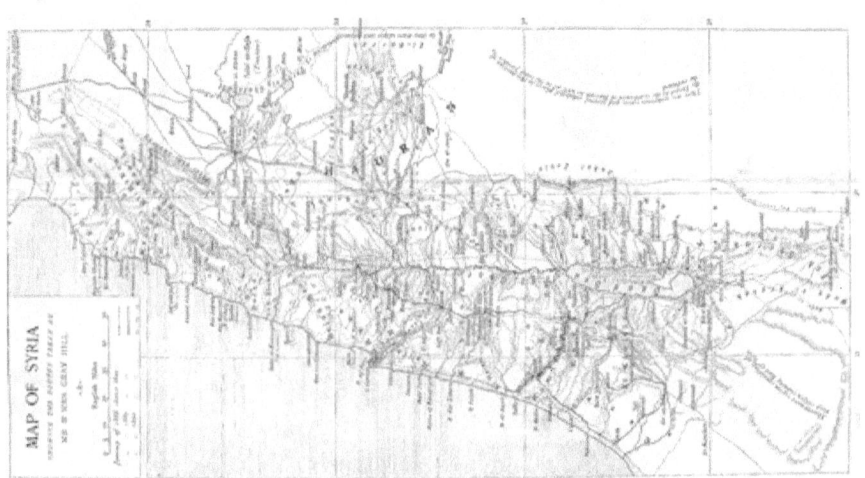

APPENDIX.

As this book is going through the press we have received a letter from Mrs. Lethaby, the wife of the Missionary of Kerâk (see page 204), dated September 15, 1890, from which the following extract may be of interest. At this date that brave woman and Miss Arnold were left alone in Kerâk, Mr. Lethaby having been obliged to go on the affairs of his Mission to England, when we had the pleasure of seeing him.

"Yesterday Sheik Khalîl sent Musa [the eldest of the young Christians depicted at p. 224], saying Sheik Khalîl wanted me to write to Mrs. Gray Hill and to the English Consul at Jerusalem. So I appointed to meet him at the house of Musa, where in half an hour we met. He, Sheik Khalîl, was very cordial, and said he would tell me himself—though, of course, Musa interpreted for the satisfaction of the Sheik. Almost literally the Sheik's words were, 'I wish to be friendly with the Howadjah and Sitt' [gentleman and lady] who came here, and with yourself and Howadjah' [Mr. Lethaby]; and though Musa was very much afraid of my saying a word too much, I asked some plain questions to assure the Sheik that if he expressed wishes for peace to these persons he must keep faith. 'Yes,' he said, 'he knew that we spoke truth and he wished me to write' (and Miss Arnold did for me in the presence of Sheik Khalîh, expressing in English what Musa said repeating the Sheik's words). I was quite astonished at the evident desire for peace, and can only suppose some fear is still felt that reprisals will be demanded for their treatment of yourselves. Only last Saturday, Nimmr [Leopard], the son of Ibrahim [the greedy Ibrahim, see p. 218], came to our gate—a grown lad of, say, seventeen, and demanded to be let in. I refused, and ordered him and his uncle off; when he took out his knife and, looking as fierce as he could, said he would cut my throat! This was his first visit to our gate, and he little knew that I was not to be daunted by a wild beast like that. I told him that his name was true (Leopard), and asked him if he knew what nobility meant. 'Yes.' 'Then act like a prince, not like a robber and wild beast.' Then he seated himself in our landlord's porch, and proceeded to eat the bread and leben [sour milk] they had provided for these noble guests! I stayed and lectured him on his conduct to yourselves and to us, and entreated him to tell his father and grandfather [Ibrahim and Sheik Khalîl] that God was a faithful Judge, and such conduct as theirs was written and remembered. The older man rebuked the lad for his violence to me, and seeing such conduct did not profit, he turned most politely and asked me to sit down and eat with them! I courteously declined the honour, and he became quite confidential, asking me if I was sure you, Mrs. Hill, were the Queen's daughter (!) I did not satisfy his curiosity on that and other points. He then took out some cartridges and showed them, saying, 'If the soldiers come to Kerâk we will give them these.' . . . We parted friends with salaams. Then on Tuesday comes this desire of Sheik Khalîl for letters to you and the Consul. Our friend . . . says we may not trust even this word and seal of the Sheik Khalîl. He thinks it is only to gratify his desire to override the ruling Sheik and get money from us and others. He will get none from us, and I trust he may never have the opportunity of serving other friends as you were treated. . . . Our dear scholars are very good, and their Moslem parents are very kind, sending us grapes, figs, tomatoes, as long as they lasted."

Sheik Khalîl's letter referred to in that of Mrs. Lethaby is as follows:—

"From Sheik Khalîl to Mr. and Mrs. Gray Hill. Sheik Khalîl wishes to say to Mr. and Mrs. Gray Hill that if they or their friends come on a visit to Kerâk, he will protect and care for them; and that if Mr. or Mrs. Lethaby or their friends wish to establish a church or school in Kerâk, or build a house or hospital they may depend upon his protection and friendship both in Kerâk and on the road to Kerâk.

"SHEIK KHALÎL MEJELLI his seal.
"Sheik Khalîl wishes his salaams to Mr. and Mrs. Gray Hill."

From these communications I infer that the Turkish Government are still intending to take possession of Kerâk, and with this object in view have made our adventure an excuse, and that the Eastern imagination has conferred on us the exalted position inquired about by the "Leopard." I do not, however, advise any of 'my readers to accept the invitation of Sheik Khalîl as long as the Mejelli rule over Kerâk.

www.ingramcontent.com/pod-product-compliance
Lightning Source LLC
Chambersburg PA
CBHW020230240426
43672CB00006B/470